REINVENT YOUR WORK

HOW TO REJUVENATE, REVAMP, OR RECREATE YOUR CAREER

FELICIA ZIMMERMAN

Dearborn™
Trade Publishing
A **Kaplan Professional** Company

Acquisitions Editor: Mary B. Good
Senior Project Editor: Trey Thoelcke
Interior Design: Lucy Jenkins
Cover Design: Design Solutions
Typesetting: Elizabeth Pitts

Published by Dearborn Trade Publishing, a Kaplan Professional Company

Printed in the United States of America

01 02 03 10 9 8 7 6 5 4 3 2 1

Library of Congress Cataloging-in-Publication Data

Zimmerman, Felicia.
    Reinvent your work : how to rejuvenate, revamp, or recreate your career / Felicia Zimmerman.
        p. cm.
    Includes bibliographical references and index.
    ISBN 0-7931-4551-1 (pbk)
    1. Career changes—Handbooks, manuals, etc. 2. Vocational guidance—Handbooks, manuals, etc. I. Title.
    HF5384 .Z56 2001
    650.14—dc21

                                             2001003145

DEDICATION

To Mary Zimmerman, my mother, who has always believed in and encouraged me.

CONTENTS

"**You**'ll never be a success in your eyes." Fearful that my supervisor's comment might come true, I initiated a career odyssey to find my ideal position.

Over the course of the next six years, I held five different jobs in three different companies. Although I enjoyed some aspects of my work and even earned several promotions, I didn't consider myself a success and, in any event, wasn't fulfilled. Sensing that I needed to create my own role and taking into account my talents and motivations, I envisioned myself as a communication coach. I launched my own business in 1987.

Although demanding, the following years were satisfying. With numerous corporate clients, I earned a reputation as a professional who was able to handle communication problems quickly and effectively. By 1993, however, I perceived that I needed a new challenge. Transforming my job and business simultaneously, I became a consultant who helps organizations operate more effectively. By collaborating closely with my clients, I witnessed firsthand that, like me and my firm, other managers and businesses were searching for their work ideals. Indeed, through my consulting engagements, professional contact, and even friendships, I helped individuals and companies rejuvenate, revamp, and recreate their jobs and businesses.

In 1998, I realized that I was ready for another change. Seeking to move to a new role—as professional speaker and media personality—I undertook the writing of this book. About this time, a business magazine did a story about me, which described how I "reinvented" myself and enabled companies to do likewise. Thanks to this article, I put a name to the phenomenon that I had observed, experienced, and coached others through. Because my reinvention odyssey has been long and challenging, I've written this handbook to facilitate the reshaping of your job or business. Whether you're an experienced worker, manager, executive, or entrepreneur, you'll find the help you've been looking for.

Reinventing your work—the subject of this book—is a process that's unique to you. You'll select its scope, which may include your job, the business you work for or own, or both. You may reinvent because of a problem or opportunity you discern, your motivations—such as wealth, power, fame, or personal fulfillment—your need or desire to change your situation, or a mixture of these elements. Your reinvention ideal will embody your skills, preferences, interests, and ambitions, and you'll select the reinvention option that will enable you to achieve your goals. To complete your reinvention, you'll employ an intuitive yet logical approach that involves your awareness and resourcefulness as well as your practicality and ability to execute. At any point, if you need or want to do so, you may again change your career or business. In other words, reinventing your work is repeatable.

Reinvent Your Work will coach you through choosing one of five reinvention options and employing seven steps to accomplish your reinvention. You'll read about eight individuals who've used these steps to reinvent their careers, companies, or both. You'll also receive guidance in implementing your reinvention. Unlike some career books, *Reinvent Your Work* won't make you play psychologist with yourself or your people. You won't have to determine which of numerous personality types you fit into. Nor will this book lay out canned rules on how to land a terrific job. Instead, this book will talk to you—whether you're male or female, relatively young or more mature, whatever your race, and whether you're an experienced worker, manager, executive, or entrepreneur. Now let's take a closer look at the book's features.

Of the five options, two will enable you to reinvent your career, and three will assist you in reinventing your area or company. To reinvigorate your job, you may rejuvenate your performance or revitalize your attitude. To change jobs in your company, you may switch to a new position, move to a new department or function, or create a new role for yourself. To enhance your business, you may improve your offerings or approach. To transition your business, you may refocus your organization, introduce new offerings, make acquisitions, or move into a new market sector. To start a new business within your company, you may launch a new venture that parlays a skill at which your company excels.

The seven steps will allow you to complete your reinvention option and, as a result, reach your work ideal. In Step One, Sense Your Timing, you'll assess your situation and decide whether or not to reinvent at all. Through Step Two, Visualize Your Reinvention, you'll craft a mental image of your goal that incorporates your abilities and motivations. Using Step Three, Verify Your Ideal, you'll confirm whether or not your vision matches what you're able and willing to accomplish. Employing Step Four, Be Resourceful, you'll be able to deal skillfully and promptly with problems and opportunities in your job or business. In Step Five, Be Practical, you'll develop the game plan that will guide your reinvention and the mission and milestones that will direct your future work changes. Using Step Six, Execute Flawlessly, you'll discover how to stay focused yet agile while you reinvent. And through Step Seven, Manage Your Attitude, you'll understand how to remain humble, confident, and patient throughout your reinvention journey.

The stories will demonstrate that the seven-step approach works, and therefore, the profiled individuals will give you hope. Gregg Engles, CEO of a Fortune 500 dairy company, continually senses his timing. Paula Madison, NBC executive, regularly visualizes her career and business reinventions. As she traversed the worlds of government, business, and academia, Evelyn Granville, celebrated mathematician, verified her ideals. Nelson Carbonell, high-tech entrepreneur, is resourceful in dealing with the vicissitudes of the new economy. Jimmy Ridings, ceiling fan entrepreneur, is practical in how he manages his business. Jim Farrell, CEO of a Fortune 500 machinery company, epitomizes flawless execution. Albert Black, corporate products and services entrepreneur, deftly manages his attitude. My story reflects how I've applied all of the steps.

You'll also learn how to implement. You'll choose your reinvention option by deciding whether or not your (or your business) circumstances line up with those that typify a particular alternative. You'll discover the requirements — such as networking and juggling your current work and reinvention-related activities—associated with your option. You'll find out how to engage in two reinventions—such as reinvigorating your job and enhancing your business—simultaneously. You'll also gather why and how you might reinvent your work again and again over the course of your career.

To obtain the most benefit from this book, first read Chapter 1, which provides an overview. Next, examine Chapters 2 through 8, which discuss the seven steps and include the eight stories, and answer the questions that appear throughout these sections. When you're ready to implement, move on to Chapter 9. Then peruse Chapter 10, which concerns reinventing anew, and use this information as you find necessary. If you want to learn more about the profiled individuals, their biographical sketches are included in the back of the book, as is a bibliography of helpful resources and a brief guide to troubleshooting your reinvention. You may use this book as written—to reinvent your job or business where you currently work—or you may employ this knowledge to reinvent your work somewhere else. In either case, *Reinvent Your Work* will be your handbook for reinventing your work—both today and in the future. If you enjoy this book, let me know, or if you've applied what you've read and are pleased (or displeased) with your results, please share your stories with me at <www.zimmbiz.com>.

Months ago, when I spoke with Norm Brinker, entrepreneur and chairman emeritus of Brinker International, the parent company of Chili's and other restaurants, he suggested that I write a book of hope. This is it, and you'll need it. As I and millions of others can attest, reinventing your job, business, or both isn't easy. Even so, it's almost always rewarding.

If you're ready, let's get started on your reinvention journey.

ACKNOWLEDGMENTS

As has been true of much of the rest of my career, writing this book wasn't easy, but like my past endeavors, this effort has been a journey of self-discovery. I've learned more about my abilities and what's important to me.

The stories of eight professionals provide *Reinvent Your Work* with credibility and also a human touch. I extend my sincere appreciation to seven remarkable individuals who allowed me to interview them and include their profiles in this book: Albert Black, Nelson Carbonell, Gregg Engles, Jim Farrell, Evelyn Granville, Paula Madison, and Jimmy Ridings. I also thank my editor, Mary Good, for convincing me to include my story.

Numerous professional contacts and clients—many of whom are also friends—provided me with invaluable entrees, ideas, and encouragement. I extend my special thanks to these folks: Sandy Allen, Trish Ballard, Mike Bell, Jill Bertolet, Teri Brooks, Janis Browning, Doug Campbell, Jim Champy, Joel Fontenot, Dan George, Drew Goodbread, Andrew Harman, Mike Krall, Darrell McKenna, Ed Morgan, Peg Neuhauser, Dean Al Niemi, Mike Nissenbaum, Ted Pappas, Sue Payne, John Podowski, Greg Renwick, C.D. Sabathier, Norma Adams Wade, Margaret Watson, Steve West, Dudley Wolf, and Steve Wolf.

I also send along a hug to my friends who gave me encouragement whenever I needed it: Art, Charlene, Elaine, Fusum, Gwen, Ivory, Jessie, Jim, Lillian, Richard, Tammy, and Yana.

I may have been resourceful or just lucky in connecting with my publisher, Dearborn Trade. Either way, as a first-time author, I've been truly blessed to work with such a dedicated team. My editor, Mary Good, is an exceptional human being who is wise beyond her years. I appreciate all that I've learned through my association with her.

My sister Carey provided both encouragement and food for thought. More than anyone else, however, I thank my mother. Without her unwavering support, I'm not sure that I could have achieved this goal or, for that matter, many of my previous work ideals.

CHAPTER ONE

Reinvent Your Work

Life is too short to squander. So work only at what really matters.[1]

—MARK ALBION, AUTHOR, FOUNDER, YOU & COMPANY, AND 20-YEAR
VETERAN OF HARVARD UNIVERSITY AND ITS BUSINESS SCHOOL

An employee rejuvenates his performance, while a colleague revitalizes her attitude. A worker changes jobs in his department, and a manager moves to a position in a different area. An owner improves her firm's approach and later enhances her products and services. An executive restructures his company and refocuses his organization. A marketing professional introduces a new offering and, with the success of this item, inaugurates a new line. A businessperson transitions her firm into a new sector. A CEO starts a new business within his company. By enhancing his department's offerings, a worker simultaneously reinvigorates his job. Dissatisfied with her new position, an individual switches to a more challenging job. Following the successful launch of a new venture, a leader shifts gears and creates a new role for himself.

You may admire the people in these examples. These folks have reinvented their careers, businesses, or both simultaneously, but because you're an experienced worker, seasoned manager, rising executive, or accomplished entrepreneur, you're not particularly concerned about changing your work. You've made improvements before, and consequently, you'll probably do so again. Yet, what if you're not certain whether you're satisfied with your work or need or want something new? What if you're not sure of your goal for your career or business? What if you don't know what actions you'll take to accomplish your objective? What if you're not aware of how you'll complete these actions? What if you don't understand how to engage in two work transformations at the same time? Or, what if you don't perceive that, over the course of your career, you'll reinvent again and again?

No doubt, you grasp the intent of these questions. Like other savvy businesspeople, you may need or want to rejuvenate, revamp, or recreate your work, and therefore, you have to understand what reinvention is and how to do it. Reinventing your work is a process that's unique to you—the reinventor. You'll determine its scope, which may include your position, the business you work for or own, or both. You'll be motivated to reinvent because of your situation, a problem or opportunity you discern, your ambitions—such as wealth, power, prestige, or personal fulfillment—or a combination of these factors. You'll formulate a reinvention goal that embodies your talents and what's important to you, and you'll choose a reinvention option that will help you attain this aim. To complete your reinvention, you'll use an intuitive yet logical approach that involves your awareness and resourcefulness as well as your practicality and ability to execute. At some point, if you need or want to do so, you may change your work again. Reinventing your career or business is repeatable.

This chapter will provide an overview of *Reinvent Your Work*. You'll preview the five options for reinventing your career or business and explore why you might engage in a particular alternative, what actions you might take, and the requirements associated with each option. You'll survey the seven steps for accomplishing these alternatives and consider what each step is, how to perform it, and why it's essential to reinventing your work. You'll hear about eight individuals who are profiled throughout this book and why their stories might be helpful to you. You'll take a glance at how to implement your reinvention by selecting the option that best fits your goal, and you'll get a glimpse of how to perform two reinventions simultaneously or reinvent anew.

Now let's begin our trip to your ideal career or business.

PREVIEW THE OPTIONS

A worker reinvigorates his job by participating in a corporate project. Seeking a faster-paced role, a manager changes positions in her company. Driven by continuous improvement, employees reengineer their firm's processes. An executive refocuses his people in order to improve his company's performance. Applying her customers' feedback, an entrepreneur successfully launches a new offering. A leader establishes a new venture within his firm by capitalizing on what his business excels at.

These scenarios illustrate why and how you might reinvent your work, but you may be fairly confident about reshaping your job or business and, therefore, don't need such information. Yet, what if you aren't sure why you're reinventing? What if you choose an option for revamping your career or business but don't know what this alternative entails? What if you don't learn about the requirements associated with this option and, as a result, don't reach your work ideal? Or, what if you aren't aware that a particular reinvention might lead to another reinvention?

You see where this discussion is headed. To choose the option that's appropriate for your career or business, you must recognize what's causing you to reinvent your work and, in turn, identify how you'll satisfy this motivation. You need to assess whether the option you select might lead to or be performed simultaneously with another reinvention. You also have to learn about the requirements associated with your alternative. Now let's briefly evaluate the five work reinvention options.

REINVIGORATE YOUR JOB

If your work has deteriorated or isn't acceptable or you're not performing up to your potential, you may rejuvenate your performance by bolstering your skills, taking corrective action, or both these efforts. If you're not as satisfied as you had been or hoped to be, or your interest in your work has waned, you may revitalize your attitude by taking on additional responsibilities, such as participating in a corporate project or teaching a class at your company. If such an opportunity doesn't exist, you may create one for yourself, such as initiating a task force to solve a problem or take advantage of an opportunity. Or, if you seek greater challenge or responsibility, you may both maximize your performance and assume additional tasks and, by doing so, build your reputation, enhance your prospects for advancement, or both.

Reinvigorating your job is a modest career reinvention that frequently results from a business reinvention. If you enhance your firm's approach, introduce new offerings, or establish a new venture, as a by-product, you may refresh your outlook. Conversely, if you opt

Compared to the previous alternative, transitioning your business is a more extensive reinvention, which may lead to reinvigorating your job or changing positions. For example, by rebuilding your business, you may reenergize your attitude. If your involvement in your firm's transformation impresses your CEO, you may receive a promotion. If you launch a new product or service, you may revitalize your demeanor. Or, if you introduce an innovative offering that generates substantial revenues, your management may promote you to a new position. Conversely, by changing jobs, you may initiate a business reinvention, such as improving a process in your new area or introducing a new item in your current department.

Four requirements are associated with this alternative. As you've seen with the previous options, you must maintain an equilibrium between your current work and reinvention. If you undertake a turnaround of your business, you have to know the specific problems you'll address and how you'll resolve these dilemmas. If you're inaugurating new offerings, you must be sure that you're launching the correct products at the right time. If you're transitioning into a new sector, you need to understand this segment and feel confident that this move makes sense for your firm.

START A NEW BUSINESS WITHIN YOUR COMPANY

If you seek to capitalize on something that your business excels at—your firm's competitive edge—you may create a new unit that will generate additional revenues and even enhance your firm's stature.

Compared to the previous two business reinvention alternatives, this option is typically more difficult and risky, and therefore, you have to be ready to initiate this endeavor. That is to say, if you haven't enhanced your offerings or approach even though your customers or suppliers have suggested that you do so, if you haven't restructured your firm and refocused your people even though you should, or if you haven't introduced the new offerings that your market demands, you may need to complete such activities before you attempt this more demanding effort. On the other hand, if this is the right option for your business and you pursue this alternative, you may rejuvenate your perspective. Or, thanks to your leadership in launching a new venture, you may receive a new job—manager of this business.

Besides your readiness to undertake this option, there are three requirements related to this alternative. As was the case with the previous four options, you have to manage your ongoing work and neer their firm's processes. An executive refocuses his people in order to improve his company's performance. Applying her customers' feedback, an entrepreneur successfully launches a new offering. A leader establishes a new venture within his firm by capitalizing on what his business excels at.

These scenarios illustrate why and how you might reinvent your work, but you may be fairly confident about reshaping your job or business and, therefore, don't need such information. Yet, what if you aren't sure why you're reinventing? What if you choose an option for revamping your career or business but don't know what this alternative entails? What if you don't learn about the requirements associated with this option and, as a result, don't reach your work ideal? Or, what if you aren't aware that a particular reinvention might lead to another reinvention?

You see where this discussion is headed. To choose the option that's appropriate for your career or business, you must recognize what's causing you to reinvent your work and, in turn, identify how you'll satisfy this motivation. You need to assess whether the option you select might lead to or be performed simultaneously with another reinvention. You also have to learn about the requirements associated with your alternative. Now let's briefly evaluate the five work reinvention options.

REINVIGORATE YOUR JOB

If your work has deteriorated or isn't acceptable or you're not performing up to your potential, you may rejuvenate your performance by bolstering your skills, taking corrective action, or both these efforts. If you're not as satisfied as you had been or hoped to be, or your interest in your work has waned, you may revitalize your attitude by taking on additional responsibilities, such as participating in a corporate project or teaching a class at your company. If such an opportunity doesn't exist, you may create one for yourself, such as initiating a task force to solve a problem or take advantage of an opportunity. Or, if you seek greater challenge or responsibility, you may both maximize your performance and assume additional tasks and, by doing so, build your reputation, enhance your prospects for advancement, or both.

Reinvigorating your job is a modest career reinvention that frequently results from a business reinvention. If you enhance your firm's approach, introduce new offerings, or establish a new venture, as a by-product, you may refresh your outlook. Conversely, if you opt to reinvigorate your job, you may bring about another reinvention, such as enhancing your business' approach.

There are two requirements associated with this alternative. You must be certain of your objective. If you receive feedback that your performance is inadequate and, consequently, you're discouraged, your primary goal must be to improve how you do your work. By doing so, you may also enhance your attitude. If you're assuming additional duties to reenergize your outlook, you also need to manage these tasks and your regular job. If you don't, you might create a new problem for yourself—poor performance—and, as a result, have to change your reinvention aim.

 ## CHANGE JOBS IN YOUR COMPANY

If you want a position that's a better match with your skills or motivations, you may change jobs within your area. If you seek new colleagues, different or more demanding responsibilities, or a faster-paced or more visible department, you may change both your job and area, such as moving from finance to sales or from operations to strategic planning. If you're looking for a greater challenge and haven't identified a position that might provide this stimulation, you may create a new role for yourself. For example, if you discover that your department doesn't have a strategy, you may volunteer to build a plan, or if your company doesn't effectively assimilate workers from the companies it acquires, you may offer to develop an approach to handling this situation.

In contrast to the previous career option, changing jobs in your company is a more ambitious endeavor that sometimes results from a business reinvention. For instance, if your company creates a new venture and your management thinks that you're the person to lead this unit, you may move to a new position. On the other hand, by changing jobs, you may initiate a business reinvention, such as enhancing your area's approach or inaugurating a new product or service.

Three requirements are associated with this option. As with the prior alternative, you need to juggle your regular job and reinvention-related activities. Often, to find the best positions, you must network effectively with coworkers throughout the company. If you're changing areas or functions or your role, you frequently have to reposition how others view you. That is to say, you need to persuade potential colleagues that your skills and motivations are similar or complementary to their talents and ambitions.

ENHANCE YOUR BUSINESS' OFFERINGS OR APPROACH

If you want to hold onto your business' competitive edge or even elevate your firm's status, you may make improvements to your division's or company's products, services, or processes—such as purchasing, manufacturing, fulfillment, or hiring. For example, if one of your competitors has eliminated certain additives from its products, you may do likewise, or if your people have found a way to expedite the delivery of your firm's services, you may enhance this process. If you and your employees perceive a chance to keep yourselves challenged and, at the same time, help your business, you may also initiate improvements, such as streamlining, modernizing, or customizing your processes or offerings.

Enhancing your business is a moderate business reinvention, and as you've read already, this option is often associated with reinvigorating your job. In other words, one of these options can lead to the other, or these reinventions can occur at the same time, but as you'll learn later in this chapter, if you engage in simultaneous reinventions, you need to know which is the primary endeavor.

There are three requirements associated with this alternative. You have to stay on an even keel in order to handle your existing business and reinvention efforts. You need to be sure that you're making the right enhancements at the appropriate time. As you'll discover, one of the best ways to verify that you're improving the proper item or process is by soliciting and applying input from your marketplace. But, no matter the enhancements, you must also be able to complete the improvements you undertake.

TRANSITION YOUR BUSINESS

If your department or company isn't performing acceptably or up to its potential, you may restructure your business, reengineer your processes, and refocus your people and, through these actions, rebuild your division or firm. If market conditions are conducive to expanding your operation and, in turn, improving your standing in the marketplace, you may introduce one or more new offerings, inaugurate a new line, or acquire other firms. If you need to reposition your business from a slow-growing or low-margin market sector or you want to expand into an additional part of the market, you may segue into a new segment.

Compared to the previous alternative, transitioning your business is a more extensive reinvention, which may lead to reinvigorating your job or changing positions. For example, by rebuilding your business, you may reenergize your attitude. If your involvement in your firm's transformation impresses your CEO, you may receive a promotion. If you launch a new product or service, you may revitalize your demeanor. Or, if you introduce an innovative offering that generates substantial revenues, your management may promote you to a new position. Conversely, by changing jobs, you may initiate a business reinvention, such as improving a process in your new area or introducing a new item in your current department.

Four requirements are associated with this alternative. As you've seen with the previous options, you must maintain an equilibrium between your current work and reinvention. If you undertake a turn-around of your business, you have to know the specific problems you'll address and how you'll resolve these dilemmas. If you're inaugurating new offerings, you must be sure that you're launching the correct products at the right time. If you're transitioning into a new sector, you need to understand this segment and feel confident that this move makes sense for your firm.

START A NEW BUSINESS WITHIN YOUR COMPANY

If you seek to capitalize on something that your business excels at—your firm's competitive edge—you may create a new unit that will generate additional revenues and even enhance your firm's stature.

Compared to the previous two business reinvention alternatives, this option is typically more difficult and risky, and therefore, you have to be ready to initiate this endeavor. That is to say, if you haven't enhanced your offerings or approach even though your customers or suppliers have suggested that you do so, if you haven't restructured your firm and refocused your people even though you should, or if you haven't introduced the new offerings that your market demands, you may need to complete such activities before you attempt this more demanding effort. On the other hand, if this is the right option for your business and you pursue this alternative, you may rejuvenate your perspective. Or, thanks to your leadership in launching a new venture, you may receive a new job—manager of this business.

Besides your readiness to undertake this option, there are three requirements related to this alternative. As was the case with the previous four options, you have to manage your ongoing work and reinvention initiative. You and your colleagues need to have the competitive edge that you'll parlay into a new business. You and your people must also have the mind-set necessary to set up and run an entrepreneurial venture.

The preceding options are discussed in the second to the last parts of Chapters 2 through 8, where you'll compare how various aspects of these alternatives line up with your (or your business') situation. Now let's move on to how you'll accomplish the alternative you select.

SURVEY THE STEPS

A manager perceives that she's ready for a new challenge. A business owner envisions inaugurating a new line of services. A worker confirms that his abilities and ambitions correspond well with his career ideal. Applying an approach that a colleague used successfully, an entrepreneur revamps his business. An employee employs a sensible plan to obtain the role she wants. Staying focused yet agile, an executive transforms his company. A leader attains her work ideal by remaining humble, confident, and patient.

These scenarios demonstrate how businesspeople bring about their reinventions, but you think that such a complicated process isn't necessary. Yet, what if you don't reinvent even though you should? What if you shape a job or business goal that doesn't fit your or your workers' skills and motivations? What if you miss out on an idea or approach that might help you to reinvent your career or business? What if you engage in the wrong actions or use a flawed technique and, as a result, don't achieve your work ideal? What if you're not diligent or nimble or can't manage your reinvention and regular job or business, and consequently, your work revamp fails? Or, what if your arrogance or restlessness makes your reinvention difficult or even causes it to fizzle?

The astute recognize that reinventing their work requires an approach that's intuitive yet logical. That is to say, these businesspeople employ their awareness and resourcefulness as well as their practicality and ability to execute in order to complete their chosen reinvention option and, in turn, attain their work ideal. Consequently, these individuals realize their timing and, therefore, decide whether or not to reinvent. These managers devise their reinvention goals and validate that their (or their people's) abilities and ambitions correspond to these aims. In both their reinventions and regular work, sharp professionals employ concepts and methods that they learn about or even devise. Pragmatic leaders develop a carefully thought-out course of action. Successful executives, entrepreneurs, and employees follow through on their reinvention plans but stay alert to problems and opportunities, and they effectively juggle their reinvention and current work. These people also make sure that their attitude facilitates—not hinders—reaching their work ideal. In other words, these folks use seven steps to reinvent their work. Let's briefly assess what these stages are, how you'll perform these maneuvers, and why these deeds are essential to your reinvention.

SENSE YOUR TIMING

Step One is the critical starting point for your reinvention and, through this stage, you'll develop (or hone) your awareness of your (or your business') situation. To do so, you'll examine the industry in which you work. You'll look at the company you own or work for. You'll evaluate how you're doing—your performance—and your attitude toward your job or business. From your assessment, you'll develop a comprehensive and integrated picture of your circumstances, which you'll use to decide whether or not to reinvent your job, business, or both. Let's look at how this step can lead to a career or business reinvention.

Perhaps you're frustrated by something that your industry is doing or not doing. You see opportunities to improve how your company operates. You're making mistakes that you wouldn't have made before. You're having trouble staying motivated, or you want to learn something new. You may opt to reinvigorate your job. Or, you see how your industry can improve. You perceive ways in which your company can enhance its products or methods. You and your people have a track record of improving your offerings or approach. You and your workers lose interest when you have to maintain the status quo. You may elect to enhance your business.

VISUALIZE YOUR REINVENTION

Step Two represents the foundation for reshaping your work and, through this stage, you'll develop (or refine) your awareness of yourself or your business. By doing so, you'll shape your reinvention goal. You will assess your preferences and interests. You'll examine your (or your business') skills and strengths. You'll analyze what drives you or your workers. Pulling together the components of your assessment, you'll craft an image of your reinvention—the destination of your reinvention journey—which becomes your goal. Here's how this step can lead to a reinvention.

Maybe you're interested in learning new things and working with new colleagues. You've developed and applied the skills necessary to do another job. Factors that have been important to you—such as wealth or recognition—still matter, but now you're moved to seek a new challenge, and you're prepared to make compromises so that you'll attain your aim. You may decide to change departments within your company. Or, you and your people enjoy developing new offerings. Your organization has the skills necessary to fulfill your business objective. You and your colleagues like being recognized as an innovative firm. You may choose to launch a new product or service.

VERIFY YOUR IDEAL

Step Three examines whether the picture you developed in Step Two corresponds with what you're willing and able to accomplish and, by finishing this step, you'll validate (or won't validate) your reinvention goal. You'll make sure that your abilities match those required by your ideal work. You'll certify that what's important to you (or your workers) is similar to the motivations of individuals engaged in your imagined job or business. Bringing together what you've discovered, you'll decide whether (or not) you'll proceed with your reinvention or whether you'll revise your goal or make adjustments—such as improving your skills or making compromises in your preferences, interests, or ambitions—before you commence your work transformation. Let's examine how this step can lead to a reinvention.

Perhaps you've decided that your talents correlate well with those necessary to perform your ideal job. You've also concluded that your ambitions correspond closely with those associated with your goal. Having confirmed your vision, you may move to another department in your firm. Or, you've determined that your people's abilities line up with those related to your business goal. Further, what drives your employees typically motivates workers who are involved in new product launches. Having verified your reinvention ideal, you may introduce one or more new offerings.

BE RESOURCEFUL

Step Four reveals how to develop (or hone) your ability to deal skillfully and promptly with your work situation. By completing this step, you'll understand how to use your quick-wittedness to recognize and address problems or opportunities, set (or refine) your reinvention objective, pursue and attain your goal, and perform well thereafter. You'll learn how to become (more) resourceful. You'll find out how to incorporate your ingenuity in your current job or use it to find a new role or position. You'll discover how to employ your sharpness in your business in order to make modest improvements or even significant changes. You'll also examine the downsides of being too resourceful and how to avoid these perils. Here's how this step can guide a reinvention.

Maybe you've made an effort to stay informed about your marketplace or you've been open to and have even experimented with new ideas and approaches. You see an opportunity to expand your role. Employing your brightness to identify and participate in projects, you may reinvigorate your job. Or, you and your people have remained alert to your marketplace or have been receptive to and have often utilized new concepts and techniques. You and your workers seek to better your firm's products or services. Using your inventiveness to determine which improvements you'll make and how you'll make them, you may enhance your offerings.

BE PRACTICAL

Step Five assists you in building short-term and long-term work strategies. That way, you'll bring about the right reinvention and at a time you determine. Through this stage, you'll devise a clear statement of your work's mission and you'll define the milestones you'll attain to fulfill this purpose. You'll also build a game plan for your current reinvention, which will include the actions you'll take and the means you'll employ to accomplish these activities. Let's evaluate how this stage can guide a reinvention.

Perhaps you're aware of your highest goal and the stages you must pass through to satisfy this purpose. You've listed the actions you'll take to obtain the new position you want. You've developed a method that's efficient and effective. You've finished your strategy and are confident that you'll be able to stick with your plan. You may change jobs in your company. Or, you're sure about your business' mission and the events that must occur to fulfill this long-term aim. You've documented the actions necessary to restructure your organization and refocus your people. You've devised a pragmatic approach to improving your organization's performance. You've completed your game plan, which is integrated and easy to follow. You may transform your organization.

EXECUTE FLAWLESSLY

Step Six provides you with the fundamentals of carrying out a task. That is to say, by detecting and addressing problems and opportunities, persevering, and maintaining an equilibrium, you'll safeguard, expedite, or enhance your reinvention and, by doing so, you'll achieve your ideal. In this step, you'll learn how to stay focused yet agile. You'll grasp how to strike the appropriate balance between your concentration and nimbleness and between your regular work and reinvention. You also will learn how to adjust your approach according to your situation. You'll anticipate the challenges that you might encounter during your implementation. Here's how this step can facilitate a reinvention.

Maybe you usually follow through. You're generally able to spot and resolve problems or discern and take advantage of opportunities. You're capable of working on two distinct projects simultaneously. You've identified your potential execution hurdles and have asked your mentor to help you handle these obstacles. Because you can carry out a task, like expanding your job responsibilities, you may reinvigorate your job. Or, you and your workers regularly complete the required activities. You and your people have a good track record in perceiving possibilities and going after them. You and your personnel are more agile when you launch a new line and more focused after you've refined your offerings to meet your customers' requirements. You and your team have documented the dilemmas you might have while you implement. Thanks to your ability to accomplish the necessary activities, you may inaugurate a new line.

MANAGE YOUR ATTITUDE

Step Seven shows you how to handle your outlook and demeanor so that these factors will assist—not adversely affect—your reinvention. Through this step, you'll remain (or become) humble. In other words, you won't hurt your reinvention by being haughty or fail to reinvent because you're smug. You'll stay confident and won't allow a negative perspective, fear, envy, or insecurity to hold you or your business back. You'll be patient with your reinvention strategy and won't pursue unrelated or unsound ideas and, in turn, bring about the wrong reinvention. You'll be tolerant of your colleagues so that you won't alienate your coworkers and thereby delay or even derail your work reshaping. You'll also identify your potential attitudinal difficulties. Let's assess how this step can facilitate a reinvention.

Perhaps you're usually modest and receptive to others' suggestions. You try to be self-assured. Typically, you're composed and, therefore, carefully assess an idea or approach before you use it. Because you might have difficulty remaining confident as you reposition your image, you'll seek your mentor's support. Aiding your effort by your attitude, you may move to a new function. Or, once in a while, you and your people are arrogant. You and your team rarely envy other firms' accomplishments. You and your workers are generally collected. Because you and your people might have trouble remaining open to new ideas and not becoming smug, you'll seek other leaders' advice on how to avoid this problem. Easing your endeavor by your demeanor, you may launch a new business.

These seven steps are detailed in Chapters 2 through 8. At the end of each of these chapters are two stories that illustrate how businesspeople have used a particular step. Let's take a peek at the individuals profiled in these anecdotes.

HEAR ABOUT THE STORIES

Using his sense of timing to make acquisitions, a CEO builds a dairy company. After visualizing her work ideal, a media executive aggressively pursues her goal. A celebrated mathematician verifies her path and, as a result, seamlessly traverses the worlds of academia, government, and business. A high-tech entrepreneur cleverly repositions his company. Employing a sensible approach, an entrepreneur builds a ceiling fan and lighting company from scratch. A manufacturing company's CEO strikes the right balance between staying focused and being agile. By effectively managing his attitude, a corporate products and services entrepreneur builds a successful business. Reshaping her career, a manager becomes a business owner, and subsequently, this entrepreneur revamps her firm and again reinvents her career.

The above scenarios aren't hypothetical. These examples refer to the stories that appear in *Reinvent Your Work*. By reading these anecdotes, you'll understand how other businesspeople have applied the seven-step approach to reinvent their careers, businesses, or both— often at the same time. You'll also appreciate that you're not alone in rejuvenating, revamping, or recreating your work. Now let's get a glimpse of the people in these narratives.

Gregg Engles is chairman and CEO of Suiza Foods Corporation, a Fortune 500 dairy company. Entering the milk business in 1993 and completing 43 acquisitions in eight years, this executive has created the nation's largest dairy processor and distributor. Engles' acute sense of timing has contributed to both his career reinvention—from lawyer to entrepreneur to CEO—and the transformation of his company and industry. (In April 2001, Suiza Foods agreed to acquire Dean Foods in a deal valued at $1.5 billion. This transaction is expected to close before the end of 2001. Engles would serve as CEO of the combined firm.)

Paula Madison is president and general manager of KNBC, the Los Angeles–based affiliate of NBC. After nearly two decades in television news, this executive has established premier newscasts at several stations and, consequently, she and the stations she's worked for have won prestigious awards. Thanks to her exceptional awareness of her abilities and ambitions, Madison has visualized her goals and then achieved them. As a result, this media professional has reinvented her career—from newspaper editor to television news director to station manager—and the businesses with which she's been associated.

Evelyn Granville is a celebrated mathematician who continues to lecture and teach. With a career that spans five decades, this National Academy of Sciences honoree has worked in government, business, and academia. Wherever she's gone, this perceptive individual has made sure that her skills and motivations matched those associated with her ideal positions and, therefore, Granville is living proof that verifying your path can lead to reinvention.

Nelson Carbonell is president and CEO of Cysive, Inc., a software firm that builds systems to support e-business operations of companies like AT&T, Cisco Systems, and DaimlerChrysler. This businessman has worked as both corporate manager—at TRW, Oracle, and Litton Industries—and entrepreneur. By employing his resourcefulness, Carbonell has reinvented his career and reengineered his company—in 1998 and again amid the 2000–2001 high-tech meltdown.

Jimmy Ridings is founder, chairman, and CEO of Craftmade International, a ceiling fan and lighting company that generates annual revenues in excess of $200 million. Like Carbonell, this one-time plumbing supplies salesman has been both employee and independent businessman. Because of his practical plan, which includes sensible actions and a down-to-earth approach, this *Forbes*-honored entrepreneur has built a market powerhouse.

Jim Farrell is chairman and CEO of Illinois Tool Works (ITW), a Fortune 500 company that manufactures engineered products, like nails and fasteners, and specialty systems, such as plastic packaging and industrial strapping. While advancing his career—from sales representative to general manager to executive vice president—this longtime ITW employee helped lead the reinvention of his company. Farrell skillfully maintains a balance between staying focused—running his existing businesses—and being agile—starting new divisions. And consequently, this executive continually reinvents his company.

Albert Black is founder, president, and CEO of On-Target Supplies & Logistics, a provider of office products and supply chain management services to large corporations, including SBC Communications, Texas Instruments, and Electronic Data Systems. Like Carbonell and Ridings, this businessman has been both employee—a doorman and computer operator at a utility company—and entrepreneur. By being patient and remaining humble yet confident, Black has reinvented his career and recreated his company—from custodial service to office products vendor to leading corporate supplier.

I'm founder and owner of F.A. Zimmerman Consulting, Inc., a firm that helps companies rejuvenate, revamp, or recreate their approach so that they operate more effectively. Like several of the profiled individuals, I've been both employee—banker, corporate planner, internal consultant, and sales manager—and independent businessperson. As you'll learn, I've employed (and continue to employ) the seven steps to reinvent my career—from worker to entrepreneur to author to professional speaker—and my business—from communication coaching to management consulting.

Once you finish the steps and accompanying stories, you'll proceed to Chapters 9 and 10, which deal, respectively, with implementing your reinvention and reinventing again. Let's briefly examine these topics.

TAKE A GLANCE AT IMPLEMENTATION

Before she begins her reinvention, an employee makes sure that she's sensed her timing, visualized and verified her ideal, developed a practical plan that includes resourceful moves, and determined how she'll execute and also manage her attitude. After concluding that his situation lines up with a particular reinvention option, a worker commences his reinvention. A businessperson makes sure that she handles her current responsibilities while she searches for a new position. A manager simultaneously revamps his department's processes and reinvigorates his job. Before reinventing anew, a business owner evaluates this endeavor against her firm's mission and related milestones.

These examples depict various aspects of implementing a reinvention, but you think that if you get through the steps, you'll be able to put your plan into action. Yet, what if you're not ready to reinvent but do so anyway and, as a result, your reinvention fails? What if you carry out a reinvention option that doesn't fit your circumstances and, consequently, you're dissatisfied with the outcome of your effort? What if you don't pay attention to the requirements associated with your reinvention alternative and, therefore, your reinvention flops? What if you don't know how to engage in two reinventions at the same time and, as a result, you miss out on an opportunity for your career or business? What if you don't know how to reinvent your work again and, because you need to make a change but don't, you're miserable? Or, what if you launch another reinvention, even though this move is inconsistent with your mission and related milestones?

You get the drift of these questions. Smart executives and employees ensure that they're fully prepared to implement their reinventions. Pragmatic businesspeople confirm that their situation corresponds with the reinvention option they select. These professionals stay alert to the requirements associated with their chosen alternative. These managers understand how to perform career and business reinventions simultaneously. Perceptive workers realize that they might need or want to reinvent again and, therefore, these individuals learn why they might reinvent anew and how to do so.

As you already learned, in the second to the last sections of Chapters 2 through 8, you'll assess how various aspects of the five reinvention options line up with your (or your business') situation. In Chapter 9, you'll review this information and, in turn, finalize your choice of option. You'll also examine how to use the seven steps to carry out your job or business reshaping and how to undertake two reinventions simultaneously. Using this information, you'll be able to implement effectively. In Chapter 10, you'll evaluate why you might reinvent again and how you'd accomplish this aim. Now let's consider some examples: a career change, a business transition, simultaneous reinventions, and reinventing again.

Maybe you're ready to reinvent your job. You sense that you want to work in a faster-paced department. You visualize changing areas within your company. You verify that your skills and motivations correspond well with your goal. You review whether (or not) your situation correlates with a particular option and, based on this assessment, you choose to change jobs in your company. To facilitate your move, you cleverly reposition your image. You craft a practical plan that ensures that you'll take the right actions and use the most productive approach. You anticipate that not striking the right balance between staying focused and being agile or becoming impatient might negatively impact your effort. Mindful of the requirements associated with your option, you juggle your current position and reinvention activities and you skillfully network with colleagues throughout your company.

Perhaps you're prepared to reinvent your business. You perceive that your company isn't performing acceptably or up to its potential and, consequently, you envision restructuring your firm and refocusing your people and, in turn, rebuilding your organization. You confirm that you and your employees have the collective abilities and ambitions to accomplish this sweeping change. You reevaluate whether (or not) your circumstances line up with a particular option and, because of this analysis, you decide to transform your company. You ingeniously apply the practices that have enabled other companies to reengineer their operations and redirect their workers. Spelling out your actions and approach, you develop a sensible strategy. You predict that if you and your workers fail to stick with your plan or become smug about your progress, your corporate transition might flop. Alert to the requirements associated with this option, you make sure you understand your company's problems and how you'll address them and you manage your existing business and reinvention tasks.

Let's briefly examine concurrent reinventions. By engaging in a project, you may simultaneously reinvigorate your job and enhance your company's approach. After you change positions, you may initiate the revamp of your department's processes. Or, before you refocus your organization, you may have to rejuvenate your own outlook. In other words, you may engage in two reinventions at the same time, or one reinvention may lead to another or be the prerequisite for a subsequent work recreation. Whatever the combination, you need to determine which is the primary initiative and whether you might need to make a trade-off concerning your job or business. For example, if you're the manager who's responsible for spearheading a new venture, until you complete this task, this assignment is your priority and, consequently, you may have to delay changing jobs.

You may opt to reinvent again. Because you're miserable in your new role, you're aware that you need another job. Imagining a new position that will meet your objectives, you confirm that your abilities and motivations fit this ideal. You review whether (or not) your situation correlates with a particular option and, based on this evaluation, you opt to change jobs again. By networking skillfully, you identify the position you want and, in turn, develop a practical plan for reaching your goal. You also foresee that if you don't balance your current position and reinvention endeavor or become discouraged about your progress, you might doom your latest career maneuver. Attentive to a requirement that's associated with your reinvention alternative, you move prudently so that your colleagues won't see you as volatile.

Conversely, even if you're pleased with your business' recent transformation, you may want to reinvent anew. You now perceive an opportunity to expand your firm. You visualize introducing a new product or service. You verify that your people's skills and motivations line up with your objective. You reevaluate whether (or not) your circumstances correspond to a particular alternative and, because of your review, you decide to introduce a new offering. You inventively apply input from your marketplace and, in turn, devise a sensible plan. You also anticipate that if you and your people don't stay on an even keel between your current business and reinvention or become anxious about your new item's potential, your reinvention might fall short. Aware of the requirements associated with this business transition, you choose the right person to lead your business' latest transition. In other words, you recognize that launching a new offering typically requires different skills than rebuilding a business. You also guard against involving your organization in too much change, such as indiscriminately inaugurating new offerings.

At this point, you're probably eager to begin the next chapter but, even if you are, let's quickly review how you can read this book and profit by doing so.

FIND OUT THE BENEFITS

Aware of her situation, an employee decides to reinvent her career and, using her self-awareness, this worker crafts an image of her ideal job that matches her skills and motivations. A resourceful entrepreneur incorporates new ideas and approaches in his business. An individual uses a practical plan to guide her career change. Staying focused yet agile, a leader and his people execute their reinvention—almost flawlessly. An executive who's reshaping her area ensures that she remains humble and patient with her colleagues. Before he engages his organization in an extensive reinvention, a CEO verifies that his company's circumstances correlate well with a particular option. After enhancing his firm's offerings, a business owner inaugurates a new line. Inspired by others' success in reinventing their careers, businesses, or both, a leader completes the reinvention of her work.

Do you see yourself in these scenarios? If so, you grasp the benefits you can derive from reading and, in turn, applying this book's information. With *Reinvent Your Work,* you'll develop (or hone) your awareness of your situation and yourself or your business. You'll inventively employ new concepts and techniques in your job or business and you'll devise a pragmatic plan that will guide your current and future reinventions. You'll execute your work reshaping without a hitch and keep your ego, insecurity, and restlessness under control. You'll choose the reinvention option that's right for you or your business and you'll implement effectively, even if you're engaged in concurrent reinventions or you're reinventing anew. You'll also parlay what you've gathered from other businesspeople's experiences to help you persevere and, as a result, you'll be more likely to achieve your goal.

Now let's move on to the first step in your reinvention journey.

CHAPTER TWO

STEP ONE
Sense Your Timing

Leaders . . . all share a gift for what we call "sensing,"
meaning that they are adept at spotting trends and
seizing opportunities ahead of their competitors.[1]

—JAMES CHAMPY, CHAIRMAN, PEROT SYSTEMS CONSULTING, AND
NITIN NOHRIA, PROFESSOR, HARVARD BUSINESS SCHOOL

Do you wonder why individuals change their work? Do you question how they know whether and when to do so? What causes workers to change jobs? How do managers discover it's time to revamp their businesses?

If you've asked yourself these questions, you're not alone. Businesspeople everywhere want to learn what leads their colleagues to reinvent their work. What's the spark or the catalyst? Does a midlife crisis, even a life-changing experience, drive their actions? Are these professionals responding to a problem or taking advantage of an opportunity? Do these employees fear that they'll fail if they don't change? How do these managers recognize when to act—reinventing neither too soon nor too late?

To transform their jobs, their businesses, or both, perceptive individuals sense their timing—an activity that gets people through their "career inflection points."[2] That is to say, owners and employees are aware of their situation—whether they're happy, unhappy, or somewhere in between—because they know that you can't know where you're going if you don't know where you are. These managers examine the industries they're in and the companies they work for or own.

These professionals evaluate their performance and also examine their attitude about their work. From their assessment, astute workers create a comprehensive and integrated view of their job, their business, or both. With this picture, these folks decide whether or not to reinvent their work.

But maybe you're not convinced that a sense of timing is really necessary. You've made good choices before and, consequently, you've been fairly successful. Besides, such an analysis would require a lot of effort. Yet, what if by not sensing your timing you don't detect and deal with a problem? You may end up with a dilemma that's impossible to fix. What if you don't discern and take advantage of an opportunity? You may regret that you didn't help your career or business. What if you reinvent your job or business at the wrong time? You may be unable to do a new job or a business improvement might flop. Or, what if you don't reinvent even though you should? You may later regret your inaction.

By this point, you're probably nodding. Sensing your timing is the critical starting point for any work reinvention. This awareness will help you identify and address problems before it's too late to resolve them. This knowledge will guide you in seeing and going after opportunities before someone else does. Understanding your situation will enable you to respond in a manner and at a time that's right for you, your business, or both and, throughout your reinvention journey, this consciousness will steer your decisions and actions.

This chapter will show you how to develop (or hone) your sense of timing. You'll examine the industry in which you work. You'll look at the company you work for or own. You'll evaluate how you're doing—your performance—and your attitude toward your work. Based on this analysis, you'll develop a complete and integrated picture of your situation and, with this view, you'll be in a position to conclude whether you need or want to reinvent your job, your business, or both. By comparing how your circumstances line up with various reinvention options, you'll also learn how to apply your sense of timing. Then you'll read about two businesspeople who used their sense of timing to reinvent their careers and businesses.

Let's first consider the field in which you work.

ASSESS YOUR INDUSTRY

Seeing the signs of a dramatic industry shift, a business owner concludes that his firm's problems reflect this phenomenon and, therefore, he pursues the appropriate solutions. Observing industrywide excess capacity, an executive acquires several of his company's competitors. Perceiving new opportunities in his industry, an employee decides to change jobs.

These scenarios illustrate how companies and individuals employ their awareness of their industries in order to act. You have a general sense of the industry in which you work. You know whether it's traditional, like manufacturing, or newer, perhaps offering Internet-related software and services. You see whether it's thriving or declining. You also hear whether it's popular with the media, executive job seekers, and recent graduates. Most likely, a cursory understanding of your industry will suffice. Yet, what if you're not fully informed about your industry? You or your business may be surprised by developments in your field. What if you mistake your company's weak performance for an industrywide decline? You may fail to turn around your operation. What if you're not apprised of your industry's challenges? You or your firm may not recognize why you have problems. Or, what if you don't respond to industry circumstances even though you should? You may lament that you didn't rejuvenate, revamp, or recreate your career, business, or both.

By fully assessing your industry, you'll grasp the context of your work. That way, you or your business will be prepared and, consequently, able to address industry problems or capitalize on opportunities in your field. From your analysis, you'll also discover whether your industry is the right one for you, your business, or both. If you're not in the proper field, you may elect to make a change. Or, if you discover that you're ill-prepared for a sweeping industry change, you may opt to bolster your (or your people's) skills. Let's consider how an individual and a business can benefit by examining their industry.

Maybe you're a manager who's assessed your relatively new industry. In the past, firms in this field have performed well because they provided new products, but as these companies satisfied market demand, industry sales slowed. In response to these conditions, leading firms in your industry are developing overseas markets for their products and moving into services, which are growing more quickly than their current offerings. From your analysis, you determine that your industry will offer excellent opportunities for professionals with the appropriate skills and motivations.

Perhaps you're an executive who's evaluated your traditional industry. Previously, companies in this field performed adequately because they applied technology to reduce their costs, but now your industry has excess capacity and neither your firm nor your competitors are responding to this situation. Through your assessment, you conclude that the time is ripe for an industry consolidation.

Examining your industry makes sense. Here are some questions that will guide you in your assessment.

- Is yours a traditional or brick-and-mortar industry or is it a newer, even Internet-related field? In what businesses is your industry involved? Do these areas provide growth opportunities or are they cyclical or even stagnating? Do developments in other industries strongly affect your field?

- How has your industry performed? Has it grown and been profitable? Which companies have led your industry and why were these firms able to do so? Did these firms develop new products or services, acquire other businesses, or apply new technologies? Conversely, which firms fell behind and why? Was your company among the winners or losers?

- What challenges does your industry face? Does your industry have excess capacity? Are pricing pressures escalating? Is global competition intensifying and, if so, how is the competitive landscape changing? Are regulations becoming more stringent? Are new technologies changing how your industry produces, delivers, or markets its offerings? Is your industry going through a dramatic shift? How are companies in your industry responding to these challenges? Are these firms enhancing their efficiency or effectiveness? Are these companies outsourcing various parts of their operations and, as a result, eliminating certain tasks and the people who perform them? Are firms in your industry merging or moving their operations to lower-cost countries? Are these companies transitioning into faster-growth sectors or focusing on particular areas of the world? According to industry analysts and your company's management, what is the outlook for your industry, and is this view generally positive or negative?

- From your evaluation, do you conclude that your industry is a good fit for you or your business? Do you believe that in the future your industry will provide outstanding opportunities for businesses like yours or individuals with your talents? Or, have you determined that your industry will continue to shrink and, consequently, become less important in the global arena? Have you decided that you (or your business) need to transition into another field?

Once you've evaluated your industry, you must examine your company.

ASSESS YOUR COMPANY

Because his business is losing ground to a competitor, an owner overhauls his offerings and approach. Recognizing that his firm's sales and profit margin are starting to decline, an entrepreneur launches a new offering. Excited about a new venture in his company, a worker moves to this area.

The individuals in these examples use their awareness of their companies to make career and business decisions, but you generally understand your company's situation and, therefore, probably have sufficient information to conclude how your company is doing. Yet, what if you're not completely knowledgeable about problems with your company's lines of business or difficulties that your firm's customers face? You may be caught off guard and, consequently, be unable to respond. What if you don't detect that your business' sales and earnings are declining, inventory velocity is slowing, return on assets is shrinking, or cash is depleting? As a result, you may confront serious—even insurmountable—obstacles. What if you don't see that a new competitor is capturing market share at your firm's expense? Seemingly overnight, your company may become a second-rate player. Or, what if thanks to your lack of knowledge about your company's situation, you don't reshape your business, career, or both? You may be sorry that you weren't informed.

Prudent workers learn as much as possible about their company. These people are thoroughly acquainted with their company's lines of business and its customers. Smart managers carefully examine all aspects of their company's performance and also stay alert to competitive developments. Once they've completed a thorough assessment, these employees are prepared and, as a result, are able to decide whether or not to reinvent their businesses or jobs.

As was true with your industry analysis, an in-depth assessment of your company's circumstances helps you understand the context of your work. By knowing your company, you also recognize the implications of your firm's situation for your job or role. For example, if you're aware that your company is trying to establish itself in global markets and you speak several languages and have lived overseas, you may change jobs. Or, if you perceive that your firm's sales force is having trouble using a new system that you're familiar with, you may set up a coaching program to help your colleagues and, by doing so, rejuvenate your role in your company. Let's return to the previous examples and consider how assessing your company can affect your work.

The first scenario describes a manager who works in a relatively new industry that needs to rejuvenate its growth. By evaluating his company, this individual concludes that his firm has performed well. He also realizes that his company's global expansion and new services could generate significant incremental sales and, therefore, help the company respond effectively to industry conditions. Because of his assessment, this employee begins to consider how he might assist the firm in meeting its goals.

In the second example, an executive senses that her traditional industry must consolidate. By examining her company, this leader determines that her firm's single line of business isn't growing quickly, but this professional also recognizes that because her business has performed better than its competitors, her company could lead an industry reshaping. Thanks to her evaluation, this manager starts to develop a strategy for acquiring other firms.

Knowing your company is a vital component of sensing your timing. Here are some questions that will show you how to broaden and deepen your comprehension of your firm's situation.

- Does your company have multiple lines of business? If so, do these areas provide opportunities for growth? Are these businesses cyclical and, if so, how have economic conditions affected your firm? Who are your company's customers? Does your firm have few clients or are these customers concentrated in one or two industries? What problems do your clients or suppliers face and could these difficulties have negative implications for your business?

- Compared to companies in and outside your industry, how has your firm performed? Are your business' sales and profits growing, declining, or stagnating? How does your firm's inventory velocity compare to that of its competitors? What is your company's return on assets? Is this measure acceptable? How effective is your business in generating cash? Has your firm merged with another company in order to achieve cost savings or has your company acquired businesses that fill gaps in its offerings? Has your company applied technology to its business(es) and, if so, has your firm been successful in these efforts? Has your firm introduced new products or services and, if so, have these offerings generated new growth and earnings? Does your company usually lead the market or is your firm frequently behind the competition?

- What challenges does your company face? Does your firm need to accelerate its growth or improve its earnings or other aspects of its financial performance? Because it confronts new or more agile competitors, does your business need to operate more effectively? Does your company have to improve its efficiency in response to industry conditions? Might your corporate culture impede your firm's progress or might your company's practices endanger your firm's success? How is your business responding to these challenges? Has your company developed and implemented the appropriate strategies and, if so, is your company now positioned to take advantage of future opportunities? How is your firm viewed by your company's customers and employees? How do industry experts view your company and are they optimistic (or not so optimistic) concerning your firm's outlook? What concerns do these analysts have?

- What have you concluded about your company? Do you perceive that your firm will be successful? Or, do you have concerns? Are these serious reservations? Do you see opportunities to assist your firm in improving its offerings or approach, launching new products or services, or expanding to new sectors?

Now let's move on to the next key element of your timing—your performance at your company or business.

ASSESS YOUR PERFORMANCE

Because she works in a dynamic industry and for a successful company, a manager assumes that she's performing well. A colleague believes that his future work will be consistent with his past accomplishments. Based on her evaluation of her track record and how her colleagues view her, an aspiring executive creates a new role for herself.

In these scenarios, business professionals allow their understanding of their performance to influence their thinking or actions, but you don't think it's essential to examine how you're doing. You work in an exciting, high-growth industry, or your company is expanding and, therefore, you probably know enough. Yet, what if you work in a fast-paced industry or for a premier company but you're not considered a top performer? You may pursue a job that you won't get. What if your performance has deteriorated or has even become unacceptable? You may have trouble holding onto your current position or obtaining a new one. Or, what if your assessment of your performance or image doesn't match that of your colleagues or customers? This dichotomy may signify that there's a problem you need to address.

Sensible managers fully evaluate their performance. These professionals recognize that how they're doing and how their industry or company is performing may not correlate. That is to say, these folks realize that if they work in a leading industry or company, they may not share this field's or firm's attributes. These people appreciate that even if they've been a strong performer in the past, they may not have what it takes to excel in the future. Pragmatic individuals also carefully examine their track record and how their colleagues and customers perceive them and, by doing so, these businesspeople begin to sense what fits (or doesn't fit) their abilities. For example, if an engineer has developed visionary products but hasn't managed people effectively, he may not pursue a management position. On the other hand, if an executive determines that her colleagues or customers see her as unmotivated, she may revitalize her attitude before she goes after a new job. Let's go back to the earlier examples and see how assessing your performance can impact your job or business decisions.

In the first example, a manager has evaluated both his relatively new industry and his company. From his assessments, this individual has concluded that he might be able to assist his firm in its overseas expansion, its launch of a new line of business—services—or both these efforts. By examining his performance, this worker determines that he's done well and that his track record includes several notable achievements, including the inauguration of a new product, and this employee also realizes that he's perceived well both within his company and among his industry peers. Because of his evaluation, this professional starts to think about a job change.

The second scenario involves an executive who's examined both her traditional industry and her company. Through her evaluation, this leader has decided that her firm might be able to lead her industry's consolidation. By assessing her performance, this individual concludes that she's been highly effective and that her track record includes far more achievements than failures, and this businessperson also recognizes that she's viewed favorably within her company and throughout her industry. As a result of her analysis, this executive begins to discuss an acquisition strategy with her board of directors.

An in-depth evaluation of how you're doing professionally can enhance your sense of timing. Here are some questions to get you started on your assessment.

- Have you made an effort to learn about your performance? If so, what have you learned? At your company, have you had an annual performance appraisal or other review? If so, what have you learned? Have you recently received a promotion, a raise, or additional responsibilities, or has your company or board given you additional perks, such as a bonus or stock options? If your company doesn't have a formal evaluation process, have you discussed your performance with your supervisor, management, board, business partners, customers, or employees? Have you received positive feedback? Did your reviewers state any concerns or point out areas that need improvement? If you're performing well, what will you do to continue or enhance how you're doing? Are you realizing your full potential? If not, how will you do so? If you're not performing acceptably, what will you do to address your deficiencies? Will you bolster your skills, take corrective action, or both these moves? Or, will you refresh your interest or outlook?

- Overall, how would you evaluate your professional track record? Are there more successes than failures or vice versa? How serious are your defeats and how significant are your achievements? Have you consistently performed well (or not so well)? What are your specific accomplishments? Did your coworkers play a role in your achievements and, if so, how important were your colleagues to your success?

- How are you perceived inside your company—by your board, management, colleagues, and employees? Are you viewed positively? If not, why do others have a negative opinion? Are you unsure of how you're viewed because you're not particularly visible because you don't attend important meetings, present to senior management, participate in corporate projects, or network with your coworkers? How are you perceived outside your company—by your industry, customers, or peers in other companies? Are you unaware of these individuals' views because you don't meet with customers, attend industry events, or otherwise network?

- Can you draw any preliminary conclusions about whether and how you'll reinvent your work? Will you improve your attitude or strengthen your performance and, by doing so, enhance others' perceptions? Or, will you help reshape your business or company and, as a result of this effort, improve your prospects for advancement?

Now you must come to grips with what you think about your job or business.

ASSESS YOUR ATTITUDE
TOWARD YOUR WORK

Even though his industry is exciting, his company is a market leader, and he's a rising star, an employee isn't completely satisfied. On the other hand, even though her industry is growing modestly, her company is performing only adequately, and her performance isn't outstanding, a businessperson is basically content.

Do these scenarios sound familiar? If so, you'll grasp why you need to evaluate how you view your work. Your attitude doesn't always mirror the state of your industry, company, or performance. Moreover, at any point, something else—such as spending more time with your family—may be more important to you than your business or career. Still, you may not be convinced that you have to examine (or reexamine) what you think about your work. Yet, what if you're missing something? You may repress your true feelings about your job or business and, therefore, not realize whether or not you're satisfied with your work. Or, you may convince yourself to spend another year or two doing a job you dislike or running a business that you're bored with.

Sharp professionals fully and honestly evaluate their attitude toward their work and, that way, these people sense their overall satisfaction (or dissatisfaction) with their job or business. In turn, these workers begin to identify whether they might need or want something new. For example, if an employee acknowledges his unhappiness with his position or his desire to move to another area of his company, this person may think about changing jobs. Or, if an entrepreneur recognizes her basic satisfaction with her business but also a need to obtain new clients, she may consider launching additional offerings. By being aware of their attitude toward their work, insightful managers also get a sense of whether or not they're ready to pursue a work reinvention. Now let's return to the previous examples and consider how assessing your attitude toward your work can lead to a career or business reshaping.

In the first example, a manager has evaluated his relatively new industry, successful and expanding company, and his own strong performance. Based on these assessments, this individual is contemplating a job change so that he can participate in his firm's launch of new services. By examining how he views his work, this professional concludes that he'd like a new challenge and that he's ready to go after a new position.

The second scenario involves an executive who's examined her traditional industry, her relatively successful company, and her own outstanding performance. Because of these evaluations, this leader is considering the acquisition of other firms in her industry. Through assessing her attitude toward her work, this professional decides that she wants to transform both her company and industry and that she and her colleagues are prepared to undertake this extensive endeavor.

Understanding your attitude toward your work is critical to your sense of timing. The questions in the next section will guide your assessmen.

- Do you realize whether you're basically satisfied, dissatisfied, or somewhere in between these extremes? (If you typically repress your thoughts about your job or business and, therefore, aren't sure of your attitude toward your work, you may want to answer the following queries.) Are you excited about facing a new project at work? Are you hopeful that you'll receive a promotion or grow your company to become a market leader? Or, are you unhappy, even depressed? Do you dread another day at your job or business? Are you bored or frustrated with what you do? Do you resent a colleague's job success or are you jealous of the area or firm that another individual manages? Have you examined why you envy a coworker's career or a peer's business?

- Do you allow yourself to think about your ideal job or business—the work you might need or want? If you'd like a new challenge, a more visible or faster-paced area, or greater responsibilities, do you allow yourself to contemplate how you might fulfill this goal? Or, do you avoid thinking about your circumstances and, as a result, ignore your preferences and motivations? (As you'll discover in Steps Two and Three, you must acknowledge these factors in order to reinvent.)

- If you think that you might want to make a change in your career or business, how strong is this inclination? Do you think about this work reshaping constantly or only once in a while? If you conclude that you need or want to reinvent your work, do you sense that you (or your employees) are ready to do so? If you're not prepared, what's holding you (or your workers) back?

Now let's synthesize what you've learned through your assessments of your industry, company, performance, and attitude. That way, you'll have a complete sense of your timing.

PULL TOGETHER YOUR SENSE OF TIMING

After moving to an expanding industry, a businessperson discovers that he works for a troubled company. Unaware of how he's perceived, an employee changes areas and, subsequently, has trouble getting along with his new colleagues. An entrepreneur decides to expand her business even though she's tired of running her firm.

If you've had these experiences, you're not alone. Many people aren't fully aware of their situations and, as a result, these individuals make decisions about their work that they later regret. You don't want this to happen (or happen again) to you. Therefore, you'll develop a comprehensive and integrated sense of your timing and, by using this knowledge, you'll be more likely to make the best decisions for you or your business.

In order to prepare to pull together your situational awareness, review your earlier assessments of your industry, company, performance, and attitude. Be sure that you've answered the questions as thoroughly and honestly as possible. Then read the three scenarios that follow. Each paints a complete and integrated picture of a businessperson's sense of timing. From your assessments, you'll select the scenario—1, 2, or 3—that best describes your work situation, but don't expect a perfect match. Identify the sketch that most closely fits where you are in your work. Once you've determined your situation, you'll choose whether to accept your circumstances or take steps to change your situation. In other words, you'll decide whether or not to reinvent your work.

Scenario 1: Basically, you're satisfied with your work.

- Whether your industry is traditional or newer, it's involved in businesses that provide solid, if not outstanding, growth opportunities. Your industry has performed adequately to well. Overall, your industry's challenges don't appear insurmountable and its outlook is good to excellent. You feel comfortable, if not pleased, to be part of your industry.

- Your company has strong lines of business and a diversified customer base. Because your firm has performed acceptably or better, your company stacks up well within your industry and compared to companies outside it. Your firm is positioned to handle its current and future challenges and your company's outlook is generally positive. You think that your firm will be moderately to extremely successful.

- You've received positive feedback about your performance or, if you've gotten negative input, you've determined how you'll improve. Your track record includes significant successes and few failures. You're visible in and outside your company and others perceive you more or less positively.

- You rarely envy your colleagues' careers or businesses. You let yourself think about what you might need or want from your work but, at this point, you're not inclined to make a change.

Scenario 2: You're somewhat satisfied but need or want something more or different.

- Whether your industry is old-line or less established, some or all of its businesses present growth opportunities. Your industry is performing acceptably to well. Most of your industry's challenges aren't overwhelming and your field's outlook is fair to good. You see how your industry could improve.

- Your company has one or two strong lines of business and its customers are concentrated in a couple of industries. Because your firm has performed adequately, your company stacks up fairly well within your industry and compared to firms outside it. Your firm has strategies in place to address its challenges and your business' outlook is generally positive, but you have concerns about whether your business will achieve its goals. You'd like to play a larger or different role in helping your company.

- You've received mostly positive feedback about your performance. Perhaps you've also gotten negative input but you're not sure how to improve. Or, you've received promotions but not as quickly as you wanted. Your track record includes both successes and failures. You're not as visible in or outside your company as you'd like to be or your coworkers perceive that your interest in your work has waned.

- You're sometimes jealous of your colleagues' jobs or businesses. You allow yourself to contemplate your ideal work and, consequently, you have an idea of how you'd like to change your job or business. You're ready to reshape your work.

Scenario 3: You're miserable and need to do something about it.

- Whether your industry is established or brand new, only some or none of its businesses present growth opportunities. Your industry is performing adequately or poorly. Your field's challenges are relatively manageable or insurmountable and its

outlook is fair to poor. In your fast-paced industry, you're struggling to keep up or you recognize that your industry needs to
improve.

- Your company has a few strong lines of business and a somewhat
diversified customer base or your firm doesn't possess these elements. Because your company has performed only adequately or
even poorly, your firm doesn't stack up well within your industry
and compared to companies outside it. Your firm has strategies
that may or may not address its challenges and your company's
outlook is more negative than positive. You have serious concerns whether your business will achieve its goals. You want to
play a larger or different role in helping your company.

- You've received disappointing or negative feedback about your
performance and, in your current situation, you're not able or
willing to improve. Or, you're dissatisfied with your progress or
track record. You're not as visible in or outside your company
as you'd like to be. Your coworkers perceive that you're not
committed or that you're frustrated, bored, or depressed.

- You often envy your colleagues' careers or businesses. When
you let yourself think about it, you realize the work you want.
You're eager to reshape your work.

Which scenario best describes your situation? If you're unsure
which sketch fits your circumstances, see if these guidelines help you
decide. If you work in an industry that's performing poorly but your
company is performing acceptably, Scenario 2 or 3 may fit your circumstances. Conversely, if you work in a firm that's performing mis-
erably in an industry that has a great outlook, Scenario 3 may well be
a match. Wherever you work, if you're not performing well or you're
unhappy, Scenario 3 may define your circumstances. If your situation
lines up with Scenario 2 or 3, you're probably ready to consider how
to reinvent your work, but even if Scenario 1 is a fit, you may want to
read the next section. In it, you'll learn even more about how timing
affects whether and how you'll reinvent. So even if you're basically
content, you may discover that you could increase your satisfaction
by reshaping your work.

APPLY YOUR SENSE OF TIMING

Now let's explore why you might choose one of the reinvention
options you read about in Chapter 1. But don't expect that your circumstances or reasons for selecting a certain alternative will match

precisely with the descriptions below. Obviously, no two human beings are exactly alike. Also don't worry if more than one option fits your situation. As you read this book, you'll refine your thinking so that you'll make the choice that's right for you.

REINVIGORATE YOUR JOB

Your work may reflect the components cited below:

- *Your industry or company.* You're frustrated by something that your industry or company is doing or not doing. You see opportunities to improve how your industry or company operates or how it's perceived.

- *Your performance.* You're sometimes late for work or meetings. You make mistakes that you wouldn't have before.

- *Your attitude toward your work.* You're somewhat satisfied, but you're having trouble concentrating, staying motivated, or getting your work done as quickly as you used to. You'd like to learn something new. You feel that there are gaps in your knowledge. You admire, even envy, people who've solved an important problem and, as a result, gained recognition for their efforts.

If some or most of the above sound like you, here are a couple of reasons you may choose to reinvigorate your job:

- You'd like to improve your performance or your prospects for advancement in your company.

- You want to feel better about your work and how others perceive you.

CHANGE JOBS IN YOUR COMPANY

Your situation may include the following components:

- *Your industry or company.* You're excited about your industry's latest developments or outlook. You're eager to participate in a new business that your company is launching.

- *Your performance.* You believe that in your current position, you've proven yourself. You feel that if you had a different role, you might contribute more to your company. Or, you think that if you worked in a different area, you might do better.

- *Your attitude toward your work.* You're dissatisfied. You feel that you could handle more responsibility. You think that you've learned all there is to know about your work. You're bored.

If some or most of the above describe your timing, here are several reasons you may opt to change jobs within your company:

- You want to be on the cutting edge of your industry. You want to work in the newest, highest-profile, or most exciting areas of your company. You seek a new and greater challenge. Or, you'd like a job that's a better fit for you.

- You're anxious to move on, or you're concerned that if you remain where you are, your attitude and performance might deteriorate.

 ## ENHANCE YOUR BUSINESS' PRODUCTS, SERVICES, OR APPROACH

Your business may embody the components described below:

- *Your industry or company.* You see ways in which your industry can improve its offerings or approach. You hear, see, or sense ways in which your company can improve its internal processes, its products or services, or how it delivers its offerings.

- *Your performance.* Your management, employees, and customers have recognized your innovativeness. Or, they're clamoring for you to make improvements.

- *Your attitude toward your work.* You're basically satisfied but see room for improvement.

If the preceding components illustrate your sense of timing, here are several reasons you may choose to enhance your business:

- You want the business you manage or your company or industry to be the best it can be.

- You expect top-notch performance from yourself. You'd like to keep your people challenged and motivated.

TRANSITION YOUR BUSINESS

Your business' status may include the following components:

- *Your industry or company.* You see your industry or company struggling to adapt to changes in the marketplace. You fear that your company's growth, profitability, or customer service is declining. You're concerned that your business could miss out on opportunities.

- *Your performance.* Your board, management, employees, or customers are disappointed in you. Or, even if others are pleased, you sense that you could be performing better.

- *Your attitude toward your work.* You're not as satisfied as you could be. You're consumed with turning around your situation. You're driven to make your firm the market leader.

If some or most of the above sound familiar, here are reasons that you may elect to transition your business:

- You want to fix problems and take advantage of opportunities.

- You demand first-rate performance from your company. You seek to build a preeminent reputation for your company and possibly yourself.

START A NEW BUSINESS WITHIN YOUR COMPANY

Your circumstances may incorporate the following components:

- *Your industry or company.* You observe an industrywide gap. You recognize that your company has the ability to fill this void.

- *Your performance.* You have a track record of significant successes. You excel at managing people and businesses.

- *Your attitude toward your work.* You're not as satisfied as you'd like to be.

If the preceding statements sound like you, here are a couple of reasons you may choose to pursue starting a new business at your company:

- You seek to produce additional revenues for your company.

- You're eager to create a new venture that capitalizes on your firm's special skill.

Are you convinced about the importance of sensing your timing? It's the gateway to any reinvention. Without it, you won't able to decide whether or not to reinvent your work. If you haven't completed your assessment, I urge you to do so before you start the next chapter. In the meantime, here are stories about two individuals who've applied their sense of timing in order to reinvent their careers and businesses.

LIVE YOUR SENSE OF TIMING

Gregg Engles has a remarkable sense of timing and he's used it to build a multibillion-dollar dairy company.[3] Engles is chairman and chief executive officer of Fortune 500 Suiza Foods Corporation. (In April 2001, Suiza Foods agreed to acquire Dean Foods in a deal valued at $1.5 billion. This transaction is expected to close before the end of 2001. Engles would serve as CEO of the combined firm.) As you'll learn, this executive's sense of timing has guided his reinventions—whether of his career, company, or industry.

Early in his career, this future businessman assessed his attitude toward his work. A chemistry major at Dartmouth College, Engles was going to become a doctor, like his father and three uncles, but in his junior year, his mother died suddenly. As he says, it was a watershed event. Prior to her death, he had doubts about whether a medical career would satisfy his tremendous curiosity about life. From this experience—especially his dealings with a detached medical establishment—he knew that he no longer wanted to pursue medicine. He switched his major, graduating with a degree in economics. After attending Yale's School of Management and graduating from Yale Law School, Engles also recognized that, at least for the near future, he didn't want to be a corporate executive or a lawyer. Instead, he sensed that he wanted to "have ownership, do something creative, and make a tangible difference." As he says of his decision, "Going into a large company or a law firm was fraught with danger for what I wanted to accomplish."

Following several difficult business experiences, Engles assessed his performance and, as a result, redirected his career. After law school and a clerkship for a judge, Engles traveled around the country trying to obtain funding for a business plan that involved airplane time-sharing. In Dallas, he learned that his idea wasn't viable, so he did a three-year stint with an investment firm. Subsequently, he and a colleague founded their own real estate company, but in the mid-1980s, the Texas real estate market collapsed and, as a result, Engles had to clean up his operation and move on.

At this point, this lawyer turned entrepreneur assessed which industry appealed to him and, consequently, decided it was time to jump into a new arena—buyouts in the food industry. During the next several years, this young businessman purchased Reddy Ice and other food companies. In 1993, Engles was interested in acquiring Suiza Dairy of Puerto Rico and, at this time, also met "Tex" Beshears, the former head of Southland Corporation's dairy business. The unlikely duo—the Ivy League–educated Engles and the self-made dairyman—hit it off over a game of golf and Suiza Foods was born. Of that day, Engles says, "I have a good sense of what opportunity is." With Beshears' input, Engles concluded that the dairy industry was ripe for consolidation. During the past six years, the executive has acquired more than 40 regional dairies across the country and, by doing so, Engles has maximized plant and distribution efficiencies and generated substantial cost savings.

Notwithstanding his acquisition activities, Engles also assessed his company and, consequently, recognized it was time to innovate. Thanks to Engles' leadership, Suiza has introduced a host of milk brands. The company also makes coffee whiteners, nonyolk egg products, and specialty milk products, including soy and lactose-free milks. In naming Suiza Foods as the 1999 Processor of the Year, *Dairy Foods* magazine paid tribute to Engles' exceptional sense of timing: "Suiza has undeniably and unalterably changed the course of dairy history."[4]

Like Engles, my sense of timing has led me on a reinvention journey through which I've transformed my career—from corporate employee to entrepreneur to author and speaker—and my business—from communication coach to management consultant.

Over a 13-year period, I assessed (and reassessed) my attitude about my work. During this time, I was a manager at five different companies—Hartford National Bank, Positions, Inc., Citibank, TransWorld, and Frito-Lay—that were involved in four different industries—banking, executive recruiting, transportation, and food. Recognizing that I hadn't found my niche, I searched for an opportunity that fit my talents and interests and, in 1985, I realized a breakthrough. To facilitate my transition from finance to sales, I attended my company's sales training program. On the first day, the instructor said that I, not he, should be teaching the course. After evaluating this professional's view of my abilities, I concluded that it was time to start my own business, which I launched in 1987.

During the next several years, I regularly assessed both my performance and company. By coaching corporate executives and managers on how to communicate effectively, I became proficient in solving my clients' communication problems and helping my customers take advantage of their communication opportunities. As my business grew, I sensed that thanks to my performance, my business was on the right track.

In 1992, a meeting with an executive client led me to reassess again—the industries in which I worked, my company, and my performance. Also present at this event was a management consultant whose latest report projected astronomical growth for my client's business. After listening to this consultant, my client asked my opinion of the report and I told him that I didn't buy it. Angered by my comments, the consultant proceeded to defend his model. Exasperated by his theoretical comments and condescending tone, I interrupted, "Model, schmodel, I'm talking reality." From this experience, I sensed that I was ready for another change. The communication skills that I had been teaching weren't what certain clients wanted from me. Because the energy industry was consolidating and technology companies were scrambling to keep pace with the growing demand for their products and services, firms in these fields needed practical help in showing their managers how to operate as effectively as possible. Based on my assessment, I transitioned my business into consulting and, by doing so, assisted professionals who worked for oil and high-tech companies.

In 1998, after reassessing my attitude anew, I discovered that I was ready for another move. Stay tuned. I'll tell you more in the upcoming chapters.

CHAPTER THREE

STEP TWO

Visualize Your Reinvention

The conviction of your vision is the sine qua non for its achievement.[1]

—MICHAEL USEEM, AUTHOR, DIRECTOR OF THE CENTER FOR LEADERSHIP AND
CHANGE, AND PROFESSOR OF MANAGEMENT, THE WHARTON SCHOOL

How do managers identify the roles they'll be able to perform? Can businesspeople find positions that they truly enjoy? How do employees get jobs that are consistent with what's important to them?

Have you asked yourself these questions? If so, you, like millions of others, want to understand how to obtain work that will ensure your success and satisfaction. Is there a book, course, or computer program that gives the answer? Do businesspeople dream their ideal jobs or businesses, or do employees stumble upon their work and hope for the best? Are managers who discover work that's right for them luckier than most? How do these folks get what you've been looking for?

Individuals who get their ideal work first envision it. Visualizing your reinvention is the foundation for reinventing your work, or as Intel Chairman Andrew Grove points out, you visualize your goal before you "traverse the career equivalent of the valley of death."[2] By completing a comprehensive and objective evaluation of themselves, experienced workers make sure that they're aware of themselves. Even so, these folks don't play psychologist, dwelling on their fears or using complicated behavioral models to analyze their actions. Instead, businesspeople assess what they prefer and what they don't and what interests them and what doesn't. Experienced workers evaluate what enabled them to accomplish their greatest feats and also examine what motivates them, such as wealth, power, prestige, or challenge. Based on their assessment, savvy employees develop a mental image—a visualization—of their reinvented job, business, or both. That is to say, managers and entrepreneurs determine the goal—the destination—of their reinvention journey. Then these people decide how they'll get there—which reinvention option they'll pursue.

But, you may think that developing your ideal is a waste of time. You've found fulfilling jobs online or through executive recruiters or friends. Or, you've developed a viable business by emulating other managers or entrepreneurs. Why should you bother to visualize what you do with the rest of your life? Yet, what if you become dissatisfied with your work? If you're not aware of your preferences, interests, and motivations, you may not be sure what's missing from your current work or what you might want instead. What if you're having trouble performing? If you don't understand your skills, you may not recognize why you're struggling in a particular job or what position might better fit your talents. Or, what if you reinvent your job or business and end up with work you can't perform, don't like, or that's incompatible with your ambitions? You may be sorry that you didn't assess what you're able to do and what's important to you.

Visualizing your reinvention is essential to crafting a picture of the work you need or want. With this image, you'll more likely attain your reinvention goal, perform well, and be satisfied thereafter. You'll pursue work that you (or your people) are able to do. You'll seek a job or business that you (or your workers) are interested in and by which you're inspired. In other words, your reinvention will incorporate your unique talents and motivations and, consequently, won't surprise or disappoint you. You'll also employ your self-assessment as a database that you'll periodically update to reflect changes in your preferences, abilities, and ambitions. Then, if you become dissatisfied, you can use this knowledge about yourself (or your employees) to again reshape your work.

This chapter will show you how to visualize your reinvented job, business, or both. You'll consider your preferences and interests. You'll examine your (or your people's) skills and strengths. You'll analyze what drives you in your work. Pulling the components of your assessment together, you'll decide what your reinvention looks like. You'll also determine which reinvention option will help you reach your ideal. You'll then read about two individuals who've visualized and pursued their work ideals.

ASSESS YOUR PREFERENCES AND INTERESTS

An employee takes a job in strategic planning even though he doesn't enjoy thinking conceptually, while a colleague becomes a salesperson despite her distaste for making cold calls. Because he's passionate about politics, an articulate manager pursues a lobbyist position at his company. An organization that's interested in protecting the environment uses recyclable materials to revamp their products' packaging. Because his hobby is learning about different cultures, an individual teaches his coworkers how to do business in other countries.

These examples portray how workers use (or don't use) their preferences and interests to change their jobs or businesses, but you generally know what you like (or don't like) about your work and you have some sense of what interests you. You enjoy being employed by a large company that can offer you numerous opportunities or you prefer working for a smaller firm that allows you a lot of autonomy. You thrive on being part of a team or you shine when you operate independently. You're interested in turning around troubled businesses or growing new ones or you like developing people who haven't reached their potential. You dislike sitting through meetings, despise making presentations, or hate doing any job that involves numbers. In any case, you probably have sufficient information to reinvent your work.

Yet, what if you're not fully aware of what you dislike? You may take a job or start a business that you're not happy with. For example, you may take a position that involves extensive travel even though you don't like being away from home. Or, you may centralize your business' decision making even though you have an aversion to headquarters calling the shots. What if you're not completely informed about your interests? You may miss a career or business opportunity. For instance, you may fail to investigate a job working for your company's chief technology officer even though you're fascinated by technology. Or, you may decline a chance to launch a new business in your company because you don't realize your curiosity about start-up ventures.

Alert businesspeople perceive what they like and dislike about their work. That way, if these managers aren't satisfied or, because of a change in their situation, they become dissatisfied, they can identify the factors that might be causing their discontent. In turn, if these workers decide to reshape their careers or businesses, they use their knowledge of their preferences to shape their work ideal. These employees and executives are also conscious of what interests them and, as a result, if they want their work to involve this concern or passion, these folks incorporate this factor in their visualization. Let's consider two examples of how an individual and a business use their awareness of their preferences and interests to craft their reinvention goals.

Perhaps you sense it's time to change jobs. In your current position, you basically work alone and used to enjoy this autonomy but, because your company moved most of your colleagues to a different building, you miss the interaction you used to have in the hallways or lunchroom. Your workload has also increased and, therefore, you have to sacrifice time with your family. Whenever you have time, you engage in one of your favorite pastimes—teaching a course at a community college. After assessing your preferences and interests, you may imagine a position in a slower-paced area of your company that lets you work with others and also serve as a trainer. Given your work ideal, you may pursue opportunities in your firm's human resources department.

Or, you perceive the need to change your organization. Your people dislike attending meetings and prefer to communicate informally—by phone, e-mail, or getting together in each other's offices. Many of your workers are also concerned with the healthiness of the products they consume. Based on your assessment, you may envision revamping your firm's approach by eliminating long meetings and making your communication more casual. You may also redesign your business' food products so that these items contain less fat, sodium, or additives.

By this point, no doubt, you grasp why assessing your preferences and interests is a logical move. With this analysis, you'll begin shaping your work ideal. Here are several questions to get you started in your evaluation.

- What do you enjoy about work? Do you like leading new projects or task forces or do you prefer being a participant? Are you excited by the chance to present to senior management, customers, or an industry group? Do you delight in solving problems? Are you partial to leading, managing, or mentoring others, or do you relish operating as an individual performer? Are you attracted to large organizations or smaller firms? Are you inclined to manage an established business or is innovating, taking a risk, or starting a new business what you're keen on? Do you enjoy overcoming seemingly insurmountable challenges or are you more comfortable maintaining the status quo?

- What do you dislike about work? Do you detest attending meetings? Are you frustrated by bureaucratic processes or slow-moving corporate cultures? Do you loathe managers and executives who don't face and resolve their problems or don't recognize and seize opportunities? Is working 18-hour days a schedule you abhor? Do you dislike the lack of diversity in your company?

- Do you have interests that affect (or could affect) your work? Would you welcome the chance to travel or live abroad? Do you desire to learn new skills—another language, the hottest technology, or the latest approach to strategic planning? Are you thinking of incorporating a hobby or favorite pastime, such as teaching or mentoring, into your work?

Now let's move on to the second component of your visualization—how you'll perform your work ideal.

ASSESS YOUR SKILLS AND STRENGTHS

An employee doesn't know whether she'll be able to perform her ideal position. Having established a goal of launching a new line, a leader isn't sure that his people will be capable of fulfilling this objective. Based on her assessment of her people's skills, an entrepreneur is confident that her employees will be able to enhance her firm's offerings. A businessperson's ideal job incorporates his best skill, which is also one of his strengths.

These scenarios demonstrate how individuals use (or don't use) their skills to craft their reinvention ideals, but you're pretty clear about your skills and strengths or innate talents and, therefore, don't think you need to assess your abilities. For the most part, you realize why you've accomplished what you have. You understand finance and accounting. You're able to think conceptually. You're capable of managing people, businesses, or both. You communicate effectively. Or, you sense why the business you manage has attained what it has. Your people apply technology effectively, operate efficiently, or satisfy your firm's customers. Your workers are resourceful and agile—getting new offerings to market before the competition, discovering new uses for existing products, or spotting trends and taking advantage of them.

Yet, what if you're not sure whether your skills are also your strengths and, therefore, your best abilities or competitive edge? For example, you may have a solid financial skill because you studied accounting, finance, and statistics in school and you've used these disciplines in your job or business. Even so, your financial skill may not be among your strengths because you have to work hard to use this capability, you don't enjoy using it, or it doesn't come naturally to you. In contrast, you may find it relatively easy to utilize your communication skill because you enjoy speaking, you have an inherent capacity to communicate well, or both. If through training and experience you've developed and honed this innate talent, communication has become both your strength and skill. On the other hand, if you have a strength but haven't applied it—you have a flair for marketing but don't use it at work—this inherent capability won't become one of your skills.

What if you're mistaken about which skills and strengths enabled you (or your business) to achieve what you have? Because you sold a new line of products to your firm's customers, you may think that you're inventive, but if your company's research and development department created these items, you may have been successful because of your sales ability. Similarly, if your business expanded globally and you attribute this achievement to your firm's products or services, you may be overlooking your organization's knack for adapting to different cultures.

Or, what if your lack of awareness about your skills and strengths leads you to create a reinvention goal that doesn't correspond to your (or your people's) abilities and, as a result, you (or your workers) can't perform your ideal job or business? You may regret that you didn't fully and objectively examine your (or your employees') talents.

Assessing your abilities will help you discover which of your skills are also your (or your people's) strengths. In all probability, you (or your workers) employed these skill-strengths—your competitive edge—to bring about your most significant achievements. Using this awareness about yourself (or your employees), you'll craft a reinvention goal that embodies your capabilities and, as a result, you (or your business) will likely attain this ideal and perform well thereafter. Let's look at examples of how an individual and a business carry out their assessments.

Maybe you're a manager who's not satisfied with your work. Thanks to a recent corporate reorganization, you don't find your current position as challenging as your previous role and, consequently, you're contemplating a job change. To visualize your ideal job and be sure that you'll be able to perform this role, you evaluate your strengths and skills. You possess financial know-how and the ability to communicate, but because you view numbers as a necessary evil and don't enjoy presenting, your financial and communication skills aren't your strengths. In contrast, two of your strengths—resourcefulness and negotiating—are also your skills, and you've used these skill-strengths or competitive edge to accomplish your most significant achievements—closing major global deals. You'll make sure that your ideal position embodies these skill-strengths.

Perhaps you're basically satisfied with the business you run but think that your firm could improve its performance and, consequently, you're thinking about enhancing your firm's offerings and approach. To develop a picture of your goal and ensure that your people will be capable of fulfilling this objective, you assess your organization's abilities. Your sales and marketing team's skill-strengths include ingenuity and communication, and these workers have used this competitive edge to develop new products and ways of delivering these items. Your technical staff possesses an analytical skill-strength and has employed this ability to streamline your firm's manufacturing process. You conclude that your company's collective talents will help you attain your reinvention aim.

The following questions will guide you as you examine your abilities. Before you answer these queries, briefly review your track record or your business' or company's performance (Step One) and make a list of your (or your business' or company's) most significant achievements. You'll use these accomplishments to help you pinpoint your skill-strengths or competitive edge.

- What are the skills that you've developed through your education, management training, experience, or a combination of these elements? Do you understand finance and accounting? Are you able to analyze quantitatively? Are you knowledgeable about technology and how to apply it? Can you think conceptually about business situations? Do you know how to devise new products, services, or approaches? Can you develop a strategy? Do you know how to market your business' offerings? Have you attended training programs and used your knowhow? Do you have experience managing businesses or organizations? If so, how effective have you been according to the feedback you've received? Are you a strong communicator, able to persuade others to adopt your ideas or recommendations? Have you presented to your company's senior management or board of directors, security analysts, or regulatory authorities?

If so, how well did you perform? Have you worked with people from diverse backgrounds or cultures? Write down your strongest skills.

- What are your strengths or innate talents? Do you possess an aptitude for analyzing situations? Are you a financial whiz? Do you have a knack for selling products, services, or ideas? Are you able to discern trends or opportunities before anyone else? Does your intuition guide you in making decisions and acting on them? Are you able to perceive relationships that your colleagues fail to see? Do you have a natural talent for managing businesses, people, or both? List your greatest strengths.

- If you have inherent abilities, have you applied them in your work? Have any of your strengths also become your skills or competitive edge? Have you employed these talents to bring about your greatest achievements? Are you using your best skills and strengths or competitive edge in your current position? If not, have you determined why this is the case? Is it possible that your present job doesn't fit your talents? In any event, write down your skill-strengths.

- What are your business' collective skills? Do your workers have capabilities in finance, marketing, sales, technology, and operations? How effectively does your organization manage its operations, finances, customer relationships, and employees? List your business' best skills.

- What are your business' collective strengths? Do your people appear to have a knack for something—satisfying your customers, achieving growth, delivering returns on investment, or innovating new products or services? Are individuals in your firm technologically savvy? Does your company have a flair for acquiring or partnering with other firms? Write down your business' greatest strengths.

- Have your people's innate talents become your business' collective skill-strengths or competitive edge? Has your organization used these talents to accomplish your most important achievements? If so, how have you parlayed your abilities? List your workers' skill-strengths.

Now that you understand how your awareness of your abilities will help you create your work ideal, you need to evaluate what motivates you to pursue this goal.

ASSESS YOUR MOTIVATIONS

An executive values money and financial security, while a peer relishes the power of managing a division within his company, being his own boss, or serving as a captain of industry. A leader thrives on being recognized for her accomplishments by her peers, her management, the who's who of business, or even the media. A worker is motivated by challenge or realizing his potential, while a colleague is drawn to helping others or making the world a better place. An employee is committed to spending time with his family or pursuing his hobbies. An organization is dedicated to generating revenues, increasing market share, or improving profitability, efficiency, or effectiveness. A firm exists to deliver the highest level of quality or customer satisfaction. A group is inspired to turn its company into a technological leader or provider of leading-edge products and services, while a team is galvanized by the publicity it receives.

These examples show why people and organizations choose (or remain in) their jobs or businesses, but you perceive what drives you. Why should you analyze your ambitions? Yet, what if you haven't been objective or totally honest about what motivates you or your workers? A reinvention ideal that incorporates this flawed information won't reflect your (or your people's) true motivations and, as a result, you may not be satisfied with your reinvented job or business. For example, do you claim that you're predisposed to helping others because the truth—you're eager to build your reputation or you're driven by money—sounds less honorable? Or, does your business assert that it's dedicated to satisfying its customers even though your organization doesn't really care about its clients or your people are primarily motivated by public recognition?

Or, what if you've overlooked key factors that drive you or your employees? If you're dissatisfied with your job or business but don't complete a thorough assessment of your or your workers' ambitions, you may not recognize what's missing from your work. Without this information, you may not develop an ideal that fits what's important to you and, therefore, you (or your employees) may remain discontent. For example, if you don't fully analyze your motivations, you may assume that money is the be-all and end-all of your existence, but if you're making a lot of money and you're still unhappy with your job, you need to reassess what motivates you. By doing so, you may discover that you also seek challenge. With this awareness, you may choose to reinvigorate your current job or change to another position within your company. Conversely, if you don't thoroughly assess your people's ambitions, you may believe that your workers are driven by challenge, but if your employees aren't performing well and your business isn't meeting its targets, you have to reevaluate what drives these folks. When you do, you may learn that these individuals are also inspired by monetary rewards. Using this knowledge, you may decide to expand your firm's offerings and provide your people with financial incentives to accomplish this aim.

Aware employees and executives pay close attention to what leads them to make decisions about their work and they also stay alert to changes in their ambitions. To be certain that their evaluations are accurate, sharp businesspeople complete an objective and thorough examination of their (or their people's) motivations. That is to say, these folks are candid with themselves and they evaluate every factor that might be important in their career choices. Let's look at two examples of how an individual and a business assess their motivations.

In the past, you've chosen jobs because they challenge you but, now that you have children, you're more concerned with earning enough money to send your offspring to college and provide for your retirement. Through your assessment, you conclude that money and financial security have become more important to you than being challenged. By coming to grips with your motivation, you may decide to pursue a higher-paying position even if this job isn't as demanding as your current assignment.

Maybe you manage a business that's done well but, recently, you and your workers have identified ways to improve your firm's services. Based on an objective and complete evaluation, you determine that because you and your team are stimulated by delighting your customers, you may opt to enhance your offerings and, by doing so, improve both your clients' and employees' satisfaction.

Evaluating what motivates you is essential to creating your visualization. As you'll learn in Chapter 4, you must verify that both your (or your business') skill-strengths and what's important to you (or your people) match your ideal. If you incorporate only the former and exclude the latter, you'll craft an image that won't fit and, therefore, won't please you or your workers.

The following questions will assist you in your assessment.

- What propels you to act? Is it primarily one factor or a combination of factors? Throughout your career, have these elements remained fairly constant or have these factors changed?, If so, do you understand why? Are you motivated by money, power, or fame? Does seeking a new challenge or realizing your potential move you? Is achieving financial security your sine qua non? Does helping others or volunteering in your community inspire you? Do your values, such as integrity, humility, or fairness, or your personal objectives, such as learning new things or meeting new people, lead you? Are you determined to have a positive impact on your hometown or possibly the world? Does your commitment to your family or outside interests strongly influence your work decisions and actions? Have you been honest with yourself? Have you completed a thorough assessment?

- What fires up your employees? Is there one principal element or a combination of them? Have these factors remained relatively constant or has there been a change? Do one or more of the following induce your workers to excel: generating revenues, expanding market share, increasing earnings, improving operational efficiency or effectiveness, maximizing quality or customer satisfaction, or becoming (or remaining) the market leader? Is your organization excited about developing new technologies and applying them or innovating new products or services? Do public recognition and rewards rouse you and your team? Have you been objective and is your evaluation complete?

Now let's synthesize what you've learned through the preceding assessments. You'll utilize what you've learned about what you're able to do—your strengths and skills—and what's important to you—your preferences, interests, and motivations—to develop an integrated picture of your work ideal. Because your visualization is based on an objective and inclusive assessment, you'll be confident that your goal fits you (or your people) and, consequently, you (or your people) will be capable of performing this ideal work. In turn, you (or your employees) will enjoy this job or business.

PULL TOGETHER YOUR VISUALIZATION

Can you imagine changing positions only to discover that your work includes elements that you intensely dislike? Would you stay in a role that's not consistent with your motivations? How would you perform a job that you're not qualified to do? Could your business fail if its success depends on skills that your people don't have? Would managers who don't like structure do well in a company that's highly regimented? Why would employees remain with a firm that doesn't appreciate their need for challenge, money, or recognition?

You see the point of these questions. Your visualization must integrate all the information you've learned through your evaluation. Assuming you're ready, let's get started. First, review the assessments you've completed. Be sure that you've fully and honestly answered the questions. If you haven't or if you need to revise your assessments, do so before you move on.

Next, create a picture of your ideal job or business. When you establish your reinvention objective, you identify what your (or your business') success and satisfaction will look like and, therefore, you'll be able to measure whether your reinvented work is successful and satisfying as you define these terms. In a word, you'll know success and satisfaction when you see them.

The examples that follow will show you how to pull together your visualization, but there's a caveat. Understandably, your circumstances won't be exactly the same as those described and, therefore, your picture of your reinvented work won't perfectly match the ideal presented. With this admonition in mind, let's move on.

Let's say that you're a manager in your company. You've evaluated your preferences and your interests. From your assessment, you've determined that you enjoy working for a large company that can afford you a wide range of opportunities, and you also prefer to work in a new or a high-growth business. But, you don't like managing an existing business that has limited growth opportunities. Your principal interests are traveling and learning new languages.

You've examined your skills and your strengths. From your analysis, you've determined that your natural talents are managing people and discerning and pursuing opportunities. Because you've used your strengths throughout your career, these innate abilities are also your best skills. Through your review of your most important achievements and through feedback you've obtained from your colleagues, management, and customers, you've concluded that these two skill-strengths constitute your competitive edge.

You've also considered your motivations. You value power and, therefore, you're driven to manage large organizations. You acknowledge that you thrive on being recognized by your peers, management, and customers, but spending time with your family is also important to you. Sometimes, you worry whether you'll be able to juggle your professional and personal lives.

From your comprehensive assessment, you may imagine starting up and growing a new global business within your company. Doing so would incorporate your preferences (working in a new business in a large company) and your interests (traveling and learning new languages) and avoid what you dislike (maintaining the status quo). Based on your evaluation of what you're able to do (managing people and capitalizing on opportunities), you believe that your ideal is a logical career move. Perceiving what's important to you (power and recognition), you sense that your goal will be consistent with much of what drives you.

Overall, you've been objective about yourself. Because you've attributed your achievements to the combined efforts of you and your people, you've neither overestimated nor underrated your accomplishments or capabilities. You've viewed a past achievement—starting and growing a small business—as an important accomplishment even if ultimately you seek to run a larger operation. You've also sought feedback from others concerning your talents.

Perhaps the most significant concern about your visualization relates to your inclination to balance your professional and personal lives. Although your reinvention ideal is consistent with your ambitions for power and recognition, your new work may lead you to make a trade-off that you might not like. That is to say, you may have to work when you'd rather spend time with your family. If you won't want to make this compromise, you may need to modify your goal.

Or, let's assume that as a division leader, you've examined your people's preferences and interests. Based on this assessment, you've decided that your employees like organizing their work into projects and using a team approach to complete these endeavors. Your employees also enjoy brainstorming, but you and your workers dislike conventional solutions. You and they hold a common interest publishing a newsletter for your customers.

You've evaluated your collective skills and strengths. Through this assessment, you've concluded that you and your team are naturally resourceful and able to think conceptually. Because you and your folks have consistently used these strengths, these inherent capabilities are also your strongest skills. From carefully examining your business' most significant accomplishments, you've decided that these two skill-strengths constitute your firm's competitive edge.

You've also considered your collective ambitions. As a group, you're stimulated by challenge, but you're also motivated by money. In other words, you and your workers are driven to achieve by the thrill of doing so as well as the associated financial rewards.

Based on your thorough assessment, you may envision developing a new line of offerings for your firm. This effort would incorporate your preferences (working as a team on projects and brainstorming) and your common interest (you'll solicit ideas through your newsletter) and avoid what you dislike (conventional solutions). Through your examination of your collective talents (resourcefulness and thinking conceptually), you think that your goal makes sense for your organization. Because building a new line would provide a challenge and offer financial rewards for achieving certain growth targets, you perceive that your aim fits your employees' motivations.

In general, you've been objective. You haven't overvalued or underestimated your people's achievements or the abilities they used to accomplish these feats. Because you've also sought input from several of your clients, you've assessed your people impartially. A potential obstacle associated with your goal involves how your people will balance their ambitions. If these workers become preoccupied with challenging themselves—engaging in too many brainstorming sessions—they may not attain the financial rewards that are associated with the new line as quickly as they might have otherwise. Conversely, if these employees become too focused on getting this line to market and reaping the related financial rewards, they may later conclude that their project didn't adequately challenge them and, therefore, wasn't satisfying. As the manager of this area, you'll encourage your people to manage their motivations so that they'll fulfill both ambitions.

Let's move on to how you'll implement your goal.

APPLY YOUR VISUALIZATION

Now it's time to examine how the components of your visualization line up with various reinvention options. You'll consider why you might choose a particular option to attain your objectives. Because the components listed under each option aren't all-encompassing, the components of your assessments may not match exactly with the descriptions below. You may find that more than one option correlates with your ideal and, if this happens, don't worry. In Chapter 4, you'll reexamine your reinvention destination and, by doing so, you'll narrow down the options that are most likely to help you. As a result, you may choose a different alternative to reach your goal.

 ### REINVIGORATE YOUR JOB

Your visualization may include the following components:

- *Your preferences and interests.* Basically, you like your job, department, or both. You enjoy your colleagues. You relish participating in special projects. You dislike adjusting to a new department or colleagues. You're interested in learning new things.

- *Your skills and strengths*. You have the skills necessary to do your job. You want or need to improve your skills. You have a strength that you'd like to become a skill. Making improvements or working well with others is your competitive edge.

- *Your motivations*. Status matters to you. You're excited by new challenges. You don't want a job that results in your spending less time with your family or on your hobbies.

If the above sounds like your situation, here are a couple of reasons you may choose to reinvigorate your job:

- You'd like to keep the job you have.

- You want to make a modest change that will help you improve your performance, learn something new, enhance a business, or a combination of these elements.

 ## CHANGE JOBS IN YOUR COMPANY

Your ideal work may incorporate the components cited below:

- *Your preferences and interests*. You like some aspects of your job but dislike others. Some of what you like is absent. Your preferences have changed. You're interested in learning new things or working with different colleagues or customers.

- *Your skills and strengths*. You've developed and applied the skills needed to do your job. You have the innate talent to do a different job. You've demonstrated your competitive edge and you'd like to use it in a new area.

- *Your motivations*. Factors that have been important to you, such as money, power, or recognition, still matter, but now you're moved to seek a new challenge. You're inclined to pursue work that allows you to have a personal life. Or, you accept that you might have to make compromises that could negatively impact your personal life.

If the preceding elements describe your circumstances, here are some reasons you may elect to change jobs:

- You've performed well (or relatively so) where you are.

- You seek to make a substantial change in your work so that you'll realize your full potential or satisfy your inclination for a better work-life balance.

ENHANCE YOUR BUSINESS' OFFERINGS OR APPROACH

Your reinvention goal may be based upon the following components:

- *Your preferences and interests.* You and your colleagues like improving your company's offerings or processes. You dislike not responding quickly to your customers or competitors. You're interested in applying something you've observed through your outside activities.

- *Your skills and strengths.* Your organization's collective skills have enabled your business to achieve its objectives. Your business will continue to parlay its competitive edge. You and your colleagues could use your skills in new ways. Your organization could turn a collective strength into a skill.

- *Your motivations.* Your business is driven to maximize quality, performance, or customer satisfaction or become (or remain) the market leader. Your organization is stimulated by change.

If some or most of the above sound familiar, here are a couple of reasons you may opt to enhance your firm:

- Overall, your business is performing acceptably to well.

- You want to make one or more moderate changes that will allow your business to maintain its status or elevate it.

TRANSITION YOUR BUSINESS

Your visualization may include the components described below:

- *Your preferences and interests.* Your organization likes fixing its problems or taking advantage of its opportunities. You and your colleagues take pleasure in innovating. You or your people dislike procrastinating.

- *Your skills and strengths.* Your business has the collective skills needed to address its problems or pursue its opportunities.

Your organization has the inherent talents to attain its goals. Your business' competitive edge is being able to adapt.

- *Your motivations.* You and your colleagues are driven to become the best you can be. Being recognized as a premier firm rouses your organization.

If the preceding factors resemble your situation, here are some reasons you may choose to transition your business:

- You expect more from your business.

- To meet your expectations, you need to make substantial changes, such as overhauling your approach or augmenting your offerings.

START A NEW BUSINESS WITHIN YOUR COMPANY

You've developed a picture of your ideal work that may incorporate the following components:

- *Your preferences and interests.* Your organization prefers innovating and taking risks. You and your colleagues dislike maintaining the status quo.

- *Your skills and strengths.* You or your colleagues have demonstrated an aptitude for launching new businesses. Your organization has the innate ability to initiate a new venture. Your business' competitive edge is moving quickly and accurately.

- *Your motivations.* Becoming a market or global leader induces your business to excel. Public recognition and financial rewards energize you or your colleagues.

If most of the above components describe your ideal, here are some reasons you may want to start a new business at your firm:

- Your business has met its goals but wants to pursue a new direction.

- You seek to capitalize on your business' competitive edge.

Do you grasp that creating an image of your work is critical? It's the foundation of any reinvention. If you haven't shaped your ideal, you'll want to do so before you start the next chapter. In the meantime, here are stories about two individuals who visualized their ideal work and then pursued it.

LIVE YOUR VISUALIZATION

Paula Madison continually visualizes her ideal work and, in turn, pursues her aspirations aggressively.[3] Even as a child, she believed in the power of setting a goal and going after it, and today she acknowledges, "It never dawned on me that I'd be anything other than what I've become." Madison is the president and general manager of NBC's Los Angeles–based affiliate, KNBC. After nearly two decades in television news, she continues to establish challenging objectives, both for herself and the businesses she manages.

This broadcasting executive has reinvented her work several times. Majoring in history and black studies at Vassar, she intended to open an alternative school in Harlem where she grew up. But after a fateful nudge—she replaced a friend at a newspaper—she became a reporter. Subsequently, she has reinvented again, each time taking on greater responsibilities and moving to larger media markets—whether as a newspaper editor, television news director, or station manager.

Early on, Madison evaluated what motivated her. As a child growing up in Harlem in the 1950s and 1960s, she didn't know what career she'd pursue, but she did think that her indigent circumstances were temporary—a bump in the road. She believed that education was her ticket to success. "I made up my mind that I'd go to Cardinal Spellman High School, one of the best schools in the city, and on to an excellent college," she says. What she saw on local television provided a second incentive. She was outraged by pictures of her neighborhood—black people in handcuffs—and ever since, the disparity between what she lived and the media's portrayal of her childhood home has inspired her to correct this gross misrepresentation, show that good things are happening, and give people a means to improve their lives. During her decade at New York City's WNBC-TV, she pioneered numerous reports that demonstrated her commitment to social change.

From the beginning of her career, Madison has also evaluated her abilities objectively. "I'm always asking people questions. Tell me about this or that. I'm absorbing. I call it osmosis," she says. Over time, by applying her strengths, they've become her best skills—her competitive edge. For example, while news director at KOTV-TV in Tulsa, she used her inquisitiveness to catapult her station to the number one spot. Driving down a highway, she noticed that the school bus in front of her was swerving. "That person's drunk," she said to herself. Following up her observation with a thorough investigation, she discovered that many of the city's bus drivers had criminal records. In the early 1980s, she parlayed another key talent, her organizational skills, to transition from newspaper to television management and, by doing so, she's established premier newscasts at different stations and has won numerous awards.

Daily, Madison pursues her mission—"make the world right, to fix things"—with integrity. She knows that as long as African-Americans are portrayed primarily as criminals and viewers are tantalized but not educated or helped, she'll continue her work.

Like Madison, I've reinvented my work several times. On each occasion, I've created an image of my ideal career and then pursued it. You might say that I'm a perpetual visualizer.

After several jobs at different companies in various industries, I examined my preferences. Belatedly, I concluded that I disliked working for a large company. From my few solo experiences—training sales personnel and calling on customers—I realized that I liked operating independently.

Prior to starting my own business in 1987, I hadn't fully evaluated my skills and, therefore, didn't really value my talents. As a result, I worked hard to develop skills that required specialized training, such finance or accounting. Looking back, I now recognize that many of my achievements reflected my abilities and, therefore, pointed to my potential. For example, at 26, I regularly advised my boss, a senior executive, on what to say when testifying before Congress, speaking before industry analysts, and meeting with his management colleagues. Since being on my own, I've fully and objectively examined my abilities. By doing so, I've learned that my strengths—communicating, logical thinking, and resourcefulness—have become my best skills—my competitive edge. In 1992, after assessing my achievements as an entrepreneur and communication coach and the talents I employed to accomplish these feats, I decided to reinvent my business. I became a consultant who helps corporate business units operate more effectively.

I've also evaluated what motivates me. During the early years of my business, I was gratified by helping people meet their challenges, but as my work evolved, I was inspired by the recognition I received and the money I earned. More recently, I've discovered that I yearn to have a greater impact on the workplace and also receive recognition on a larger scale. Based on my latest visualization, I'm again reinventing my work, this time as a speaker and media personality. My self-awareness—what's important to me and what I'm able to do—guides me in my journey.

CHAPTER FOUR

STEP THREE

Verify Your Ideal

A mushy mission statement is an indication that a
company doesn't know where it's going.[1]

—JACK TROUT, AUTHOR, SPEAKER, AND BUSINESS STRATEGIST

Why can't some people perform their dream jobs and why are others unhappy in their ideal positions? Can managers ensure that their talents and ambitions line up with the skills and motivations associated with their ideal work?

Have you asked yourself these questions? If so, you're on the right track. Achieving success and satisfaction as you define these terms will require more than visualizing your reinvention. Even businesses that have well-crafted mission statements can fail to fulfill their objectives. Throughout your reinvention journey, you want to be confident that you're pursuing work that truly reflects what you're able to do and what matters to you.

Savvy workers everywhere verify their ideals. These experienced workers validate that the work they seek corresponds with their (or their employees') abilities and ambitions. By confirming that there's a match, these individuals sign off on their goals and give themselves the go-ahead for their reinvention journeys. On the other hand, if there isn't a close correlation, these managers can abandon their reinvention or reshape their goal. Or, these folks can improve this pairing by bolstering their skills or making trade-offs in what's important to them. The prudent also plan how they'll make such adjustments and consider the potential downsides of their work change.

Even so, you're not convinced that this step is really necessary. You've completed visualizing your reinvention, and to you, verifying your path is overkill. Besides, you know what your reinvented work will look like and you're fairly confident that you'll attain your goal. Most likely, you won't benefit by undertaking this step. Yet, what if you're not able to perform your dream job? You may have miscalculated the skills necessary for your work ideal. What if you're dissatisfied with your new role or business improvement? You may have misjudged the motivations associated with individuals who go after particular positions or managers who engage in certain business revamps. What if you're disappointed with the results of your work change? You may regret that you were unwilling to improve your abilities or make adjustments in your personal life. Or, what if you're unpleasantly surprised? You may wish that you had explored the downsides of your reinvention.

Successful professionals confirm that they possess the talents required by their ideal jobs or businesses. The sensible also make certain that their reinvented work incorporates what's important to them. Through this verification, managers determine whether or not their abilities and motivations correspond with those typically associated with their work ideal. If there's not a match, these individuals can abandon their ideal. Conversely, if there's a correlation, these folks can proceed with their reinvention. Or, if their match isn't close, these employees can revise their goal or make adjustments. To complete their evaluations, these leaders ensure their preparedness. That is to say, these people make plans to complete any needed adjustments and also anticipate the downsides of their career or business reshaping.

This chapter will show you how to check the ideal you developed in Chapter 3. In contrast to the previous step in which you used information about yourself or your business to craft a goal, you'll now begin with this objective and work backward and, by doing so, you'll find out whether (or not) your talents and motivations correspond to your aim. You'll make sure that your abilities match those essential to your ideal work. You'll verify that your ambitions and the motivations of people who engage in your imagined job or business line up. Bringing together what you discover, you'll decide whether (or not) to proceed with your reinvention or whether to revise your goal. If you think that there could be a closer correlation, you may opt to enhance your abilities or make personal compromises. In turn, you'll ensure your preparedness by planning such improvements or trade-offs and also foreseeing the potential downsides of your reinvention. You'll next consider how to apply your certified ideal. You'll choose the reinvention option that most closely describes your situation and reasons for reinventing. You'll then read about two individuals who've verified their ideals and successfully pursued them.

Let's start by confirming that your (or your people's) abilities match those that are connected with your ideal job or business.

VALIDATE YOUR SKILLS AND STRENGTHS

Thinking that he understands the talents necessary to perform a particular role, an executive obtains the position he wants but quickly discovers that he's unable to carry out his new responsibilities. Because she's not aware of her skill-strengths, a worker fails to get the position she sought. Having decided to introduce new offerings, a business owner is disappointed when his people can't fulfill this objective. A leader who tries to establish a new venture within her company is unsuccessful because her employees don't possess the competitive edge she sought to capitalize on.

These scenarios illustrate how individuals and businesses don't reach their work ideals because they don't have the required talents. Even so, you're not particularly concerned. Based on the assessment you completed in the previous chapter, you've concluded that you have the talents necessary for your ideal job. Maybe you have a flair for something, such as finance, selling, or managing people, and you've developed your innate abilities through your education and experience. Consequently, you think that you're ready to go after the job you've dreamed about. Perhaps you presume that your workers have the talents needed to enhance your firm's offerings and approach and, therefore, you assume that your company will achieve its goals. You don't have to reexamine your (or your people's) abilities.

Yet, what if your analysis of the skills and strengths that are critical to your ideal work isn't complete or fully accurate? You may have underestimated the abilities necessary for your reinvented job or business. For example, if you possess the talents of a business strategist, you may presume that you could become one of your company's executives. However, an executive also has to have experience in leading people. If you've served on project teams in which you've addressed your company's difficulties, you may believe that you're able to lead a project, but such a role requires more than an ability to solve problems. A project leader also has to be capable of managing others. If your business has a knack for enhancing its offerings, you may assume that your organization has the skills to start a new line. But to develop new offerings, your employees also have to understand how to innovate. Or, if your business has demonstrated its ability to introduce new products or services, you may think that you'll be able to start a new venture. However, this undertaking also demands the ability to take and manage risk.

Or, what if you're not positive of your (or your business') best skill-strengths or competitive edge? You may be overestimating your (or your workers') talents. Maybe you believe that your strongest skills are discerning opportunities and pursuing them, but because your manager has a remarkable facility for obtaining new business, your abilities may not be as strong as you think they are. Perhaps you surmise that your organization's competitive edge involves developing and selling new technologies, but because your firm partners with the company that actually creates the new hardware or software, your people's talents may not include innovating.

Before they commence their reinventions, astute businesspeople identify the skills and strengths that are needed to perform—if not excel at—their dream jobs or in their ideal businesses. Through their evaluation, these people pinpoint the abilities associated with their desired work and also make sure that they fully and accurately understand their own skills and strengths. In turn, these managers confirm whether or not their talents correspond with those required by their ideal work. If these individuals discover that there isn't a match, they may choose to abandon their aim or they may decide to revise their objective or improve their abilities so that their skills will be consistent with those essential for their goal. In any event, by verifying their talents, workers gain confidence about their reinvention decisions. Let's consider some examples of how individuals and businesses validate their skills and strengths.

Maybe you're an employee who wants to rejuvenate your interest in your work. Because you aren't ready to move to another area of your company, you're thinking about leading a project. To be sure that you understand your work ideal, you examine the skills and strengths necessary to handle this task. An individual who's overseeing a project must be able to manage people and communicate effectively. To verify that your abilities line up with those related to your goal, you reassess your skills and strengths. You have solid financial and analytical skills and, because you regularly use these abilities, these talents are also your strengths. But one of your innate talents, managing people, isn't a skill because you don't have experience supervising. Based on your evaluation, you conclude that at this point, your talents don't line up with those associated with your ideal. Consequently, you decide to participate in—not lead—a project.

Perhaps you're a manager who'd like a new challenge. You work in planning, but you'd like to change areas and move into sales. To fully comprehend your desired work, you assess the skills and strengths necessary for the sales position you'd like to obtain. A sales representative must be able to communicate effectively and have a knack—if not a skill-strength—for selling. To confirm that your abilities correlate with those connected with your dream job, you reevaluate your skills and strengths. You have outstanding financial and analytical skills that, because of your work, are also your strengths. By regularly presenting to your company's senior management and persuading them to accept your recommendations, you've developed and honed two innate talents—communication and selling—and as a result, these strengths have become skills. Through your assessment, you determine that your abilities correlate well with those needed to excel at your ideal job. But as you'll learn later in this chapter, if you need to reposition how your colleagues view you, you may also need to be resourceful.

Let's say that even though you're a successful entrepreneur, you'd like to improve your firm's approach. After examining the talents necessary to enhance your business, you conclude that this effort will require communication skills to obtain input from your suppliers and customers, analytical skills to reengineer your company's processes, and resourcefulness in order to make the required changes as efficiently and effectively as possible. To be certain that your talents fit this objective, you reassess your organization's collective abilities. Your employees who are involved in operations possess sound analytical and managerial skills, which, over time, have become their strengths. Your sales force has skill-strengths in selling and communicating. Your greatest talent is your resourcefulness. Based on your examination, you decide that you and your people are ready to take your firm to the next level.

Maybe you're the leader of a large division in your company, and at this point, you want to inaugurate a new service. By assessing the capabilities needed to launch a new offering, you conclude that this endeavor will demand marketing know-how—a talent for spotting and going after opportunities. To validate that your workers' abilities correspond to those typically associated with this effort, you reexamine your collective talents and based on your division's most significant achievement—introducing several successful products—you determine that your people's competitive edge is discerning and pursuing possibilities. Through your evaluation, you conclude your team has demonstrated the necessary talents and, therefore, you choose to proceed with your reinvention.

Perhaps you're the CEO of your company and, because you've seen colleagues establish new ventures within their firms, you'd like to do likewise. After a careful evaluation of the abilities required to launch a new business, you determine that an organization involved in this initiative must excel at some activity and, therefore, possess a unique competitive edge. Individuals engaging in this endeavor also need an entrepreneurial mind-set. To verify that your people's abilities line up with those related to this effort, you reexamine your collective talents. Overall, your employees possess an array of skill-strengths, including finance, selling, and conceptual thinking, but because your organization doesn't currently excel at a particular task, you decide that this option doesn't make sense for your company. If, subsequently, your people develop a competitive edge, you may hire a manager with an entrepreneurial outlook to help you start up a new business within your firm.

By now, you recognize why it's critical to understand both your (or your workers') talents and those necessary to perform your work ideal. To assist you in your analysis, here are several questions.

- How much do you know about the abilities that are critical to performing your dream job? Have you identified these talents correctly? Could you have underestimated the abilities necessary for this role? Or, are you aware of the capabilities that are needed to achieve your business reinvention? Are you certain that you've identified the right skills? Could you have left out any talents? According to the type of reinvention you've imagined, do businesses that succeed possess a particular competitive edge? If so, what are its usual components?

- Do you really understand your skill-strengths? Are you fully confident of your assessment? Could you be mistaken about your talents or have you overrated your abilities? Or, are you certain that your business has the capabilities you think it has? Has your organization demonstrated these talents in the past? Could you be wrong about your firm's competitive edge?

- Do you believe that your talents line up adequately or even well with those needed to perform your reinvented job? If so, what does your match look like? Do you have all of the capabilities associated with your ideal? If not, which skill-strengths don't you possess? How important are these abilities to performing your dream position? If you don't have these talents, will you be able to excel? Or, have you concluded that your organization's abilities correspond acceptably or even closely with those necessary to achieve your business reinvention? If so, how does this pairing look? Do your people have all of the skills essential to your reinvention? If not, which skills does your organization lack? Could this deficiency cause your business to fail in its reinvention or perform poorly thereafter?

- If your (or your people's) talents don't match those related to your ideal job or business, how will you respond to this situation? Will you abandon your job or business goal? If so, why will you make this choice? Or, will you revise your aim or improve your (or your organization's) skills? If you decide to make adjustments, how will you do so?

Next let's consider whether what matters to you is compatible with your ideal job or business.

CONFIRM WHAT'S IMPORTANT TO YOU

An individual thinks that salespeople are motivated exclusively by money, while a peer believes that executives are always driven by power and prestige. Not perceiving that his ambitions have evolved, a worker goes after a position that no longer matches what's important to him. A business owner concludes that employees who are involved in launching new offerings are propelled by money, when, in fact, such workers are also stimulated by challenge. Not realizing that her people's ambitions have changed, a leader undertakes a reinvention that's inconsistent with what matters to her employees.

These examples portray how people and businesses sometimes misread their own motivations or those of individuals engaged in particular jobs or businesses. More or less, you sense what matters to you. Perhaps you enjoy working for a large company or you prefer being employed by a small firm. Maybe your pastimes include helping the needy or serving on your city council. Possibly you thrive on making money, receiving awards for your achievements, the thrill in challenging yourself, or mentoring other people. Or, you understand your organization's collective motivations. Perhaps your people delight in serving their customers or innovating new offerings or approaches. Maybe your workers are driven to beat your firm's competitors or attract and retain the industry's best talent. In other words, you understand what moves you or fires up your employees.

Yet, what if you're mistaken about the ambitions that are typically associated with your ideal job or business? You assume that money and power propel corporate executives, but taking on new challenges or having a positive impact on their company, their industry, or the world is sometimes more important to these individuals. You're convinced that an entrepreneur is roused primarily by taking risks, but an owner is often more interested in building a business that endures. You presume that organizations that make revolutionary discoveries are galvanized exclusively by money, but these firms may also be induced to make a difference in the world—finding cures for deadly diseases or making life easier for millions of people.

Or, what if you've made incorrect assumptions about your (or your workers') motivations or your ambitions have changed? Maybe you assume that money stimulates you because you've made a lot of it. Perhaps you confuse your organization's pride in its accomplishments with a hunger for publicity. Or, you don't realize that the factors that propelled you or your employees in the past aren't important to you now. For example, years ago, getting ahead at your company stirred you, but now that you've reached your career goals, you're inclined to spend more time on your outside interests or with your family. Or, years ago, your workers were driven by challenge and money, but today they're motivated by financial security.

Perceptive businesspeople discover what moves people in particular jobs or businesses. Clever folks also verify what motivates them or their workers. If professionals determine that their (or their employees') ambitions line up with those typically associated with their work ideals, they may decide to pursue their reinvention. Conversely, if they detect a significant disparity, these managers may opt to abandon their goals. Or, these individuals may revise their aims. For example, if an executive concludes that a promotion requires that he live away from home, he may choose to go after a different role. On the other hand, workers may elect to make one or more trade-offs in what's important to them. If a professional finds that in her new position she'll have to travel abroad every month, she may decide to proceed with her reinvention but cut back on her outside activities. Here's an example that illustrates how to use your awareness to determine whether or not your motivations match those related to your ideal work.

Let's say that you're a manager at your company. Because you impressed your CEO with your leadership of a task force, you have an opportunity to take on a new role that involves greater responsibilities. From speaking with colleagues in similar positions at other companies, you learn that this job would require long hours and extensive international travel. Assessing your ambitions, you conclude that you're driven by challenge, money, and power. As a result, you decide that the motivations typically attributed to individuals in this job and what's important to you correlate well and, therefore, you proceed with your job change.

Now assume that it's years later. You've become a senior executive in your company and you earn a lot of money and manage thousands of people. At this point, you have another opportunity to change positions. This new role involves leading negotiations in developing countries and, therefore, requires that you live away from home for extended periods of time. Reevaluating your ambitions, you determine that although you're still motivated by challenge, acquiring money or power has become less critical to you. Developing talent and spending time with your family have become more important to you and, consequently, you choose to remain in your current position.

No doubt, you see the importance of understanding whether or not your motivations and those associated with your reinvention correspond. To facilitate your assessment, here are some questions to ask yourself.

- Do you fully comprehend what stimulates people who have the job you desire? For your evaluation, have you relied on just one source or person or have you spoken to various individuals at your company and elsewhere? Do you believe that you've developed an accurate picture? Or, have you carefully considered what usually excites people who work in your ideal business? In your assessment, did you speak with employees in several such businesses? Did you also take the time to read about this business in the media and industry publications?

- Are you confident that you understand what's important to you? Do you sense that your preferences, interests, or motivations have evolved? If so, have you modified your evaluation? Or, are you sure about your employees' collective ambitions? Has what drives your people changed? If so, have you adjusted your assessment?

- Do your (or your people's) motivations and those that typify your ideal correlate acceptably, even strongly? If so, how confident are you about this pairing? If you have concerns, what are these doubts and are these serious reservations? Or, do your (or your people's) motivations and those connected with your goal differ substantially? If so, why isn't there a match? How will you respond? Will you abandon your reinvention? Will you revise your goal? Or, will you make trade-offs in what's important to you so that your ambitions correlate better with those associated with your ideal?

Now let's synthesize what you've discovered.

PULL TOGETHER YOUR VERIFIED IDEAL

Can you envision being able to perform a particular job or business but not being motivated to do so? Will you land your ideal work but not have the skills you'll need to excel at this position or in this business? How can you be confident about your reinvention if you're not sure whether your talents and ambitions are similar to those associated with your dream job?

You grasp the intent of these questions. You need to bring together the components of your verification. That way, you'll understand both yourself and your ideal job or business and, as a result, you'll be able to determine—precisely and confidently—whether or not your goal fits you or your people. If you conclude that there's a match, you may choose to proceed with your reinvention. If you determine that there's not a match, you may elect to abandon your goal. Or, you may opt to revise this objective or improve this pairing.

Now let's pull together the components you've reviewed. Review the assessments you've completed in this chapter. Be sure that you've answered the questions as thoroughly and honestly as possible. If you haven't responded fully or need to revise your answers, do so before you proceed.

Using the examples you read about in Chapter 3, let's examine how to verify your ideal. As before, bear in mind that your circumstances won't be exactly the same as those described and, therefore, your confirmed goal won't exactly resemble the ones that follow. With this caveat in mind, let's proceed.

The first scenario describes a manager who imagines starting up and growing a new global business in his company. If you're this individual, you're positive that you fully and accurately understand the abilities required to accomplish your desired role. Establishing and expanding a worldwide business for your company would involve managing an organization, generating revenues, and coordinating with your firm's existing businesses. You've also reexamined both completely and objectively your skills and strengths. From your analysis, you're confident that you understand your abilities. Managing people and discerning and pursuing opportunities constitute your competitive edge. Based on your evaluation, you've concluded that there's only a partial match between your abilities and those required to perform your ideal job. To succeed, you'd need to improve how you coordinate with your colleagues.

You're certain that you comprehend what matters to people who have the job you desire. You've validated that such individuals often value power—being responsible for a huge organization—and recognition—money and other awards for their achievements. You've also reevaluated thoroughly and honestly what's important to you. You've confirmed that you prefer working for a large company and in a new or high-growth business and enjoy traveling and learning new languages, but you're also strongly inclined to spend time with your family. Because of your assessment, you've decided that your motivations aren't fully compatible with those associated with your ideal job. You fear that your new work might adversely impact your personal life.

Based on your review, you'll probably respond in one of these ways:

- You choose to abandon your reinvention. You decide that going ahead doesn't make sense or is even risky because neither your abilities nor your motivations fully conform to those connected with your ideal. Besides, you're not able or willing to make any adjustments.

- You revise your reinvention goal. You decide to start up a smaller business that requires less coordination with your colleagues. Or, you launch a U.S.-based business and, that way, you travel less and, consequently, have more time to spend with your family. Possibly you make both of these changes.

- You elect to make adjustments before you begin your reinvention. You improve your ability to coordinate. Or, you make a trade-off in what's important to you. In other words, you'll spend less time with your family. Possibly you take both these actions.

In the second example, a division leader envisions developing a new line of offerings. If you're this businessperson, you're sure that you grasp the skills essential to this endeavor. Launching new products or services would require designing the right items and then positioning these offerings in the marketplace. You've also fully and impartially reevaluated your people's abilities and, by doing so, you're sure that you view your workers' talents correctly. Being resourceful and able to think conceptually constitute your firm's competitive edge. Based on your examination, you've decided that your workers' abilities correspond closely with those essential to your aim.

You're positive that you recognize what's important to individuals involved in introducing new offerings. You've verified that challenge and money drive these workers. You've also reassessed fully and objectively what matters to your employees and, consequently, you're certain that your people have similar motivations. Through this evaluation, you've concluded that your employees' ambitions correlate well with those associated with your objective.

Because there's a good match between your people's skills and motivations and those associated with your goal, you decide to proceed with your reinvention.

At this point, you're almost ready to determine how you'll reach your verified ideal, but first, you have to plan the adjustments you've decided to make and also explore the downsides associated with your reinvention.

ENSURE YOUR PREPAREDNESS

A worker decides to bolster his skills, but because he doesn't plan how he'll improve his abilities, this individual doesn't follow through and, as a result, this employee's performance in his new job is barely adequate. Because an executive doesn't determine how she'll make trade-offs between her position and personal life, this once-rising star doesn't make these compromises and, consequently, she falls off the fast track. A manager is taken aback by his new coworkers' coolness, while a colleague is surprised that she's dissatisfied with her new job just weeks after starting this position. A business owner doesn't assess the opportunity cost of enhancing his firm's approach and, as a result, he misses out on a chance to introduce a new product. Having recently transformed his company, an executive inaugurates new lines, reengineers his processes, and starts a new venture within his firm. The fallout of these successive revamps is a shell-shocked work force that's not as productive as it was before these changes.

These scenarios depict individuals and businesses that didn't properly prepare for their reinventions. In other words, these businesspeople didn't plan how they'd make the necessary adjustments—such as improving their abilities or making trade-offs between their work and personal life—or didn't consider the potential downsides of their work reshaping. Even so, you're not especially worried. You're pretty good at getting ready for upcoming endeavors. Yet, what if you don't develop a specific plan on how you'll bolster your skills or make work-life compromises and, consequently, you don't make the adjustments you should? You may perform poorly in your new position or be miserable in your dream job. Or, what if you don't consider the potential downsides of your career or business move? You may be unpleasantly surprised by your own or your colleagues' reactions, or you may be disappointed that you weren't able to pursue a different opportunity.

Sensible business professionals ensure that they're fully prepared for their reinvention journeys. These employees and executives develop specific plans concerning how they'll make adjustments in their abilities or personal lives. These folks also consider the potential downsides of reinventing their careers or businesses. For example, an individual who's changing jobs assesses whether he might not want his new position once the honeymoon is over. If a worker is moving to another area of her company, she examines whether her colleagues will accept her. Similarly, a business leader evaluates the opportunity cost associated with his firm's reinvention. That is to say, this manager contemplates whether engaging in a particular effort—like enhancing his business' approach—might cause his company to lose out on another opportunity—such as introducing a new product. If he determines that pursuing a certain reinvention might hurt more than help his firm, this person won't undertake this effort. Along the same lines, an executive who's thinking about undertaking another reinvention assesses whether such an endeavor might lead her workers to become weary or demoralized and, consequently, less productive.

To help you evaluate your preparedness, here are some questions to ask yourself.

- If you've decided to improve one of your (or your workers') abilities, have you developed a plan that details how and when you'll do so? If you realize that you'll have to make trade-offs in what's important to you (or your employees), have you determined who or what will be affected by your actions? Are you or your loved ones, such as your spouse, children, or significant other, willing to make these compromises?

- What are the potential downsides of your career move? That is to say, if you obtain your dream job, what factors might cause you to become unhappy with your new role? For example, if shortly after you start your new job, you discover that your new supervisor is less supportive of your work-life balance than you thought she'd be, will you become dissatisfied and want to change positions? If you change functions within your company, do you foresee that your new colleagues might not welcome you or find you credible? If so, how will you deal with such a problem? Or, what are the potential downsides associated with your business reinvention? If you undertake the enhancement of your products, services, or approach, might you miss out on an exceptional opportunity, such as introducing a new offering, or might you fail to address a problem? If so, would such an outcome be acceptable to you? If you initiate a new reinvention even though you've just completed several business revamps, might you negatively affect your workers' morale or productivity? If so, would such a result be a risk you're willing to take?

Now you're ready to determine how you'll reach your reinvention destination.

APPLY YOUR VERIFIED IDEAL

Let's assess how your situation stacks up with the various reinvention options. You'll determine why you might select a particular alternative to fulfill your aim. As was true in the previous chapters, your circumstances won't correlate precisely with the characteristics of the following scenarios, nor will they include all of these features. If you're still not able to finalize your choice of option, don't be concerned. You'll do so in Chapter 9.

 ### REINVIGORATE YOUR JOB

Your confirmed ideal may incorporate the following components:

- *Your skills and strengths.* You've reexamined your abilities and those needed to rejuvenate your position. You've concluded that your abilities fit those associated with your ideal.

- *Your motivations.* You've reviewed what's important to you. You've determined that your ambitions align adequately or well with those related to this reinvention.

- *Your preparedness.* As necessary, you're prepared to spend less time on your outside interests. You don't project any particular downside to your engaging in a project or taking on a new responsibility.

If the above sounds like your situation, here are a couple of reasons you may choose to reinvigorate your job:

- You'd like to keep the job you have but want to make a modest change that will help you enhance your performance or reputation, revitalize your interest, learn something new, improve a process or offering, or a combination of these elements.
- You're sure that such a move will be the right one for you.

 CHANGE JOBS IN YOUR COMPANY

Your validated goal may incorporate the components cited below:

- *Your skills and strengths.* You've reevaluated your talents and those essential to perform the position you're seeking. You've decided that your abilities are basically consistent with those associated with your ideal job. Or, you've determined that your skills don't fully match your reinvention.
- *Your motivations.* You've reassessed what matters to you and concluded that your ambitions agree with those connected with your work ideal. Or, you're aware that you'll have to make trade-offs between your new job and personal life.
- *Your preparedness.* You've planned to strengthen one or more of your capabilities. You and your family are ready to make compromises. Because you anticipate that your new colleagues might have trouble accepting you, you're prepared to reposition how they view you.

If the preceding elements describe your circumstances, here are some reasons you may elect to change jobs:

- You've performed well (or relatively so) where you are, but you seek to make a substantial change in your work so that you'll realize your full potential.
- You're confident that your abilities, preferences, and motivations match those associated with your ideal job. Conversely, you've developed a plan to strengthen your talents. You've decided to make compromises concerning what's important to

you. Or, you've identified how you'll improve your skills and also make trade-offs between your work and personal life.

ENHANCE YOUR BUSINESS' OFFERINGS OR APPROACH

Your confirmed objective may be based upon the following components:

- *Your skills and strengths.* You've reexamined your organization's collective talents and those required to undertake your ideal. You've concluded that your people's abilities fit satisfactorily or even closely with those connected with this goal. Or, you've decided that your skills aren't as compatible as they could be.

- *Your motivations.* You've reassessed your organization's passions. What excites your workers also stimulates individuals going after this type of reinvention. You've determined that there's a match.

- *Your preparedness.* You've developed a plan to improve your workers' capabilities. You and your people are ready to make adjustments in your personal lives. You don't foresee any particular downside to your reinvention, although you'll remain alert.

If some or most of the above sounds familiar, here are a few reasons you may opt to enhance your firm:

- Your business is performing acceptably to well, but you want to make one or more moderate changes that will allow your business to maintain its status or even elevate it.

- You believe in your organization's commitment to and capacity for continuous improvement. Your people are prepared to do whatever's necessary to fulfill your business' objectives.

TRANSITION YOUR BUSINESS

Your verified ideal may include the following components:

- *Your skills and strengths.* You've reexplored your organization's capabilities and those critical to undertaking this reinvention. You've decided that your business' skills correspond acceptably with those affiliated with this ideal. Or, you've determined that your organization's abilities don't exactly match the talents you'll require.

- *Your motivations.* You've reappraised your organization's ambitions. What drives your people also stirs workers involved in business transitions. Or, you've concluded that this pairing could be better.

- *Your preparedness.* Your workers have made plans to improve their abilities. Your employees have decided to make work-life compromises. Your people will bolster their skills and also make trade-offs between their work and their personal lives. Because you expect that your people might become weary or demoralized from undertaking successive reinventions, you'll pursue such changes prudently.

If the preceding factors resemble your situation, here are some reasons you may choose to transition your business:

- Because you expect more from your business, you need to make substantial changes, such as overhauling your approach or augmenting your offerings.

- You're convinced that your people will strengthen their skills, make trade-offs in what's important to them, or both. Accordingly, your workers have (or will have) the collective abilities and motivation to fix your business' problems or expand your firm's focus.

START A NEW BUSINESS WITHIN YOUR COMPANY

Your validated goal may include the following components:

- *Your skills and strengths.* You've reviewed your organization's talents and those that are vital to attaining your objective. You've determined that your organization's skills match adequately or well with those associated with this reinvention. Or, you've concluded that your collective skills don't correlate sufficiently to the abilities you'll need.

- *Your motivations.* You've reconsidered the factors that stimulate your organization. You've decided that your people's motivations correspond well with those that typify individuals starting new businesses. Or, you've determined that this pairing is less than perfect. Your organization will need to become more oriented to taking risks.

- *Your preparedness.* Your employees have developed a plan to improve their capabilities through training, or you've devised a strategy for hiring an entrepreneurial manager. Your people are ready to make adjustments in their personal lives. You expect that if you don't remain attentive, you might miss out on an opportunity in your marketplace or you might fail to address a problem in another area of your company.

If most of the above describes your ideal, here are a couple of reasons you may want to start a new business at your firm:

- Your business has met its goals but wants to pursue a new direction.

- Your organization has (or will obtain) the abilities and mind-set to achieve its goal.

Do you agree that verifying your ideal is essential? If you haven't completed your review, you'll want to do so before you move on to the next chapter. In the meantime, you'll enjoy reading about two individuals who verified their ideals and then went after them.

LIVE YOUR VERIFIED IDEAL

With a career spanning five decades, Evelyn Granville is living proof of the value of verifying your ideal.[2] She's traversed the worlds of academia, government, and business, transitioning almost seamlessly between them.

Granville thoroughly understands her abilities. Wherever she's gone, she's made sure that her talents were consistent with those required to perform her ideal position. If she concluded that a match could be closer, she improved her skills. In 1956, with a Ph.D. in mathematics, a knack for solving problems, and five years' experience in academia and government, the then 32-year-old Granville began her business career. She was part of an IBM team that formulated orbit computations and computer procedures for NASA, but because she had studied pure mathematics, she didn't know the applied methods essential to her work. Consequently, in what was to become a recurring theme of her life, she taught herself what she needed to know. Twenty-four years later, she took a sabbatical from California State University to study computer science so that she could teach an introductory class and, in 1985, while teaching at Texas College, she taught herself a new computer language so that she could stay one day ahead of her class.

This celebrated mathematician also realizes what's important to her. She's motivated by her unquenchable thirst for learning. As she points out: "I always want to know something more. I'm always going after things, but I'm not taking risks to show how brave I am. I'm doing so because there's new knowledge that I want to learn. I don't want to be left behind." Also enjoying teaching and solving problems, Granville returned to academia in 1967. Matching her passions and interests with those typically associated with her ideal, she joined California State University, where she taught computer programming, numerical analysis, and mathematics. While there, she became fascinated with something called new math because it encouraged students and teachers to learn why they are doing something rather than doing it by rote. To foster the teaching of this new discipline, Granville and a colleague published a book that showed elementary teachers how to explain this subject's new concepts.

As an African-American woman—before affirmative action, diversity, and political correctness—Granville blazed paths that were new, even to white males. By confirming her goals, this remarkable woman has succeeded in and been satisfied with the numerous endeavors she's undertaken. Thanks to her prudent approach, Granville was a frontline participant in two revolutions—information technology and space flight—that have changed the world.

Like Granville, I recognize my talents. Since becoming an entrepreneur, I've regularly reviewed my abilities and, as a result, I understand my competitive edge. Before commencing any reinvention, I assess—and reassess—whether my talents correlate with those essential to performing my ideal work. In 1987, I validated that my skills conformed with what I needed to become a communication coach to corporate managers and executives. Five years later, I verified that my abilities were similar to those required to help corporate teams operate more effectively. More recently, after fully and objectively reassessing my skill-strengths, I decided to write a business book and, in turn, launch a speaking and media career. In this situation, I determined that my talents—communication, logical thinking, and resourcefulness—would enable me to reach my goal. Even so, the match between my abilities and those connected with my ideal was not as close as it might have been and, therefore, I worked at improving my writing skills by attending writers' workshops and continually revising my work.

I'm also conscious of what drives me. As I indicated in the previous chapter, my motivations have changed. I've become more concerned with receiving recognition from a national audience. To facilitate my current reinvention, I've assessed whether my ambitions were similar to those associated with prominent public speakers and media personalities and, as a result, I've concluded that there's a correlation.

While Granville exemplifies how to improve your skills so that they correspond more closely to your ideal, I personify how to ensure that you're fully prepared to undertake your reinvention. Consequently, I often ask: "Am I ready to make sacrifices in my personal life? Do I need more training or experience? What might cause me to become dissatisfied with my new role? Will my new colleagues accept me? If I engage in this effort, might I miss out on another opportunity?"

Verifying that your career goals correlate with your talents and motivations is worth the time and effort. I couldn't have achieved my various reinventions without confirming that what I was able to do and what mattered to me was consistent with my ideal job or business.

CHAPTER FIVE

STEP FOUR
Be Resourceful

Discover who has the best ideas, and put those ideas into practice.[1]

—ROBERT SLATER ON ONE OF (FORMER GE CEO) JACK WELCH'S TRADEMARK MESSAGES

Have you marveled how colleagues have handled difficulties in their jobs or businesses? Do you stand in awe of managers who employ ideas or approaches that they see or hear about to take advantage of opportunities? Have you wondered why some businesspeople are ingenious in their work while others aren't?

If you've asked yourself these questions, you sense that resourcefulness is all around you, but what exactly is this skill or innate talent? Resourcefulness is the ability to deal skillfully and promptly with situations. Resourceful managers ably resolve problems in their work and inventively capitalize on opportunities involving their careers or businesses. If a business professional is resourceful, he or she is quick-witted, clever, or even venturesome. This person may be an employee, executive, or entrepreneur who is inherently resourceful or an individual who develops or hones their resourcefulness by being aware, informed, and receptive to new concepts and techniques. For whoever employs it, resourcefulness assists its users in performing their jobs, running their businesses, and, when necessary or desirable, reshaping their work. In other words, resourcefulness helps businesspeople succeed, no matter the endeavor.

Still, you may think that you'll be resourceful if you have to be. Yet, what if you don't utilize a particular idea or approach and, as a result, fail to address a pressing career or business problem? You may not turn around your performance or improve your firm's offerings even though you should. Or, what if you don't exploit a certain concept or technique and, consequently, don't take advantage of an exceptional opportunity to advance your career or build your firm? You may not obtain your ideal position or launch a new line.

Astute businesspeople comprehend that even if resourcefulness sounds vague, if applied, this ability can produce tangible results. By being resourceful, you can fix problems or seize opportunities and, by doing so, reinvent your job or business. You can also use your imaginativeness to set or refine your reinvention goal. In other words, your work reinvention may be the by-product of your resourcefulness or its direct result. This knack or ability can also assist you in pursuing your reinvention and, even after you've reached your goal, allow you to remain successful in and satisfied with your reinvented work.

This chapter will show you how to use your resourcefulness to deal with problems and opportunities, shape (or reshape) your reinvention objective, go after and attain your goal, and perform well thereafter. In this step, you'll learn how to become (more) resourceful. You'll discover how to apply your resourcefulness in your current job or use your quick-wittedness to find a new role or position and, if it's relevant to your circumstances, how to employ this skill in your business in order to make modest or even significant changes. You'll also find out about the downsides of resourcefulness and how to avoid these perils. You'll next consider how to apply your inventiveness. You'll choose the reinvention option that's most applicable to your situation. You'll then read about two people who've applied their resourcefulness in their jobs and businesses.

Let's begin with how to develop (or hone) this capability.

BECOME (MORE) RESOURCEFUL

An entrepreneur didn't listen to her customers' complaints. An executive didn't see that his organization was taking too long to make decisions. A professional didn't sense that her clients wanted a new service. A worker didn't read about developments in his marketplace or speak with colleagues at other companies. A manager failed to explore a new role at her company. A business owner refused to consider how to enhance his offerings.

Because the individuals in these examples aren't aware, informed, or open to new thinking, they might have trouble being resourceful at work. But you think that if you're not born resourceful, there's nothing you can do to develop this talent and, consequently, you won't bother to improve your alertness or receptivity. Yet, what if you aren't fully apprised of your (or your organization's) problems or opportunities? At some point, you may discover that a difficulty has become insurmountable or a fortuitous circumstance has changed. What if you're not attentive to developments in your marketplace? You may not identify an idea or approach that you or your business could adapt. What if you're not open to new ways of improving your job or business? You may not solve your (or your business') problems or take advantage of your (or your business') opportunities as efficiently or effectively as you might have. Or, what if you don't critically evaluate the concepts and methods that you see, hear, or read about? You may miss out on ways to reinvent your job, business, or both.

Sharp employees develop (or hone) their resourcefulness. To do so, these folks listen, observe, and tap their intuition in order to be totally aware of their (or their workers') situation. These individuals stay alert, reading about their marketplace and speaking with people in other jobs, companies, and industries and, by doing so, the perceptive uncover ideas and approaches that others have employed. These executives and entrepreneurs are also open to exploring new notions and techniques and, by regularly evaluating such information, these leaders develop or improve their analytical skills. That way, these workers can determine whether or not to employ a concept or method they've learned about. Through their actions, business professionals can become resourceful—whether or not they were born so—and, as a result, these leaders can solve their problems, pursue their opportunities, establish their work ideals, and go after and attain these objectives. If while executing their reinvention plans these people need to make a change—they have to be agile (Step Six: Execute Flawlessly)—their resourcefulness helps them respond.

If you or your employees want to become (more) resourceful, here are some questions that will assist you. Before you begin these questions, go back to Chapter 2 and quickly review the situational picture you developed. The following questions will help you become (more) resourceful and, by doing so, you'll enhance your situational awareness. In turn, you'll confirm whether (or not) you need to reinvent and how you might bring about a change in your career or business.

- In your job, have you been aware? Have you noticed whether your work has improved, remained the same, or deteriorated? What have you heard about your attitude or what does your intuition tell you? Have you discerned problems or opportunities or ways of dealing with these circumstances both skillfully and promptly? If so, have you allowed yourself to be resourceful? Have you stayed informed about the conditions, trends, and developments of your marketplace and also spoken to colleagues in different areas of your firm and in other companies? Have you also been receptive? Have you examined how other individuals have changed jobs or otherwise advanced their careers? Whom do you know in your company or elsewhere that's resourceful? What have they achieved and how have they accomplished these feats? From what you've seen, heard, sensed, or read about, have you critically evaluated ideas and approaches for rejuvenating your attitude or performance, enhancing your prospects for advancement, or moving to a different role or function?

- Based on your answers to the preceding questions, will you modify the situational picture you developed? If so, will you change your mind about reinventing your job? If you decide to reinvent, will you use any of the concepts or methods you've learned about?

- Have you been aware about your business? Has your firm or area of responsibility met or exceeded expectations or not operated as well as it could have? Have you listened to your customers, employees, management, or investors? Did you (or your people) uncover problems or discern opportunities and, if so, have you dealt with these difficulties or possibilities adroitly and in a timely manner? If not, why have you impeded your (or your workers') resourcefulness? Have you kept up to date concerning the performance, trends, and developments of your company and industry? Have you examined how competitors or companies outside your industry have turned ideas into business improvements or even new ventures? Do you understand how they've applied these thoughts or methods? Have you learned whether or not they were successful and why this was their situation? Have you also been open to emulating these businesses' strategies or methods? That is to say, have you been receptive to new ways of enhancing your offerings or approach, refocusing your organization, introducing new products or services, or starting a new venture? Have you critically analyzed the information you've picked up?

- Based on your answers to the above queries, will you revise the situational image you developed? If so, will you reach a different decision about reinventing your business? If you choose to reinvent, will you employ any of the ideas or approaches you've learned about?

In the next two sections, you'll learn how to use your ingenuity in your work.

BE RESOURCEFUL IN YOUR JOB

A professional utilizes a technique that helps him get his job done more quickly and effectively than before. Exploiting an idea that she's heard about, a manager revitalizes her interest in her job. Having detected a problem in his company's delivery process, an employee initiates a project to resolve this dilemma. By parlaying his project experience, a leader creates a new role for himself. Repositioning how others view her talents, an individual moves into a different area of her company.

You grasp that the folks in these scenarios are being resourceful, but you're not sure that being inventive in your job is really worth the effort. Besides, you're performing acceptably. You're satisfied with your current role or position. You're usually able to identify and deal with problems or opportunities. Why should you change how you deal with the challenges you face?

Yet, what if you have a performance problem? Maybe your performance has slipped and is no longer acceptable. Perhaps you're new in your position and haven't fully mastered the skills you need to perform your job or you're not performing up to your potential. Your quick-wittedness may help you rejuvenate your performance. To improve your speed, accuracy, or business know-how, you may emulate a colleague's approach or employ an idea you've read about.

What if you become less satisfied with your job? Perhaps a recent reorganization resulted in your losing several of your responsibilities. Maybe you've become bored with your work. Possibly you want to work with new colleagues or customers. Or, you yearn to learn new skills or confront new challenges. Whatever your reason, your resourcefulness may assist you in reinvigorating your current job or even changing positions in your company. For example, to reenergize your attitude or even enhance your prospects for advancement, you may augment your existing responsibilities by mentoring younger workers, teaching a class at your company, or participating on a corporate task force or in a special project. To move to a new job or area, you may capitalize on the knowledge you've gained or the contacts you've made. Or, you may imaginatively devise a new position and then cleverly convince your management that this role is critical to your company's success.

What if you need to solve a problem or pursue an opportunity as effectively and efficiently as possible? Your ingenuity may aid you in such tasks. You may initiate a project team or task force to address a difficulty or take advantage of a favorable situation and, as a result, you and your colleagues might work faster or more productively and achieve the results your company is looking for. In turn, you may parlay your experience to build your reputation, move to a new position, or create a new role for yourself.

Or, what if you decide to reinvent your role or job? Your inventiveness may enable you to set or refine your goal. For example, because of what you've seen, heard, read, or sensed, you find an idea that you'd like to incorporate in your work and, therefore, you establish your reinvention objective—helping your company assimilate the firms it acquires. If, subsequently, your company scales back its acquisitions, you may revise your goal and, instead, manage your company's alliances with other firms.

Successful professionals benefit by utilizing ideas and approaches that they've learned about or that they've devised. These individuals employ these concepts and techniques to improve their performance or satisfaction, solve problems and pursue opportunities, shape (or reshape) their reinvention goals, and pursue and attain these aims. The following scenario will deepen your understanding of how to be resourceful in your job.

Let's say that you're a manager who's lost interest in your position. Because you're not sure how to revitalize your attitude, you ask a colleague who's rejuvenated his outlook to mentor you. Applying an idea he's used successfully, you create and conduct a new course at your company and, through your brightness, you reinvigorate your job.

Several months later, you sense that you're ready for a new challenge. Because you're aware, you observe that your company's hiring process is slow and, consequently, your firm is losing talent to other businesses. With your mentor's assistance, you devise a way to address this dilemma and, by explaining the true cost of not hiring these exceptional workers, you also persuade your management to let you create a task force to implement your solution. Because of your ingenuity, you help your company and you enhance your prospects for advancement.

A year passes and you decide to change areas in your company. Because you stay informed, you've learned how other businesspeople have switched functions. Employing this knowledge, you create your reinvention goal. In order to change how your colleagues view you, you also reposition your image. You suggest that your key skill-strengths are well suited to your new position. Thanks to your sharpness, you attain your work ideal.

If you're eager to incorporate resourcefulness in your job, here are several questions that will help you:

- Have you employed an idea or approach that you've seen a colleague use in order to improve your job performance? If so, what did you do and what were the results of your actions? Have you utilized a scheme that you've heard about to revitalize your attitude about your work? Were you successful in this effort?

- Have you used a concept or method that you've read about or even devised to solve a problem or go after an opportunity? If so, did you initiate a task force or project team to deal with a particular situation? Did you experiment with a new technology or imitate another manager's modus operandi? Whatever your approach, did you fulfill your objective?

- Have you parlayed your job performance or involvement in projects to build your reputation and, by doing so, enhance your prospects for advancement? Or, did you ingeniously exploit your knowledge, experience, or contacts in order to secure a new job? If so, did you also change areas within your company? If you made such a move, did you reposition your image with your colleagues or management? Or, have you created a position or role that hadn't existed previously? Did you convince your company that this role was critical to your firm's future? Whatever you did, were you successful in your endeavor?

- Has being inventive helped you establish your reinvention goal? If so, how did being imaginative contribute to shaping (or reshaping) your ideal position or role? If you haven't finished visualizing your goal, will you use your ingenuity to assist you?

- Whether or not you've set your reinvention goal, will you use your brightness to go after your ideal? For example, will you ask your mentor to introduce you to an executive for whom you want to work? Will you exploit ideas you've learned about to develop a new technology or product for your company? Will you speak before industry groups so that you position yourself as an expert? Or, will you network with colleagues in and outside your company, whether at work, meetings, conferences, or community activities?

- Will you also utilize your resourcefulness to ensure that you remain successful in and satisfied with your reinvented job or role? Periodically, will you meet with other businesspeople to discuss novel ways of improving your performance, revitalizing your attitude, expanding your role, or changing positions? Will you also solicit feedback from your manager and colleagues concerning whether you've applied quick-wittedness and done so consistently and effectively?

Now let's look at how to put your sharpness to work in your business.

BE RESOURCEFUL IN YOUR BUSINESS

In response to his clients' input, an entrepreneur improves his services. Because they observe that their firm's processes aren't as efficient or effective as they could be, employees revamp these methods. Employing an approach used by another firm, a manager launches a new line of products. Having read about other companies' entrepreneurial ventures, a leader capitalizes on his firm's competitive edge and establishes a new business.

While you appreciate the accomplishments in these scenarios, you're not convinced that being resourceful in your business is absolutely necessary. You've effectively managed divisions for your company. Or, as an entrepreneur, you've consistently generated solid growth and earnings.

Yet, what if your organization isn't meeting its objectives? Maybe your business' products or services aren't what they were or what they could be. Perhaps your workers aren't fully applying their energies or talents. Or, your company has become complacent and, therefore, lost its competitive spirit. Your resourcefulness may help you refocus or restructure your organization. For example, you may create a monthly newsletter that communicates the values and behaviors you expect from your managers. You may reengineer your company, eliminating overlapping divisions and establishing a few clear lines of business. You may initiate cross-functional projects that encourage your managers to collaborate more closely. Or, you may establish a new compensation system that rewards enterprising behavior.

What if you hear about a problem that involves your business' offerings or how you produce or deliver them? Perhaps your customers seek improved products or services or faster delivery of these items. Maybe your suppliers recommend that you expedite your business' purchasing and payment procedures. Possibly your workers want to streamline your firm's decision making. Or, you come across a serious difficulty involving your business' manufacturing process. Your ingenuity may assist you in responding to such input and thereby enhancing your offerings or approach. For instance, you may bring together a group of customers to help you redesign your offerings or delivery methods. You may ask your suppliers for their ideas on how to revamp your processes. Your people may speak to managers in other companies about their decision making and, in turn, identify a system that suits your firm. Or, you may assemble an emergency task force to resolve your manufacturing challenge.

What if you perceive a need or an opportunity to launch one or more new offerings, enter a new market segment, or start a new enterprise within your company? Possibly one of your competitors has recently inaugurated a new line and you need to catch up. Maybe you'd like to introduce a new product or service. Perhaps your market segment is growing slowly and, therefore, you want to switch into a higher-growth area. Or, your people perform a particular activity exceptionally well. Whatever your situation, your inventiveness may help you pursue opportunities and, in turn, facilitate the expansion of your business. For example, exploiting what you see, sense, or hear, you may augment your business' offerings by launching a new product or service or introducing a new line. Employing your awareness of the marketplace, you may move into a rapidly expanding sector. Or, ably capitalizing on an activity that your workers excel at, you may establish a new business that parlays this expertise.

Or, what if you decide to reinvent your business? Your imaginativeness may help you establish (or modify) your goal. For instance, thanks to what you and your managers have learned from colleagues at other companies, you may craft your reinvention objective—revamping your company's hiring process—but if you later hear that such a method only works for new hires and not midcareer placements, you may refine your objective.

As is obvious from the preceding examples, successful managers employ their sharpness to improve their business' performance. These executives and entrepreneurs use their ingenuity to enhance their business' offerings or approach, expand their firms, or transform their organizations. Let's consider another example of how being resourceful can assist you—whether you manage a business for your company or operate your own firm.

As a quick-witted entrepreneur, you notice that your firm's sales aren't growing as fast as they used to. Based on discussions with your peers at other companies and also industry experts, you conclude that your customers seek safer products. To redesign your offerings, you obtain feedback from your clients and employees. When you introduce these enhanced items, you offer these products on a limited basis and, that way, you make additional improvements that are needed before your national rollout. Your brightness helps you pinpoint your business' problem, devise a solution, and execute flawlessly.

After evaluating the results of your business change, you decide that despite your efforts, your firm isn't achieving the growth you hoped for. You notice that other companies in your market sector are struggling and several of your competitors have merged. By exploring how companies outside your industry have responded to similar circumstances, you decide to parlay your firm's particular expertise—high-quality manufacturing—to move into a higher-growth market sector. In turn, you reposition your firm's image with your customers, suppliers, and the media. You assert that your manufacturing excellence will lead to superior products. Your enterprising approach allows you to recognize a problem, set an objective for remodeling your business, and execute your reinvention plan effectively.

If you're excited about applying resourcefulness in your business, here are some questions that will guide you.

- In your business, have you been inventive? If so, what did you do? Were you successful in your efforts? If not, do you understand why? What caused you to employ your ingenuity in your business? Was your organization performing unacceptably or not reaching its potential? Were you addressing a problem that involved your offerings, how you delivered these items, or one or more of your business' processes? If so, was your team responding to a customer demand or expectation, or did your managers or suppliers want to improve your firm's efficiency or effectiveness? Or, were you pursuing an opportunity, such as introducing a new product, inaugurating a new line, transitioning into a new market segment, or starting a new venture?

- Has being imaginative helped you set your reinvention goal? If so, how did such thinking enable you to build your ideal? Or, has your brightness aided you in refining your objective? If you haven't visualized your ideal, will you use your resourcefulness to assist you?

- Whether or not you've decided upon your reinvention objective, will you employ your quick-wittedness to pursue your goal? For example, if you're enhancing your business' offerings, will you seek feedback from your customers concerning the improvements they'd like to see? If you're expanding or transitioning your business, will you solicit other businesspeople's ideas in order to launch new offerings or move into a high-growth segment of your market? If you're starting a new business within your company, will you minimize your risk by speaking with firms that have established such ventures or by partnering with a business that's experienced in start-ups? Whatever reinvention option you undertake, will you and your people network effectively—attending conferences, participating in industry initiatives, and talking to other professionals that have reshaped their businesses?

- Will you ensure that you apply your sharpness to stay successful in and satisfied with your reinvention? Will you establish measures to track your progress? For example, to maintain your organization's upbeat or productive mind-set, will you establish particular mechanisms, such as special events, rewards, or other recognition? Will you also routinely meet with other businesspeople to discuss your experiences?

By this point, you understand the value of being resourceful in your career or business, but whether you're an employee, executive, or entrepreneur, can you be too resourceful? Let's look at the associated pitfalls.

AVOID THE DOWNSIDES OF RESOURCEFULNESS

Wrapped up in being clever, a worker utilizes an unsound approach and, consequently, impedes his job change. Unduly venturesome, an executive's idea leads to disastrous results. Because of her wiliness, a manager's colleagues mistrust her. A crafty entrepreneur loses customers and also the respect of his employees.

These examples illustrate how businesspeople can be too resourceful, but you're not worried. You're levelheaded and, therefore, won't get carried away. Yet, what if you become consumed with being ingenious and, as a result, you pursue an ill-conceived concept or half-baked technique? You may wish that you hadn't used such an unproductive plan or method. Or, what if you're so intent on your goal that you exploit any means available to attain this end? Your coworkers, customers, or suppliers may resent your Machiavellian tactics.

Sensible executives and entrepreneurs stay on an even keel. These workers are neither too clever nor insufficiently inventive and, by striking the right balance, these businesspeople aren't inclined to employ ineffective ideas or approaches that might slow their job or business reinventions or even cause these efforts to flop. These professionals also don't allow their quick-wittedness to become excessive and, consequently, these individuals don't become sly or deceitful. These folks recognize that tricky behavior can alienate people who are critical to their career or business success and, therefore, these individuals act with integrity. The following examples may help you better understand the perils of being too resourceful.

Maybe you're an employee who wants to reenergize your attitude. To accomplish your goal, you initiate a project to address a problem with your department's approach. Having witnessed a colleague's poor results from a similar undertaking, you're determined not to repeat his mistakes. Because this coworker was intent on establishing a project using whatever means were necessary, this individual deceived his fellow employees. This crafty businessperson promised several employees that in exchange for their support in launching his endeavor, he'd name them to his project team. Once this wily operator fulfilled his objective, he abandoned his commitments. Because of his trickiness, this worker's colleagues no longer trust him and many go out of their way to avoid dealing with him. Unlike this person, you'll network with integrity. If you aren't sure about what you'll be able to offer others, you won't make promises you might not be able to keep.

Perhaps you're an entrepreneur who seeks to enhance your firm's offerings. To meet this aim, you solicit your customers' input concerning the improvements they'd like to see. Because you've heard about the disastrous outcome of a like effort of a peer at another company, you're committed to applying your resourcefulness appropriately. Rather than obtaining his clients' feedback, this business owner employed what he considered an exceptionally clever technique. Without first evaluating its relevance to his firm, this individual blindly copied another business' approach and, because of his reckless action, this entrepreneur failed to improve his products. As a result, many of his clients took their business elsewhere. In contrast to your colleague, you won't employ methods that sound ingenious but that won't lead to your goal.

To assist you in avoiding the dangers associated with being too resourceful, here are several questions to ask yourself.

- Have you (or someone you know) employed an idea or approach that backfired? If so, why did this happen? Were you consumed with being ingenious or clever and, as a result, you didn't critically evaluate whether a particular move might delay your progress or even cause you (or your business) to become unsuccessful? What was the outcome of your action? Did you fail to initiate a project or obtain the position you sought? Or, did your business reshaping or expansion fizzle? In other words, did too much resourcefulness lead to the demise of your career or business reinvention? (In Chapter 8, you'll learn that being impatient can also lead you to employ an unsound approach.)

- Did you (or someone you're acquainted with) use a wily technique to reach a career or business goal? Did you state that you'd take certain actions but instead engaged in activities that contradicted your words? Have you tricked a fellow employee to get the position you wanted, or have you deceived your customers, suppliers, or employees in order to transform or expand your business? Did your approach bring about the results you planned? Even if it did, was there fallout from your being tricky or deceitful?

- If you suspect that you might become too resourceful during your career or business reinvention, how will you prevent this problem from occurring?

Now let's examine which reinvention option best fits your work situation.

APPLY YOUR RESOURCEFULNESS

In this section, you'll assess how your situation lines up with various reinvention options. You'll evaluate why you might choose a particular option to satisfy your objectives. As was true in the previous chapters, your situation won't precisely match the attributes of the scenarios that follow, nor will it incorporate all of these characteristics.

REINVIGORATE YOUR JOB

Your situation may include the following components:

- *Become resourceful.* Usually, you've used your senses. You've made an acceptable effort to stay informed about your marketplace. You've been open to listening to and occasionally experimenting with new ideas and approaches.

- *Be resourceful in your job.* To improve your performance or revitalize your attitude, you'd like to emulate a colleague's approach. You want to use a concept or technique you've read about to solve a problem or pursue an opportunity.

- *Avoid the downsides.* You won't be tricky with your coworkers.

If the above sounds like your circumstances, here are a couple of reasons you may choose to reinvigorate your job:

- You don't want to leave your current position but, by using a clever idea or technique, you seek to enliven how you handle your job, how you feel about your role, or both. Or, you need or want to solve a problem, take advantage of an opportunity, and, by doing so, reach the goal you've set for yourself.

- You're sure of your aim(s).

CHANGE JOBS IN YOUR COMPANY

Your work may reflect the following components:

- *Become resourceful.* You've utilized your senses. You've made a good to excellent effort to keep up to date about your marketplace. You've been receptive to new thoughts and methods and have sometimes applied these notions in your work.

- *Be resourceful in your job.* You see how you can use your contacts to change positions. Because you're moving to a new area, you have to reposition your image. You want to create a new role for yourself.

- *Avoid the downsides.* You won't act deceitfully toward your colleagues.

If the preceding elements describe your circumstances, here are some reasons you may elect to change jobs:

- Although you've performed acceptably or well, you're ready to leave your current job or role. Employing an inventive concept, an ingenious approach, or both, you're committed to obtaining the work you want and, therefore, attaining your work ideal.

- You're confident of your objective(s).

ENHANCE YOUR BUSINESS' OFFERING OR APPROACH

Your circumstances may incorporate the following components:

- *Become resourceful.* You and your people have employed your senses. You and your colleagues have stayed alert regarding your marketplace. You and your team have been open to new processes and have often utilized them. You and your people have developed or honed your ability to think critically.

- *Be resourceful in your business.* You seek to apply another firm's approach to improve your offerings or processes. You want to use the input you've received from your customers, suppliers, or employees.

- *Avoid the downsides.* You won't employ unproductive or even dangerous plans or methods.

If some or most of the above sound familiar, here are a few reasons you may opt to enhance your area or firm:

- Your business has performed acceptably to well but, by inventively applying what you've learned, you seek to make a moderate change in your business or achieve the goal you've established.

- You're certain about what you want to accomplish.

TRANSITION YOUR BUSINESS

Your business may embody the following components:

- *Become resourceful.* In the past, you or your people haven't applied your senses effectively. You or your managers haven't stayed fully informed about your marketplace. You or your colleagues haven't been receptive to listening to or adopting new notions or techniques. Or, you and your workers have utilized your faculties. You and your employees have been attentive to trends and developments in your marketplace. You and your people have sought and frequently exploited imaginative ideas and methods.

- *Be resourceful in your business.* You'd like to employ another leader's approach. In order to develop new offerings or move into a new sector, you want to exploit ideas you've learned about.

- *Avoid the downsides.* You won't engage in overly clever ideas and approaches that won't help you reach your goal. You won't be wily when dealing with your customers or employees.

If the preceding factors resemble your situation, here are some reasons you may choose to transition your business:

- By using your resourcefulness, you're committed to bringing about a substantial reshaping of your business. Doing so will enable you to solve a problem, pursue an opportunity, or meet a goal you've put in place.

- You're positive about what you need or want to achieve.

START A NEW BUSINESS WITHIN YOUR COMPANY

Your business' status may include the following components:

- *Become resourceful.* You and your managers have used your senses. You and your people have carefully followed trends and developments in your marketplace. You and your managers have aggressively pursued and regularly taken advantage of new concepts and modes of operating.

- *Be resourceful in your business.* You want to utilize another firm's strategy. You seek to capitalize on an activity at which your workers excel.

- *Avoid the downsides.* You won't employ unsafe means to achieve your ideal.

If most of the above describe your ideal, here are a couple of reasons you may want to start a new business at your firm:

- By exploiting what you've learned from other organizations or through your own experiences, you're determined to make a significant change in your business.
- You're committed to fulfilling your entrepreneurial objective.

By now, you're probably motivated to incorporate resourcefulness in your job or business. If you haven't finished answering this chapter's questions, do so before you begin the next chapter. Step Five will show you how to build your reinvention game plan, which will incorporate your resourcefulness. Meanwhile, here are the stories of two people who've used ingenious ideas and approaches to reinvent their jobs and businesses.

LIVE YOUR RESOURCEFULNESS

Nelson Carbonell personifies resourcefulness.[2] Now president and CEO of Cysive, Inc., a software firm that builds systems that support large-scale e-businesses, this Internet entrepreneur has continually applied his cleverness.

Throughout his life, Carbonell has honed his resourcefulness. In doing so, this entrepreneur has consistently and fully used his senses and, as a result, he's improved his ability to think critically. While still in elementary school, he questioned his principal about a rule that required students to walk on the third tiles from the wall: "Haven't you noticed that those tiles are wearing out faster than all the others?" Moreover, to become and remain a high-tech leader, Carbonell has stayed alert to marketplace trends and developments. For instance, by being active in various business groups, such as the Young Presidents Organization, this savvy businessman has remained in touch with customers. As an early participant in the Internet revolution, this high-tech manager has also been highly receptive to new concepts and methods for producing and delivering e-business solutions. Indeed, Carbonell relishes challenging the status quo and asserts that he "likes getting someone to look at their convictions and, if these beliefs are flawed, helping them abandon these views."

Before becoming an entrepreneur, Carbonell employed his resourcefulness in his job. For example, during college, this young man held down two jobs, parking cars at a restaurant and programming computers for a Washington, D.C., consulting firm. To meet the demands of his grueling schedule, Carbonell hired his friends to help him.

After starting his own business, Carbonell used his resourceful-ness to rescue his struggling young firm and put it on a path to suc-cess. Founded in late 1993 as Alta Software, the company grew from $1 million in revenues in its first full year to $5 million in 1996, but despite this accomplishment, this organization didn't possess the know-how necessary to sell to large companies. In response to his company's problem, Carbonell experimented with other companies' selling techniques and, by doing so, landed an important project—building Cisco Systems' Internetworking Product Center, which, in 1998, was the world's largest e-commerce system. But because Car-bonell hadn't fully remedied his business' deficiency, his company continued to struggle and, by 1998, Alta had grim prospects. Some of Carbonell's employees thought that the young businessman should sell his company but, because he was alert to developments concerning the Internet, this bright entrepreneur did just the oppo-site. He hired staff, opened two new offices, established a professional sales process, and retrained his people in Java—the computer lan-guage of the coming Internet boom. As he says of his enterprising approach, "When things go wrong, seize the opportunity to reshape how you operate." In 2000, because he observed disturbing trends in the high-tech sector, Carbonell again employed his sharpness to refocus and restructure his organization so that his firm would suc-ceed—regardless of market conditions.

This high-tech whiz has also avoided a downside of resourceful-ness. This business owner acts with integrity. As he says: "I'm an engi-neer. Everything's black or white. I have a strong sense of right and wrong." In contrast to some firms in the e-business arena, Cysive provides solutions that deliver on their promises. In other words, this firm's systems actually work.

Like Carbonell, I've applied my resourcefulness to my work. You may recall the statement at the beginning of this chapter that your work reinvention may be the direct result of your resourcefulness or its by-product. I've sometimes reflected upon this chicken-or-egg conundrum: Did I reinvent because I'm clever or did my inventive resolution of work problems or pursuit of opportunities lead to my reinventions? Perhaps I won't discover the answer to this puzzle. In any case, while writing this book, I was pleased to learn that my fam-ily, friends, and clients think that, although I reflect the other steps, I embody this one.

Since childhood, I've been resourceful. For example, because I observed that existing communication coaching programs focused primarily on style and not content, I started a business to help executives improve both what and how they communicated. Thirteen years later, based on what I heard from corporate managers and entrepreneurs, I began writing a book to guide these individuals in reshaping their careers and businesses. In both cases, by using my awareness, I imaginatively crafted my work ideals. Moreover, I've stayed informed. My clients can attest to my attentiveness to trends and developments in their industries. To keep up to date, I routinely read numerous periodicals and books and, through reading such publications, I identified two of this book's interviewees: Evelyn Granville in the *Smith Alumnae Quarterly* and Jimmy Ridings in *Forbes*. I've also been receptive to new notions and techniques. I regularly seek input concerning my ideas and projects from a variety of people and, while I don't always follow others' advice, I consistently listen to and critically evaluate their suggestions.

Prior to launching my business, I incorporated resourcefulness in several of my jobs. Two decades ago, as a corporate planner, I volunteered for an additional role—undercover agent. Nicknamed "G. Gordon Zimmerman," I skillfully investigated how my employer could transition into a market that another company dominated. Four years later, at a different company, I parlayed my involvement in a project into a new job, which entailed a move from my firm's finance area into sales. Cleverly repositioning how my colleagues and management viewed me was a critical factor in this job change. Eighteen months later, capitalizing on what I had seen and heard, I created a new job for myself—developer of an integrated sales strategy.

In my business, I've employed my resourcefulness to obtain new clients, develop additional offerings, and transition my firm. For example, sensing that there was a chance to provide hands-on, practical guidance to corporate managers, I segued from communication coaching to management consulting. Through ingeniously applying concepts and methods that I've used or read about, I've also helped my clients solve problems and pursue opportunities and, as a result, I've assisted companies in reinventing themselves—refocusing their organizations and improving how they delivered their products or services.

I've also endeavored to avoid the downsides of resourcefulness. Because I critically evaluate new concepts or techniques before I use them, I don't employ unsound or even unsafe ideas or approaches. I'm also not deceitful in my dealings with clients or colleagues and, consequently, I operate with integrity—whatever reinvention I'm engaged in.

CHAPTER SIX

STEP FIVE
Be Practical

Don't get swept up in grandiose visions of what you want to accomplish.
Bring the vision below the 50,000-foot level. You should be able to
explain what you need to do in clear, simple terms. . . .[1]

—RAM CHARAN, CONSULTANT AND AUTHOR

Do you envy a colleague who set successive goals for herself
and achieved them? Have you admired a businessperson who signifi-
cantly improved his business within a short period of time? Have you
been jealous of a worker who was confident of what he was doing and
where he was headed?

If you've answered yes to any of these questions, you perceive that
practical business professionals work in businesses near you or even in
your company. Pragmatic individuals usually succeed in attaining
their objectives, whether such aims involve their jobs, their businesses, or both. Perhaps you want to develop realistic ideals and go
after them in a businesslike way but you're not sure that you'd recognize a doable idea or approach when you saw it.

Practicality can take many forms. It may be a sound statement of
purpose and the sensible milestones that a manager uses to guide his
career or the business he operates. Rational actions enable individuals
to attain their goals. Down-to-earth methods ensure that organizations deliver on their expectations and workers reach their ideals. Or,
it may be a combination of these elements—a plan that makes sense

for its user. No doubt, developing and using such a strategy requires a lot of work.

Yet, what if by not utilizing a practical plan, you bring about the wrong reinvention of your job or business? As a result, you may be confused by or dissatisfied with the outcome of your efforts. What if by not employing an efficient approach, you don't accomplish your work transformation when you planned or in time to meet a deadline set by your management or investors? Under these circumstances, you may become anxious or even desperate. Or, what if because you're unrealistic, you don't obtain the new position you hoped for or bring about the business transition you wanted? In this case, you may be disappointed that you weren't effective in reaching your career or business goal.

To avoid these situations, you need to develop and apply a carefully thought-out course of action. As you've seen in the sports world, this invaluable tool—a game plan—embodies practical thinking and action. It's what major league teams employ to win. Because you are (or seek to be) among the best in your business, company, or industry, you'll create such a strategy to make sure that you succeed. Your plan will include a statement of the overall purpose or mission of your work and the milestones or specific events, like a job or business reinvention, that you'll achieve in order to realize this ambition. Your strategy will also lay out the specific actions you'll take to arrive at each milestone and the approach you'll use to do so. When you combine these elements, you'll establish an integrated scheme for yourself or your business. In other words, you'll create a road map that will help you know where you want to go and will make sure that you get there.

This critical chapter lays the groundwork for the implementation of your reinvention, a subject you'll examine in the chapters that follow. Step Five will show you how to build a game plan, the tool you'll use to pursue and obtain your ideal work—both now and in the future. You'll learn how to devise a clear statement of the mission of your work and define the milestones you'll achieve to fulfill your purpose. You'll identify the actions that you'll take to arrive at your first milestone or reinvention and the approach you'll use to accomplish these deeds. Next, you'll bring together the various components of your game plan and, in turn, choose the reinvention option that's most applicable to your situation. Then, you'll read about two people who've utilized practical plans to reinvent their careers and businesses.

DEVELOP A PRACTICAL MISSION

A sensible professional confidently pursues positions that involve increasing levels of responsibility. Anticipating the skills she'll need for a future role, a pragmatic manager obtains the necessary training. Looking back on his numerous successes, a down-to-earth executive credits the mission statement that has guided him throughout his career.

Maybe you respect the businesspeople in these examples. These individuals obtain what they want. The savvy know where they're going and prepare to get there. These practical people devise a declaration of purpose to steer their job or business choices. Even so, you're not sure that rejuvenating or revamping your work requires such a statement. Yet, what if you have an opportunity to change jobs or move your firm into a new product line? Will you be able to determine whether such a move makes sense for your career or business? Without a cogent statement of your work's purpose, you may have difficulty coming up with the correct answer. What if you assume a new role, such as the leader of a global project team or an organization that needs to refocus? Will you be ready to handle the demands of your new work? If you didn't expect this position, you may not have prepared and, therefore, may have trouble performing. Or, what if you're about to retire? Will you know whether you've fulfilled your calling if you never bothered to articulate your ambition?

Logical businesspeople realize that their job or business may involve several reinventions, with each reshaping of their work leading them closer to their lifelong goal. That is to say, these intelligent individuals understand that whatever reinvention they're undertaking is probably not their last. To be fully conscious of how their current work transformation fits within the larger picture of their career or business, these astute professionals design customized mission statements. Such practical declarations convey how managers and entrepreneurs will exploit their abilities and motivations to achieve the highest goal of their career or business.

Perhaps you're shaking your head. You've seen these vague pronouncements before. Such statements often seem unrelated to the talents and inclinations of the individuals or organizations they're intended to direct. These expertly crafted manifestos typically promise accomplishments that aren't doable by the people who must meet these commitments. These assertions usually don't convey how their users will progress from their current situation to the prescribed ideal state. You don't want such an impractical articulation for your career or business.

If, however, you devise a mission statement that truly fits your skills, motivations, and ultimate workplace objective, you'll have a highly serviceable tool that will guide your work in the coming years. That way, by the time you retire, you'll recognize whether or not you've achieved your greatest goal.

To ensure that you'll know how to proceed from where you are to your highest work ideal, you'll also develop key milestones—one of which may be your upcoming reinvention—that you must reach along the way. These events will build logically upon each other. For example, if your ultimate objective is to become your company's chief financial officer, your interim milestones may include financial analyst, corporate controller, and acquisitions advisor. Or, if your dream is to become your firm's top sales executive, your intervening steps may be sales representative, sales manager, and director of sales strategy. By identifying these future stages of your work, you'll be able to anticipate the talents you'll need and, if you choose, prepare your skills.

At this point, if you're not positive about your mission or milestones or how you'll use them, don't worry. In Chapter 7, you'll discover how to respond if your mission and milestones are wrong or need revision and, in Chapter 10, you'll learn how to evaluate a future reinvention against these tools. Meanwhile, the following two scenarios may help you crystallize these concepts.

Let's assume that you're an accomplished worker who seeks to change jobs in your company. You visualize moving from your area, which is a support function, such as finance, human resources, or information technology, into a group that has direct responsibility for selling and, in turn, providing your company's products or services to customers. You've concluded that your skills—inventiveness and working well with others—and what's important to you—recognition—match well with your current reinvention goal. Ultimately, you want to become your company's top business development executive. How will you translate this information into a declaration of purpose?

You may state that your mission is to parlay your resourcefulness and ease in working with people to spearhead your company's global expansion. By doing so, you'll receive recognition as a leader from your colleagues, customers, and industry. How will you articulate the principal stages you'll pass through in order to fulfill this objective?

You may say that you'll serve as the manager of a small division that sells your firm's offerings to a particular industry. Assuming you perform well, your next milestones (or reinventions) may include becoming the manager of a midsized division, the manager of a large division that has customers around the world, and, lastly, the senior vice president for global business development. Having identified these future opportunities, you may recognize potential gaps in your skills and begin to remedy these deficiencies.

Now imagine that you run a business. At this point, you visualize introducing a new offering in your marketplace. You've determined that your workers' skills—managing risk and selling aggressively—and their motivations—money and recognition—correspond closely with your reinvention objective. Your greatest goal involves establishing a new business within the firm. How will you employ this awareness into a mission statement?

You may assert that your business' purpose is to capitalize on your people's entrepreneurial savvy in order to launch an enterprise that provides a full range of services to companies in your industry. This venture's managers will be compensated as if they were independent businesspeople. The efforts of these professionals will win the plaudits of their marketplace and possibly the media. How will you describe the milestones related to your long-term ambition?

You may state that your firm will introduce a new service that fills a void in your marketplace. If this offering is successful, your company will subsequently inaugurate additional services. Once your business has built a critical mass of customers for its services, your business will set up a separate unit that provides a complete array of these offerings.

No doubt, you see the value of creating a mission statement and milestones for your career or business. Here are some questions that will assist you in developing these instruments.

- Do you know a businessperson who used a mission statement to guide his career? If so, what did his declaration of purpose include? Did it reflect the individual's skills, inclinations, and highest goal? If not, what were its components? Did this person also identify the key steps necessary to attain his mission? If so, did such milestones build logically upon one another? Did this worker use these stages in order to prepare his skills? Has this individual employed his mission statement and milestones to advance his career and, if so, has this businessperson been successful in his efforts?

- Are you familiar with businesses that have mission statements? If so, what do these assertions say? Do they reflect their employees' abilities and motivations and incorporate the business'

general direction or ultimate aim? If not, what do these procla-
mations include? Do these businesses also articulate the events
that have to occur before they achieve their goal? If so, do these
milestones progress sensibly? By identifying these stages, are
these businesses able to prepare their people's skills? Are these
businesses successful in utilizing their mission statements and
milestones to deliver the results they seek?

• Whether or not you've previously used a mission statement and
milestones for your career or business, will you create these
mechanisms? If so, formulate your (or your business') declaration of purpose and the key stages you (or your business) will
pass through in order to reach your highest goal. Be sure to put
these items in writing so that you can use them in Chapter 10.

PURSUE PRACTICAL ACTIONS

By undertaking activities in the appropriate sequence, a savvy
entrepreneur avoids wasting time or money. A shrewd executive turns
around his company by pursuing actions that lead to his goal.

You understand that the persons in these examples are practical,
but so are you. You're not concerned about whether you'll do the
right things. You've been fairly sensible throughout your career. Yet,
what if you forget to incorporate resourcefulness in your job or business? Without inventive deeds, you may not be able to bring about
the imaginative results you seek. What if you perform the right
actions but at the wrong time? You may have to backtrack and,
because of your inefficiency, lose time or money or miss a narrow window of opportunity to initiate a task force, introduce a new product,
or launch a new line. What if your actions don't build logically upon
each other? You may not be effective in reinvigorating your job,
changing positions, or creating a new role for yourself. Or, if you
manage a business, your illogical actions may keep you from enhancing your products or services, refocusing your organization, or starting a new venture within your company. What if your actions cause
you to become frustrated and, as a result, you abandon your reinvention journey? You may regret not identifying and completing the
appropriate tasks.

Rational business professionals pinpoint the key actions, including those using their resourcefulness, that they must complete in
order to attain their milestones or reinventions. These workers realize
that engaging in activities that don't lead to their goals is ineffective.

Pursuing impractical actions can also be inefficient because if you have to regroup, you'll lose time, money, or both. Sensible people also determine the order in which they need to perform their actions. These down-to-earth folks understand that doing the right task at the wrong time is inefficient and if their reinvention fails because they undertook actions at inappropriate times, it's also ineffective. The savvy also grasp that knowing the correct actions and their proper sequence gives you the confidence to persevere in your reinvention. Let's go back to the two examples in the previous section.

The first scenario describes a manager who wants to change jobs in his company and, by doing so, move from working in a support function to running a small division of his firm. For this worker to achieve this first milestone or reinvention, he may complete course-work that will help him develop the skills needed for his new job and also obtain a corporate mentor to advise him. He may serve on a project team that's addressing business issues and, in turn, capitalize upon his training and project experience to secure his ideal position. Because this individual will engage in actions that build logically toward his goal, he'll probably be effective and, most likely, he'll reach his reinvention ideal. On the other hand, if this worker doesn't seek guidance, whether through instruction or a mentor, and apply his learning in a project, he may not appear credible to his future colleagues and, therefore, fail to achieve his job change. But, there may be some flexibility in the order of his actions. For example, in order to select the best training, this worker may meet with his mentor before he starts his coursework. Yet, no matter which of these two actions he takes first, in all probability, this worker will be efficient. He won't lose time backtracking to acquire the training he didn't obtain at the start of his reinvention.

In the second example, an entrepreneur seeks to introduce a new service. To attain her reinvention objective, this business owner and her employees may solicit input from existing and potential customers and also consult with an industry expert. This organization may perform a market test of the new service, make the necessary refinements, and launch the new offering. Because it will complete activities that progress sensibly toward its aim, this firm will, most likely, be effective. Even so, this leader may choose to skip one of the listed activities. If she feels confident about the customer feedback she's received, this individual may not speak with a market guru. In any event, assuming that this entrepreneur obtains feedback before she introduces her new service, this business will also be efficient. That is to say, this executive and her workers probably won't waste time and money retracing their steps.

Engaging in practical actions is critical. Here are some questions to deepen your understanding of how to identify the right actions for your reinvention.

- Do you know someone who decided to revitalize her attitude or improve her performance but didn't identify the specific actions she'd take to accomplish her goal? Has she been ineffective in fulfilling her objective? Have you met a manager who sought to change jobs in his company but didn't pinpoint the activities essential to attaining his dream position? Has he become frustrated and given up his reinvention? Or, are you acquainted with a businessperson who wanted to change roles but engaged in tasks that didn't lead to her ideal? Did she have to regroup and, as a result, lose time or even her opportunity? Could she have avoided such an inefficient and ineffective result?

- Have you heard about an area of your company that had an admirable aim but didn't determine what it had to do to fulfill its objective? Was this business ineffective in delivering on its promises? Have you seen an organization that was engaged in activities that weren't headed anywhere? Did its employees become discouraged and throw in the towel? Or, have you observed a team that was involved in actions that weren't leading to its goal? Did this group have to backtrack and, consequently, waste time and money? Or, did management lose confidence in this team and shut down its effort? Could this group have prevented such an inefficient and even ineffective outcome?

- Do you know people who've completed the right actions but in the wrong order? Did these people go after jobs before they learned about the prerequisites associated with these roles? Did these businesspeople fail to network with managers who could have provided helpful introductions? Have you heard about workers who tried to change positions before they assessed their skills and motivations? Did you deduce that performing the correct task at an inappropriate time can cause you to retrace your steps and, as a result, waste time or even miss out on the opportunity you're seeking?

- Are you familiar with a business that engaged in the right actions but at the wrong time? Did this firm launch a new product before fully testing this offering and, consequently, have to pull this item from the market? Have you seen an area of your company that hired additional employees before it restructured and later had to terminate these workers? Have you heard about a business that moved into a new market segment before it fully investigated this sector? Did you conclude that a business whose actions are out of order often has to regroup and, thus, loses time or money or even fails to achieve its objective?

- Before you commence your reinvention, will you determine the specific actions you need to take to attain your ideal role or position? Will you decide upon the actions you must complete in order to achieve the revamp of your business? Will you incorporate all key tasks, including deeds that reflect your (or your people's) resourcefulness? How will you make sure that you've identified the right activities? Will you discuss your choices with your coworkers or businesspeople outside your company? Will you emulate the actions taken by people or businesses that have accomplished similar aims? Once you've identified the necessary actions for your career or business, will you decide upon the order of these activities? How will you verify that the sequence you've chosen is correct?

Take the time to write down the actions you'll take to reach your ideal job or business. Also indicate the order in which you'll pursue these tasks. In Chapter 9, you'll learn how to implement these activities.

USE A PRACTICAL APPROACH

A team accomplishes its objective on time and without incurring additional costs. By employing direct techniques, an organization becomes more efficient than before. Avoiding flawed methods, workers are effective in enhancing their firm's offerings. A perceptive businessperson operates in a manner that's consistent with her style.

You see that the individuals in these examples are pragmatic in how they approach their work, but you've gotten by in the past. Your mode of operating has usually worked for you. Yet, what if you're having trouble finishing the actions associated with your milestone but don't know why? Assuming you're performing the right activities in the proper sequence, you may discover that your faulty approach, such as being arrogant with customers or colleagues, is impeding your progress or that your circuitous technique, such as e-mailing a coworker when stopping by would be faster, is delaying your efforts.

What if your managers take too long to finish their tasks and, consequently, your business doesn't meet a deadline for introducing a new product? Your firm may lose out to a competitor who launches a similar offering before you do. What if you and your managers exceed your budget to launch a new line of services? Your company may terminate your initiative. Or, what if you emulate a colleague's job-change technique even though you're uncomfortable with their plan of attack? You may not network or interview as well as you could and, therefore, you may fail to secure your dream position.

Smart businesspeople recognize that the most efficient and effective approach usually involves direct and sensible means and that this mode of operating also costs less and is faster than an unproductive method. That is to say, these individuals are aware of the downside of using flawed or roundabout methods, not staying within their budget, or not adhering to their schedule. These professionals have seen individuals and companies pull the plug on career and business reinventions that went awry. The realistic are also conscious that if their approach doesn't fit them, they probably won't use it, and if they do, they may have trouble bringing about their work ideal. Let's return to the worker and the entrepreneur described earlier and examine how these individuals can employ practical approaches in their reinventions.

In the first example, a manager wants to change jobs in his company and, by doing so, move from working in a support function to running a small division of his firm. To complete the coursework needed for his ideal position, this individual may pursue a part-time MBA, taking classes every other Friday and Saturday. Or, in the evenings or on weekends, he may complete courses online. Either way, this individual will use his (and his employer's) time efficiently. In order to obtain a mentor, this businessperson may seek the guidance of a colleague he knows who runs a business. That way, this worker won't waste time chasing a senior manager or executive he hasn't met and, consequently, won't slow his reinvention. Once he finds an advisor, this person will avoid using an improper approach, such as not responding promptly to his mentor's messages, or one that's circuitous, such as rambling during their conversations. To obtain the project he needs, this clever professional will network effectively with his contacts throughout his company. In going after his ideal job, this aware person will also use an approach that fits his style.

The second scenario involves a business owner who seeks to launch a new service. To solicit input that they'll use to design their new offering, this individual and her employees may hold one or two meetings with customers. So that these sessions are both efficient and effective, this firm's managers may develop a carefully thought-out agenda, use a meeting facilitator, or both of these approaches. But regardless of how they operate, these individuals will act in a manner that's consistent with their corporate culture. If these businesspeople decide to seek an expert's advice, they may ask their colleagues at other firms for recommendations. That way, these savvy players won't waste time looking for a market guru or lose money by hiring the wrong consultant. If they employ an outside advisor, these people won't use an unsound approach, such as giving the consultant free rein to pursue his favorite strategies, or a roundabout means, such as allowing this counselor to interview colleagues who aren't involved with the introduction of the new service. To test their new item and make refinements, these professionals may establish a reasonable yet expeditious schedule that includes clear accountability. In this way, these individuals won't delay the launch of their new service or even fail to inaugurate this offering. When they launch their new product, these businesspeople may introduce this offering across the market or only in certain segments. However they roll out this item, these folks will choose the approach that provides the optimum combination of efficiency and effectiveness.

Hopefully, you're committed to utilizing a practical means to accomplish your actions. Assuming you are, the following questions will assist you.

- Have you known businesspeople who wanted to rejuvenate their positions or change jobs but ended up spinning their wheels? Were these people ineffective because they didn't use their time efficiently, employed a roundabout method, such as e-mailing instead of meeting with a prospective supervisor, or an incorrect technique, like trying to dominate an interview? Or, did their lack of results stem from their employing an approach that didn't fit their style?

- Have you observed businesses that sought to enhance their offerings, launch new offerings, transform their organizations, or start new ventures but failed in their efforts? Were these companies ineffective because their workers were inefficient, wasting time in unnecessary meetings or getting bogged down in unfruitful discussions? Did their managers utilize a circuitous technique, such as using a third party to contact dissatisfied customers instead of speaking with them directly, or a defective approach, such as taking dangerous shortcuts in testing a new product? Or, did these businesses fail to achieve the outcomes they planned because their approach didn't suit their collective style?

- Before you start your reinvention, will you decide upon your approach? How will you ensure that your method will be practical? Can your resourcefulness help you identify sensible techniques? Will you (or your workers) set up a schedule with clear deadlines for your actions? How will you (or your managers) stay within your budget? Will you (or your employees) avoid using roundabout or faulty techniques? Will you determine ahead of time that your method fits your (or your managers') style? Through your efforts, will you (or your business) operate as efficiently as possible? Will you (or your business) be effective in attaining your career (or business) milestone?

Write down the key elements of your approach so that you'll be ready to implement in Chapter 9.

PULL TOGETHER YOUR GAME PLAN

After spending months pursuing a job change, a manager discovers that her actions aren't leading to her goal. Just weeks before a major deadline, frustrated managers abandon their reinvention initiative.

You probably want to avoid these scenarios. You don't like unpleasant surprises, especially when they concern your work. Even so, you feel relatively confident that your reinvention plan will work. Besides, you usually achieve what you set out to accomplish. Yet, what if after you've begun your reinvention, you find that your plan's components don't mesh? As a result, you may not make progress and, because of your situation, you may become disappointed, even depressed. Or, what if by employing a convoluted plan, you have trouble following or sticking with your strategy? You may make mistakes, such as undertaking actions in the wrong order, and, if you become too frustrated, you may throw in the towel.

Practical businesspeople confirm that their game plan is fully integrated. The milestone they're working toward is consistent with their mission statement. Their actions build logically toward this milestone. To complete their actions, they use an efficient and effective approach. Because they know that a complicated plan isn't inherently better than a simple one and can even be self-defeating, these pragmatic folks also check that their plan is easy to follow and stick with. By carefully assembling their plan, these down-to-earth people are more likely to complete their plan and, in turn, achieve their career or business reinvention. Now let's return to the two examples you examined earlier.

The first scenario describes a manager who wants to change jobs in his company and, by doing so, move from working in a support function to running a small division of his firm. After assembling his game plan, this individual decides that its components fit together well. His milestone or current reinvention—becoming the manager of a small division—is his first step in fulfilling his purpose—spearheading his company's global expansion. His actions—which include completing coursework, obtaining a mentor, undertaking a project, and going after his new position—build logically to his milestone or reinvention goal. His approach—which involves studying part time, choosing a colleague as his advisor, and networking to secure a project and find his ideal job—is efficient, effective, and consistent with his style. As a result, this method will enable this individual to accomplish his actions. This sensible businessperson also concludes that his plan is relatively simple and, consequently, he'll be able to stay with his strategy.

In the second example, an entrepreneur seeks to inaugurate a new service. Having brought together the game plan for her business, this owner determines that her strategy is integrated. Her firm's milestone or current reinvention—introducing a new service—fits with her company's mission—launching a new venture that will provide a full array of services. Her business' actions, which include obtaining input from customers and possibly advice from an industry expert, testing and refining her new offerings, and launching this service, move her operation closer to its objective. Her organization's approach—which involves using an agenda and a facilitator for meetings, choosing a consultant based on recommendations from colleagues at other businesses, and developing and adhering to a clear schedule—is productive and also compatible with her employees' collective style. This entrepreneur decides that, unlike many business strategies, her game plan isn't complex and, as a result, she and her people will be capable of persevering.

Most likely, you appreciate the value of pulling together your game plan. Here are some questions to get you started.

- Did a colleague employ a plan to change jobs but didn't obtain the position he wanted? After talking with this person, did you suspect that the components of his plan didn't come together? Assuming he knew his ultimate career goal, was his ideal job inconsistent with his mission? Did his actions fail to help him progress to his desired position or was he pursuing the right actions but in the wrong order? Was his approach inefficient, ineffective, or incompatible with his style? Or, was this individual's strategy complex? As a result, did he become frustrated and abandon his goal?

- Have you known a businessperson who used a plan to transform her organization but didn't achieve her objective? After speaking with this individual, did you surmise that her plan wasn't integrated? Did her proposed reinvention not correspond to her company's stated mission? Were her organization's actions incorrect or in the wrong sequence? Did this manager and her workers utilize an approach that was inefficient, ineffective, or inconsistent with their collective style? Or, was this business' plan so complicated that this firm's workers became confused?

- Before you start your reinvention, will you assemble your game plan? If so, will you ensure that its components fit together? Will you also confirm that your strategy is easy to follow and stick with? If colleagues read your plan and don't think that it fits together or they find it too detailed, will you revise your strategy?

Assemble the components of your plan and review your strategy. You'll implement your course of action in Chapter 9.

APPLY YOUR PRACTICALITY

Now let's move on to how your circumstances correspond to various reinvention options. In this section, you'll determine why you might choose a particular option to meet your goals. As was true in the previous chapters, your situation won't precisely match the attributes of the scenarios that follow, nor will it incorporate all of these characteristics.

 REINVIGORATE YOUR JOB

Your work may reflect the following components:

- *Develop a practical mission.* You haven't determined your ultimate goal and its related milestones. Or, you've identified your career's overall purpose and contemplated how you'll achieve this aim.

- *Pursue practical actions.* You've considered what you'll have to do in order to rejuvenate your performance or revitalize your attitude. Or, you've decided upon the actions you'll take.

- *Use a practical approach.* You've thought about how you'll avoid wasting time and being unproductive. Or, you've resolved how you'll be as efficient and effective as possible.

- *Pull together your game plan.* You haven't fully developed your plan. Or, you've created a plan, which is simple and fits together well.

If the above sounds like your circumstances, here are a couple of reasons you may choose to reinvigorate your job:

- You know your immediate goal.

- Taking practical actions at the appropriate time and in a sensible way will help you reenergize your performance or attitude.

 ## CHANGE JOBS IN YOUR COMPANY

Your situation may include the following components:

- *Develop a practical mission.* You're aware of your highest career goal and the stages you must pass through to fulfill your purpose. Or, you've written down your mission and milestones.

- *Pursue practical actions.* You've thought about the actions you'll take. Or, you've documented the tasks you'll perform to change jobs or create a new role or position.

- *Use a practical approach.* You've assessed how you'll avoid being inefficient and ineffective. Or, you've developed the modus operandi you'll use.

- *Pull together your game plan.* You haven't finalized your plan. Or, you've finished your strategy, which is integrated and easy to follow.

If the preceding elements describe your circumstances, here are some reasons you may elect to change jobs:

- Your current job isn't helping you fulfill your purpose or a different position will move you more quickly toward your long-term aim. In either case, you're certain that you want to change jobs or roles.

- A pragmatic plan will assist you in accomplishing your goal and doing so faster than if you didn't have this strategy.

ENHANCE YOUR BUSINESS' OFFERINGS OR APPROACH

Your business may embody the following components:

- *Develop a practical mission.* You're conscious of your business' future direction and the goals you'll need to achieve along the way. Or, you're clear about your business' mission and milestones and have written down this information.

- *Pursue practical actions.* You have a pretty good idea of what you'll do to bring about improvements in your offerings or processes. Or, you've finalized your actions.

- *Use a practical approach.* You've evaluated how your organization can stay on schedule and within its budget. Or, you've laid out how you and your people will be efficient and effective in developing, testing, and launching your improved item or procedure.

- *Pull together your game plan.* You haven't finished your strategy. Or, you've completed your plan, which comes together well and will be convenient to stick with.

If some or most of the above sound familiar, here are a few reasons you may opt to enhance your area or firm:

- You've decided to make moderate changes.

- A doable strategy will allow you to accomplish your improvement initiative on time and within your budget.

TRANSITION YOUR BUSINESS

Your business' status may include the following components:

- *Develop a practical mission.* You perceive your business' long-term objective. Or, you're sure about your business' mission and the stages your firm must pass through to satisfy this purpose and you've developed a formal mission statement and milestones.

- *Pursue practical actions.* You understand the actions that will be necessary to refocus your organization, launch a new offering or line, or transition into a new market segment. Or, you've fully documented your actions.

- *Use a practical approach.* You've examined how your organization will maximize its efficiency and effectiveness. Or, you've written down your methods for reorganizing your people, developing and testing new items, or identifying and moving into a new sector.

- *Pull together your game plan.* You're not done formulating your strategy. Or, you've finalized your plan, which fits well and is serviceable.

If the preceding factors resemble your situation, here are some reasons you may choose to transition your business:

- You're committed to undertaking a substantial transformation of your business.

- A down-to-earth and orderly course of action will be essential to achieving your goal.

START A NEW BUSINESS WITHIN YOUR COMPANY

Your circumstances may incorporate the following components:

- *Develop a practical mission.* You grasp your business' overall direction. Or, you've developed your firm's mission statement and the milestones your business must attain to satisfy this ambition.

- *Pursue practical actions.* You recognize the actions your business will take to launch its new venture. Or, you've written down the specifics.

- *Use a practical approach.* You've considered how you'll establish and run this new unit. Or, you've documented your operating mode.

- *Pull together your game plan.* You're putting the finishing touches on your strategy. Or, you've completed your plan, which is fully integrated and functional.

If most of the above describe your ideal, here are a couple of reasons you may want to start a new business at your firm:

- You're determined to pursue this entrepreneurial route.

• A realistic game plan will be critical in taking such a risk.

By now, you understand the importance of developing and following a plan for your reinvention. If you haven't already done so, pull together your plan. In Step Six, you'll learn how to execute your game plan—almost flawlessly. Meanwhile, here are the stories of two businesspeople who've employed their plans to reinvent their work.

LIVE YOUR PRACTICALITY

Jimmy Ridings epitomizes practicality.[2] The Texan is founder, chairman, and CEO of Craftmade International, a ceiling fan and lighting company that generates annual revenues in excess of $200 million.

Aware of his selling ability and motivated to work independently, Ridings identified his purpose—to run his own business. This businessman grasped that he didn't want anyone putting limitations on him. Even so, beginning at age 19 and until he started his business 15 years later, Ridings worked for two different plumbing supply companies that regularly cut his commissions. Because he hadn't determined the milestones necessary to fulfill his mission, the future entrepreneur backed into these events. In 1985, after leaving his plumbing supply employer, Ridings became an independent sales representative whose best-selling items were ceiling fans. But when his main client changed strategies, this firm no longer needed him. Wasting no time, the young man started his own company. Subsequently, this intense businessman has established ambitious milestones for his business. Guided by these objectives, Ridings took his $12.5 million ceiling fan company public in 1990. Eight years later, by acquiring Trade Source International (TSI), the savvy entrepreneur doubled Craftmade's revenues and broadened his firm's distribution to include mass merchandising outlets in addition to the company's existing network, which caters to upscale markets.

This pragmatic business owner identifies and pursues the actions essential to meeting his goals. To launch his business, Ridings went from bank to bank until he found one that would lend to him and, during this time, also wrote orders, delivered fans to customers, and turned his sales into the cash necessary to purchase more fans. But because the astute businessman understood that his hand-to-mouth activities wouldn't catapult his company into the big leagues, Ridings scraped together the airfare and traveled to Taiwan to secure the fan supply he needed. Over the past 15 years, this entrepreneur has formalized his game plans by spelling out specific tasks, such as adding new products and undertaking acquisitions and joint ventures.

Ridings' down-to-earth approach is efficient, effective, and fully consistent with his style. For as long as possible, he used his business' cash flow to grow and, even today, asserts that "ROI is everything." This businessman also handles his professional partnerships in a sensible way. For example, Ridings made sure that he knew TSI's principals before he acquired their company, and he attributes his 15-year relationship with a Taiwanese ceiling fan manufacturer to his highly ethical modus operandi.

Thanks to his simple and well-integrated game plan, Ridings has been able to persevere and, as a result, he's built a market powerhouse.

Compared to Jimmy Ridings, I've been slower to formulate my purpose. When I started college, I planned on becoming an actress, but after taking several theater courses, I changed my mind and switched to a major in history. Because I wasn't sure of my abilities or aware of my motivations, I couldn't envision the general direction of my career and, consequently, I pursued and held jobs—executive assistant, banker, corporate planner, internal consultant, and salesperson—that didn't build toward a particular mission. After starting my business, I perceived that, even if I couldn't articulate it, my highest ambition would incorporate my talents—communication skills, logical thinking, and resourcefulness—and my desire for recognition. During the past several years, I've formalized my mission—to become a nationally recognized business authority—and my milestones, which include becoming a speaker and assuming a media role.

Whenever I've committed to a milestone or reinvention goal, I've employed my practicality to determine what actions I needed to take and in which order. For example, to transition from communication coaching to consulting, I declined coaching assignments in order to accept consulting engagements, focused on clients who could provide such opportunities, and expanded my contacts by attending business gatherings. Because of these actions, I tripled my firm's revenues in two years. In order to get published, I attended a writer's conference, sought my clients' input, and began writing full time. When I finished a book proposal and a draft of my manuscript, I searched for a publisher.

My approach to my work has usually been efficient and effective. For example, to solicit coaching work, I called on business decision makers instead of individuals in support areas, such as human resources or public relations. My direct approach, which is compatible with my style, helped me build my coaching business relatively quickly and, a few years later, segue—almost seamlessly—into consulting. On the other hand, my initial approach to getting published neither fit me nor was productive. After several months of sending one-page query letters to literary agents, I concluded that such a roundabout approach was wasting time and might fail, so I switched to a direct technique— contacting publishers by phone and in person. I realized that I was on the right track when, within days of contacting them, I received positive feedback from three publishers.

Overall, my game plans have been easy to follow and cohesive. But as you'll learn in the next chapter, I've sometimes had to revise my strategy or even regroup. Yet, even when my reinvention was difficult, I've learned, and as I reinvent my career, I draw upon my experiences.

CHAPTER SEVEN

STEP SIX
Execute Flawlessly

Winning leaders are high-energy people.
They are focused and determined.[1]

—NOEL TICHY, PROFESSOR, CONSULTANT, AND AUTHOR

Agility entails a continual readiness to change, sometimes
to change radically, what companies and people do and how they do it.[2]

—STEVEN GOLDMAN, ROGER NAGEL, AND KENNETH PREISS,
COMPETITIVENESS EXPERTS AND AUTHORS

Do you respect people who concentrate on accomplishing a course of action and, by doing so, achieve their goal? Why do successful businesses respond to some problems and opportunities but not others? Do you question how a professional can perform his regular job and change positions at the same time or how a company can move into a new market and simultaneously serve its existing customers? Are you interested in discovering how individuals and businesses can anticipate where they might have problems executing and prepare to deal with these challenges?

If you're asking yourself these questions, you're interested in how to carry out your career or business reinvention. You've witnessed managers and companies execute without a hitch and others fail to do so. You want to accomplish your reinvention but don't completely understand the ins and outs of implementation.

If they execute flawlessly, individuals and businesses tenaciously pursue their work ideals. That is to say, these people and firms perform the actions that are listed in their game plans. Business professionals and companies are attentive to shifts in their situations and, therefore, are ready to respond to both obstacles and favorable circumstances. The shrewd also maintain their equilibrium. In other words, these workers and businesses are neither so intent upon their work that they fail to perceive and react to changes nor so quick to tackle problems or take advantage of opportunities that they become distracted and don't finish their tasks.

Implementation sounds involved. Is all this effort really necessary? What if you waver in your commitment or perseverance? You may not achieve your work ideal. What if you're not alert or you're inflexible in how you operate? You may miss out on ways to safeguard, expedite, enhance, or even divert from your reinvention. What if you pursue opportunities indiscriminately? You may bring about the wrong reinvention. Or, what if you have trouble juggling your work and its transformation? You may unwittingly undermine your efforts.

Smart businesspeople know that flawless execution is critical to achieving their career and business reinventions. These individuals accept that reaching their goals will require dedication and hard work. Understanding that problems can undermine their efforts, these managers and entrepreneurs stay alert to such troubles and, if they detect an obstacle, they respond. Aware that a change in circumstances can be beneficial, the astute discern opportunities and determine whether and how they'll react. Because they recognize that not performing well in their existing work can sabotage their reinventions, professionals maintain a proper balance between their current role or business and its reshaping. Astute workers and owners also adjust how they implement. If they're involved in a new job or business, they're more agile than focused, but if these people are engaged in established roles or firms, they're more focused than agile.

This chapter will provide you with the fundamentals of execution. Step Six will show you how to stay focused yet be agile as you reinvent your work. You'll also learn how to strike the appropriate balance between your concentration and nimbleness. You'll next examine how to anticipate and prepare for the challenges that you might encounter during your implementation. Then, you'll consider how your situation lines up with various reinvention options and you'll select the alternative that best fits your circumstances. Then, you'll read about two businesspeople who've executed—almost flawlessly.

STAY FOCUSED

Determined to enhance his firm's offerings, a conscientious manager performs the actions documented in his game plan. A worker who's committed to reinvigorating her job uses the approach prescribed in her strategy to reach her ideal. Doggedly following his course of action, a businessman transitions his business into a new market sector. A manager's stick-to-itiveness enables her to create a new role for herself within her company.

You may admire the people in these examples because they're steadfast in their pursuit of their objectives. These folks don't become distracted by activities that are irrelevant to their goals. No matter the barriers, such individuals persevere and, more often than not, bring about the results they seek. But, you're not especially concerned about whether you'll persist during your reinvention journey. You usually undertake and complete the right tasks and, therefore, attain your aims.

Yet, what if you bring about the wrong reinvention, for example, introducing a new service when you planned to start a new venture that offers an array of such services? When you scrutinize your outcome, you may learn that you and your employees didn't undertake the actions written in your strategy. What if you're not progressing in your job-change endeavor or enhancement of your business' offerings? If you assess your (or your people's) performance, you may find that unrelated activities have sidetracked you. Or, what if you fail to achieve your business' objective of launching a new line or your career ambition of moving into another area of your company? After analyzing what went awry, you may discover that you (or your workers) weren't diligent.

Businesspeople who are determined to achieve their ideal work make sure that they perform the actions and use the approaches that are cited in their game plans. That way, they progress toward their objective instead of a result they didn't expect and don't want. Down-to-earth professionals don't become distracted by or preoccupied with activities that aren't connected to their reinventions and, consequently, these folks don't falter in their devotion to their goals. These practical managers and entrepreneurs also don't stint on the energy they put into their career or corporate transformations and, as a result, these persistent people complete their reinventions and usually attain their ideal jobs and businesses. The two scenarios that follow may deepen your understanding of staying focused.

Let's say that you're a manager who wants to reinvigorate your job. You visualize augmenting your current responsibilities with additional tasks, such as participating in a project, teaching a class at your company, or mentoring new or less experienced workers. Your game plan spells out the actions you'll take to pursue your goal. You'll pursue a project and also investigate opportunities to provide instruction to your colleagues and advise young professionals. Your strategy recommends that you utilize a practical approach to accomplish your activities. That is to say, you'll network effectively with colleagues to discover and go after part-time initiatives, like projects or task forces. You'll also meet directly with your company's human resources executive to explore how you can teach and with your division's general manager to discuss how you can counsel younger workers in your area. You may sense what being focused looks like, but how does its opposite appear?

Instead of doing the actions listed in your game plan, you may interview for a new job or create a position that you might want in the future. By such deeds, you may end up with the wrong result—a job change. If you don't become involved in projects, teaching, and mentoring, you may not progress toward your ideal work. If rather than using the approach outlined in your strategy, you employ roundabout techniques, such as meeting with people who don't make decisions about training or mentoring, you may not attain your aim as planned or even fail to reach it. If you become distracted by impertinent interests, you may waver in your purpose or even abandon your reinvention. Or, if you don't vigorously apply your talents, you may not reach your work ideal.

Now picture that you're a business leader who seeks to transform your organization. You visualize a company that consistently satisfies its customers and earns the respect of its industry. Your game plan delineates what you'll do to reshape your firm and the order in which you'll take these actions. You'll articulate your vision and the values that will guide your company. You'll restructure your operation, folding overlapping units into four clear lines of business. You'll also institute performance measures, such as a ranking system for managers, and establish mechanisms to enhance collaboration among your employees. As documented in your strategy, your approach will be efficient. That is to say, you won't lose time or money backtracking, such as having to explain your purpose six months after you've begun your reinvention. By addressing both the business and human aspects of your turnaround, your endeavor will also be effective. Can you imagine the impact of not aiming your attention on this major undertaking?

In lieu of performing the actions written in your game plan, you and your people may meet with customers to get their input on a potential new offering and, in turn, develop a prototype of this new item. Through such activities, you may bring about the wrong reinvention—the launch of a new product or service. If you don't explain your rationale for your corporate remodeling and put in place the structure, measures, and tools that are critical to this turnaround, you may not make progress toward your goal. If instead of employing the efficient approach laid out in your strategy, you start and stop your efforts and, consequently, have to regroup, you may waste your firm's resources, slow your reinvention, or even miss a window of opportunity to revamp your firm. If you or your managers become absorbed in ungermane activities, you may falter in your commitment and even abandon your reinvention. Or, if you and your people aren't industrious, you may not fulfill your objective.

Do you have a better grasp of why staying focused is critical to your reinvention? Assuming you do, here are some questions to help you.

- Have you ever devised a game plan and carried out this strategy and, consequently, attained your career or business goal? On the other hand, did you develop a game plan but didn't undertake the actions described in your strategy or use the recommended approach? Did you engage in unrelated activities? As a result, did you not progress or do so more slowly than planned? Were you forced to regroup and, by doing so, waste time, money, or both? Did you fail to achieve your work ideal or did you bring about the wrong reinvention?

- Throughout your career, have you usually stayed focused? Conversely, did you ever intend to reshape your work but became distracted by, or even preoccupied with, unrelated activities? Did you waver in your commitment and, therefore, give up your reinvention?

- Whether in your job or business, have you been diligent? On the other hand, did you ever plan to reinvent your career or business but weren't persistent? As a result, did you delay your reinvention or even fail to achieve it?

- Will you stay focused while executing your game plan? That is to say, will you undertake the actions and approach cited in your strategy? Will you avoid becoming distracted by or immersed in irrelevant activities and, therefore, remain resolute? In addition, will you devote the energy necessary to reshape your job or business?

Let's move on to the second essential component of flawless execution—being agile.

BE AGILE

A resourceful business professional stays informed about his company and industry and regularly networks with colleagues in and outside his firm and, as a result, this person is able to respond to situations quickly and easily. An astute worker detects and resolves problems before these difficulties can undermine her work. An entrepreneur discerns and takes advantage of opportunities to expedite his company's reinvention. Recognizing that her mission and milestones no longer fit her, a manager revamps these tools and, in turn, adjusts her reinvention game plan.

Perhaps you'd like to be as nimble as the individuals in the preceding examples, but such dexterity requires a lot of effort. Besides, you're usually alert and, therefore, address your dilemmas or capitalize on fortuitous circumstances. Yet, what if you don't cultivate the contacts you'll need to advance your career or business or don't track trends and developments in your company and industry? Because you're not resourceful, you may not be able to move yourself or your company forward easily and quickly. What if, while reinventing, you discover a problem but don't remove this obstacle? Because of your sluggishness, you may jeopardize your reinvention. What if during your work transformation, you notice an opportunity to accelerate your reinvention or enhance its outcome but don't jump on this good fortune? Thanks to your lethargy, you may miss out on a chance to help yourself or your business. Or, what if you discover that your mission, milestones, and game plan are incorrect but don't redo these tools? You may not achieve your work ideal or you may attain the wrong goal.

Whether or not they're reinventing their work, successful managers remain attentive to the world around them and continually network with colleagues throughout their company and industry. Parlaying this resourcefulness, these people respond quickly and easily—agilely. Leaders fix the problems they detect before these difficulties escalate and become impossible to solve. These executives and business owners evaluate and, as appropriate, take advantage of opportunities they discover rather than ignoring these chances and allowing other individuals or businesses to benefit instead. These folks are also brave enough to admit when their strategies are wrong or no longer work and, as a result, these nimble workers divert from their plans, make the necessary adjustments, and then continue. Let's return to the two earlier examples and consider how being agile can affect the recreation of your work.

The first scenario describes a manager who wants to reinvigorate her job. This individual is resourceful—staying alert to developments and trends in her company and industry, keeping in touch with colleagues in and outside her firm, reading industry publications, and attending key marketplace events—and that way, if she needs to do so, she'll move nimbly. If she uncovers a problem that could undermine her reinvention, she'll identify this difficulty and address it without delay. For example, if she's having trouble becoming involved in large or highly visible projects, she may instead pursue smaller endeavors. If she spots an opportunity that could enhance the outcome of her reinvention, she'll explore it. For instance, if she hears that her company is struggling to assimilate the employees of the firms it's acquired, she may suggest that she can develop and conduct an orientation program to assist these newcomers. Or, if she detects that her game plan doesn't fit her current goal—she wants to change jobs—she'll switch gears. Now let's examine the opposite behavior. She's not agile.

If she doesn't network with her colleagues, she may not find out about projects in which she could participate or develop the contacts that will help her do so. If she doesn't read about her industry and communicate with people in other companies, she may not discover marketplace needs that she could address or learn how other managers have reinvigorated their jobs. In other words, by not being resourceful, she may not move easily and quickly and, as a result, she may hamper the progress of her reinvention or even cause it to fizzle. If she detects a problem that could endanger her reinvention but doesn't address it, she may impede her progress or even irreparably damage her endeavor. For instance, if the head of human resources insists that only members of his department conduct companywide training, but this individual becomes an instructor anyway, she may alienate the department head and receive a reprimand from her management. Had she been agile, she would have recognized the obstacle she faced and sought instruction opportunities solely within her area. If she stumbles on a chance to improve the pace or result of her reinvention but doesn't evaluate and, as appropriate, pursue it, she may not help her career as much as she could have. For example, if she discovers an opportunity to initiate a project or task force but doesn't take advantage of this opening, she may have to wait a long time until another such possibility comes her way. Or, if she realizes that her game plan is wrong but doesn't revise her strategy, she may not achieve her goal or she may obtain work she doesn't want.

In the second example, a business leader seeks to transform his organization. If this executive is attentive to how his transformation is proceeding and also stays informed about how executives in other companies and industries have succeeded (or failed) in remodeling their firms, he'll probably elude the pitfalls that have trapped others. For example, if he learns that successful corporate overhauls typically involve employees at all levels, he may include such employees in the planning or execution of his initiative. If he spots a problem that endangers the outcome of his reinvention, he'll deal with it immediately. For instance, if his executives are slow in implementing a new performance ranking system and, as a result, his workers have become anxious and distracted, he may expedite this process. If he discerns an opportunity that could accelerate his company's changeover, he'll assess it. For example, if he has a chance to partner with a firm that successfully refocused its people, he'll evaluate this possibility and, if it's beneficial, pursue it. Or, if he recognizes that his game plan isn't complete—he also wants to enhance his offerings—he'll divert from his strategy, revamp his plan, and then proceed. Let's consider the reverse situation. This executive isn't being agile.

If he's not aware of why other leaders have failed in their corporate renewals, he may not avoid their mistakes. If he's not in touch with how his vision is viewed and whether his restructuring and new systems are working, he may not realize the adjustments he'll need to make and, therefore, he may not make these moves. That is to say, by not being resourceful, he may retard the pace of his reinvention or even cause it to flop. If he uncovers a problem that could imperil his reinvention but doesn't address it, he may impede his progress or even destroy his initiative. For example, if his managers tell him that his reorganization has confused his company's customers but he ignores this input, he may lose his clients. Had he been agile, he would have listened to this feedback and taken corrective action. If he comes across an opportunity to expedite or enhance his reinvention but doesn't investigate it and, if it's viable, pursue it, he may not be as successful as he might have been. For instance, if he has a chance to hire an experienced manager from a company that successfully reshaped itself but doesn't evaluate this possibility, he may regret his inaction. Or, if he determines that his game plan is inadequate but doesn't make the necessary adjustments, he may fail to fulfill one or both of his objectives.

No doubt, by this point, you appreciate the value of being agile. The following questions will help you improve your nimbleness.

- Whether in your job or business, have you usually been resourceful and, therefore, responded to situations quickly and easily? On the other hand, have you not stayed informed about your company and industry or not networked with colleagues in and outside your firm? Has your business been inattentive to customers or not kept up with marketplace trends and developments? Because you or your workers weren't resourceful, did you fail to move as quickly and easily as you should have?

- Throughout your career, have you generally dealt with your problems before these difficulties became serious impediments? Conversely, have you sought to change jobs but fell short because you didn't remedy a performance problem in your current position? Did you let a poor attitude hinder your job change? Did you fail to launch a new line of offerings because you didn't fix a serious problem with your firm's existing products? Did your company postpone resolving a dilemma with an important customer and, as a result, lose this client?

- Have you typically taken advantage of opportunities? On the other hand, did you ever want to create a new role for yourself but didn't attain this goal because you overlooked or even declined a chance to initiate an important corporate project? Did your business have an opportunity to acquire another firm but didn't explore this option and, as a result, a competitor made this purchase and became the market leader?

- Will you be agile during your reinvention of your job or business? That is to say, will you employ your resourcefulness to help you move nimbly? Will you face up to and resolve your problems and also explore and pursue opportunities?

Now that you've examined staying focused and being agile, you'll look at how to juggle these capabilities.

STRIKE THE RIGHT BALANCE

While he develops a new line, a business owner satisfies his customers with his firm's existing offerings. A manager interviews for new jobs in her company but also performs well in her current position. In his business' first year, an owner is concerned with adjusting his product mix and delivery methods to meet his customers' expectations. Subsequently, this entrepreneur focuses on fulfilling his customers' orders and providing outstanding service.

Maybe you envy people who are able to engage in different activities at the same time. Perhaps you admire how some individuals can adapt their approach according to their circumstances. Even so, you think that you'll be able to apply your focus and agility correctly. Yet, what if you're absorbed in your tasks and don't see that your actions aren't producing the intended results? Or, what if you're rigid in your activities or methods or consumed with your work and, therefore, miss out on an idea that could help you to reinvent your job or business? In these cases, your focus may be impeding your agility. What if you're so quick to tackle problems or capitalize on opportunities that you can't finish your work or complete your reinvention? Your nimbleness may be hindering your ability to follow through. What if you're changing jobs in your company but don't maintain your performance in your current position or transforming your organization but don't pay attention to your customers? Or, what if you're more focused when you should be more agile or vice versa? Under these conditions, you may be defeating yourself or your business.

Wise businesspeople are aware of their circumstances, flexible in their actions or approach, and receptive to new ideas. In other words, these individuals don't become too focused. Consequently, these workers are able to recognize and resolve critical problems, make necessary adjustments, and explore new avenues. But smart managers are also selective about which problems they deal with or opportunities they chase. That is to say, the adroit aren't too agile. These people understand that if they're engrossed in hopping from activity to activity, they won't finish their regular tasks or accomplish their reinventions. As a result, these discriminating folks undertake only those challenges that can impact, whether negatively or positively, their work or reinventions. Down-to-earth professionals know how to juggle disparate efforts, like a job or business and its reinvention, and also grasp when to be more focused than agile, and vice versa. If these individuals are involved in a new role or business, they devote more effort to learning about their new responsibilities or marketplace. On the other hand, if these people have been in their job for a while or are engaged in an established business, they direct their energies to fulfilling the demands of their position or satisfying their customers' needs. Let's go back to the previous examples and see why striking the right balance is vital to a reinvention.

In the first scenario, a manager wants to reinvigorate her job. She won't be so focused that she'll fail to notice that her actions aren't working. She also won't miss out on viable opportunities to instruct or participate in projects, but she won't pursue every training or mentoring possibility she hears about or jump from one project to another. She'll also strike the appropriate balance. That is to say, she'll do her regular job while she reinvigorates her role. She realizes that if she doesn't keep up her performance in her current position, she may not be able to change jobs in the future.

The second example involves an executive who seeks to transform his organization. This leader and his people won't be so absorbed with their endeavor that they ignore problems associated with their reinvention, such as a new system that doesn't work. They also won't overlook opportunities that could expedite their efforts or enhance their results, such as a chance to learn from another company's experience. But, this individual and his managers won't be so agile that they tackle every organizational dilemma they hear about or go after every possibility to speak with other leaders. This leader and his team will also seek to maintain an equilibrium in their work. In other words, they'll undertake a dramatic reshaping of their firm and, at the same time, meet their existing commitments to their customers and employees. They understand that if they achieve their corporate ideal but end up losing major clients and valuable workers, their reinvention may be in vain.

Keeping the proper balance between focus and agility is essential to flawless execution. Here are some questions to help you juggle these disparate capabilities.

- Throughout your career, have you usually avoided being too focused or too agile? Have you remained on an even keel and also modified your approach according to your (or your business') situation?

- On the other hand, have you ever been consumed with your job search and unaware that your negative attitude was undermining your efforts? Were you inflexible in your methods and, therefore, didn't adjust your technique even though this approach wasn't working? Or, were you (or your managers) so absorbed in introducing a new product that you didn't consider a superior idea for this offering?

- In the past, have you chased after every job opportunity you saw, whether or not these possibilities fit you? Or, did you launch so many new initiatives that your workers became confused or frustrated and, consequently, quit?

- Have you had trouble juggling your job and your participation on projects? Or, did you seek to introduce a new line but let the quality of your firm's existing products slip?

- Have you ever floundered in a new job because you didn't modify your approach and, as a result, your mode of operating wasn't compatible with the one used by your colleagues? Or, did your firm blunder in its move into a new market sector because you didn't make the requisite adjustments in your offerings or distribution process?

- Will you bring about the right balance as you reinvent your work? In other words, will you avoid being unaware, inflexible, or closed? Will you refrain from being indiscriminate in your pursuits? Additionally, will you manage your regular work and reinvention effort? Will you also adjust your equilibrium according to your situation, being more agile in a new job or business and more focused in an established position or venture?

Let's move on to how you'll anticipate and prepare for problems that might occur during implementation.

ANTICIPATE YOUR EXECUTION CHALLENGES

A worker who's reinvigorating his job seeks his mentor's advice on how to improve his concentration. Because she sometimes doesn't perceive opportunities to enhance her division's offerings, a leader asks a quick-witted employee to identify attractive possibilities. Because he's usually preoccupied with his work and, therefore, not open to new ideas or approaches, a professional schedules time to speak with colleagues. An entrepreneur who's often distracted by extraneous activities hires a diligent manager to assist her in following through. Acknowledging that he may have difficulty carrying out his current responsibilities while he searches for a new position, an individual closely monitors his performance. An owner assigns a trusted coworker to manage her business while she explores how to move her firm into a new market sector.

The businesspeople in these scenarios have anticipated and prepared for the problems that they might encounter during their reinventions. But because you're not usually caught off guard, you're not particularly concerned. Yet, what if you don't foresee that you or your employees might not be as focused or agile as you need to be? What if you don't expect that you or your workers might be too focused or agile? Or, what if you don't predict that you or your colleagues might have difficulty managing your regular work and reinvention? Under any of these circumstances, you might fail to reach your goal.

Sensible professionals anticipate where they might have problems in executing their game plans. To do so, these pragmatic folks evaluate their past performance and, as a result, recognize whether they're usually focused, agile, and able to maintain the right balance between these two capabilities. If they identify potential difficulties, these sharp managers and entrepreneurs prepare to deal with these challenges. For example, these professionals may seek others' advice or suggestions. These circumspect leaders may establish useful mechanisms, such as a monthly conference call to discuss how managers can become more pertinacious or vigorous. These wise businesspeople may also designate or even hire others to help them improve their focus, agility, or ability to juggle following through and making changes. Let's return to the previous examples and consider how the worker and the executive can anticipate and prepare for their execution challenges.

The first scenario describes a manager who wants to reinvigorate her job. Based on her self-assessment, this individual may conclude that she's usually too focused and, consequently, might not perceive the opportunities necessary to advance her career. Expecting that such behavior might slow her reinvention, this worker decides to obtain guidance from her mentor, an alert individual. To help her handle her regular job and involvement in projects and teaching, this worker will review her performance with her supervisor each month and also routinely seek a colleague's feedback.

In the second example, an executive seeks to transform his organization. After evaluating his track record, this leader may decide that he's often been too agile and, therefore, might lead his employees in too many different directions. Because of this possibility, this leader asks a steadfast senior manager to serve as his lieutenant and prevent the company from engaging in unnecessary endeavors. To ensure that his firm doesn't lose touch with its customers during the reinvention, this executive directs his sales executive to watch these relationships closely and respond promptly to any problems.

Clearly, anticipating and preparing for the challenges that might affect your execution make sense, but even after you've done so, you may still have trouble executing because of your attitude. In Chapter 8, you'll learn how to manage your outlook so that you'll be certain to achieve your work ideal. Meanwhile, here are some questions that will assist you in dealing with potential implementation obstacles.

- Has your company sought to launch a new business but didn't reach its goal? If your CEO had predicted that his workers might have difficulty finishing what they start, could he have found a way to avoid this dilemma? Or, have you wanted to reinvigorate your job but didn't fulfill this aim? If you had foreseen that you might have trouble discerning opportunities, could you have prepared to handle this problem?

- Have you wanted to launch a new line but didn't accomplish this objective? Did your workers' preoccupation with their existing offerings impede their efforts? Or, have you wanted to change jobs but didn't attain this ideal? Did your haphazard pursuit of positions hamper your progress? Could you have anticipated these implementation hurdles?

- Have you ever tried to reinvent your career or business but were unsuccessful in your endeavor? Were you (or your employees) unable to juggle your work and reinventions? Or, were you incapable of adjusting your approach according to your situation? In either case, could you have prevented these failures?

- Go back to the questions in the previous three sections (Stay Focused, Be Agile, and Strike the Right Balance) and review your answers to the questions concerning your approach. Do you anticipate that you'll encounter problems in executing your reinvention plan? If so, what are these challenges and how will you handle these difficulties?

Write down your responses to this last query, listing each hurdle and, next to it, how you'll deal with this impediment. In Chapter 9, when you kick off your reinvention, you'll revisit this information.

APPLY YOUR FOCUS
AND AGILITY

Now let's examine how your situation stacks up against various reinvention options. You'll determine why you might choose a particular option to meet your goals. As was true in the previous chapters, your situation won't correspond exactly with the characteristics of the following scenarios, nor will it include all of these features.

 ### REINVIGORATE YOUR JOB

Your status may reflect the following components:

- *Stay focused.* You periodically become distracted by events and activities that are unrelated to your work. Or, you're usually able to concentrate.

- *Be agile.* Sometimes you're not resourceful or don't deal with problems or take advantage of opportunities. Or, most times, you're bright and address your situation.

- *Strike the right balance.* You can be inflexible in your actions or approach. Or, you're conscientious about your work yet receptive to new ideas and methods.

- *Anticipate your execution challenges.* You've thought about the difficulties you might have in implementing. You'll ask a colleague to help you deal with these problems.

If the above sounds like your situation, here are a couple of reasons you may elect to reinvigorate your job:

- It's essential that you rejuvenate your performance or attitude about work.

- You'll make sure that your focus and agility will support, not impede, your effort.

 ## CHANGE JOBS IN YOUR COMPANY

Your work may incorporate the following components:

- *Stay focused.* Occasionally, you don't follow through. Or, you usually complete the actions necessary to fulfill an objective.

- *Be agile.* At times, you're not quick-witted and, therefore, don't respond to difficulties or fortuitous circumstances. Or, you're generally sharp and, thus, solve problems and investigate opportunities.

- *Strike the right balance.* You sometimes have trouble pursuing two different courses of action at the same time. Or, you're able to work on two distinct projects simultaneously.

- *Anticipate your execution challenges.* You've identified your potential execution hurdles. Your mentor will assist you in handling these obstacles.

If the preceding elements describe your circumstances, here are some reasons you may choose to change jobs:

- Moving to a new position is important to your career.

- Your diligence and nimbleness will ensure that you attain your dream.

ENHANCE YOUR BUSINESS' OFFERINGS OR APPROACH

Your business' situation may be based upon the following components:

- *Stay focused*. Now and then, you and your workers don't fully apply yourselves to your work. Or, you and your team devote your collective energy to reaching your goals.

- *Be agile*. Once in a while, you and your people aren't ingenious and, consequently, don't handle dilemmas or opportunities. Or, your organization is usually resourceful and, as a result, routinely responds to difficulties and possibilities.

- *Strike the right balance*. You and your employees chase opportunities that aren't right for your firm. Or, you and your group are generally selective about the enhancements you undertake.

- *Anticipate your execution challenges*. You and your staff have agreed upon the problems you might experience during implementation. You'll establish a board of outside advisors to help your business attain its goal.

If some or most of the above sound familiar, here are some reasons you may choose to enhance your business' offerings or approach:

- Improving your offerings or methods will enable your business to remain successful.

- Your and your workers' industriousness and deftness will allow your firm to keep its competitive edge.

TRANSITION YOUR BUSINESS

Your business may include the following components:

- *Stay focused*. Occasionally, you and your employees become distracted and don't finish the tasks listed in your business plan. Or, you and your workers regularly complete the necessary actions.

- *Be agile*. You and your team sometimes aren't inventive and, therefore, don't deal with problems or respond to opportunities. Or, you and your people are imaginative and, thus, typically resolve your difficulties and perceive possibilities and go after them.

- *Strike the right balance.* From time to time, your organization fails to adapt its approach to its situation. Or, you and your personnel are more agile when you launch a new line and more focused once you've refined your offerings to meet your customers' requirements.

- *Anticipate your execution challenges.* You and your people have documented the dilemmas you might have while you implement. You'll hire an experienced manager who'll assist you in fulfilling your objective.

If the preceding factors resemble your situation, here are a few reasons you may opt to transition your business:

- Refocusing your organization, inaugurating a new line, or moving into a new sector will transform your business from a so-so performer to a key market player.

- Your and your employees' perseverance and agility will facilitate the remaking of your business.

START A NEW BUSINESS WITHIN YOUR COMPANY

Your status may embody the following components:

- *Stay focused.* Once in a while, you and your managers undertake activities that aren't included in your strategy. Or, you and your team usually engage in and complete the right actions.

- *Be agile.* You and your people sometimes aren't enterprising and, as a result, don't deal with your circumstances. Or, you and your personnel are usually venturesome and, consequently, solve your problems and capitalize on your opportunities.

- *Strike the right balance.* Occasionally, you and your colleagues have difficulty simultaneously undertaking a new initiative and managing your regular operation. Or, you and your workers can work on two different endeavors at the same time.

- *Anticipate your execution challenges.* You and your staff have written down the potential barriers to implementing your new venture. You'll seek advice from other firms that have successfully launched new businesses.

If the above aspects describe your ideal, here are a couple of reasons you may want to start a new venture:

- Establishing an entrepreneurial unit will distinguish your company from the pack.

- Your and your managers' dedication and dexterity will make a risky move less hazardous.

You're now ready for the stories of two individuals who've employed their focus and agility to implement their reinventions.

LIVE YOUR FLAWLESS EXECUTION

As a longtime employee of Illinois Tool Works (ITW), Jim Farrell says, "I've loved everything I've done here."[3] That's no surprise. The company and its leader are a lot alike. Both have made executing flawlessly an art form, if not a science. Farrell is chairman and CEO of ITW, a Fortune 500 company that manufactures engineered products, like nails and fasteners, and specialty systems, such as plastic packaging and industrial strapping.

Throughout his career, Farrell has stayed focused. Rarely distracted or wavering in his commitment, this executive fully uses his energy to pursue his business plans. During the late 1970s and into the 1980s, Farrell helped lead the reinvention of ITW. The company simplified its product line, streamlined its manufacturing, and applied the 80/20 process—a combination of keeping things simple and concentrating on the best opportunities—to every aspect of its business. By 1990, ITW had hit its stride. This CEO also assists his people in concentrating and following through: "After two days of asking questions of almost any business, I know where we can go and what we can do."

Quick to spot and address both problems and opportunities, Farrell is extremely resourceful and, as a result, incredibly agile. In the early 1970s, he read a *Harvard Business Review* article about the true cost of a bad product. As the general manager of a start-up division at ITW, Farrell knew that he had such an item, which, unfortunately, represented a third of his revenues. Thanks to his agility, the young executive sold this line and was delighted with the result: "The whole business responded incredibly fast. My people seized other opportunities." Two decades later, when one of ITW's acquisitions was struggling, the then CEO asked Farrell to take over this new unit. Never one to decline a challenge, the nimble Farrell accepted but, by doing so, went from running the largest part of ITW to the smallest. Yet, not allowing his ego to get in the way, Farrell turned around this operation and, under his leadership, the acquisition became a roaring success. Like Farrell, his managers are remarkably agile. The company's executives regularly create new businesses from both acquired companies and existing ITW divisions and, consequently, this organization continually reinvents itself.

Farrell has a knack for striking the right balance between staying focused and being agile. While he was helping to reinvent ITW, the ambitious executive was also managing much of his company. Today, Farrell and his colleagues maintain a healthy equilibrium between running their existing operations and selectively acquiring new companies and starting new divisions. In other words, neither too focused nor too agile, these executives know how to handle two different courses of action. On balancing focus and agility, Farrell admits: "It's a contradiction. I can take credit for helping to preserve it."

This astute CEO also knows how to anticipate and prepare for potential implementation obstacles. In 1976, Farrell became the executive vice president of the fastener group, which, at the time, represented 30 percent of ITW's revenues. At this point—which Farrell calls his most difficult time in the company—the rising executive questioned whether he could add value to his general managers' efforts but, after seeking out and spending time with a consultant (who later became ITW's CEO), Farrell discovered the role he would play in his company's transformation. As he says of this epiphany: "The door was opening. There was something important for me to do."

As a director of several companies, including Allstate Insurance and Sears, and a member of numerous business and nonprofit organizations, Farrell applies his focus and agility to everything he does.

Like Jim Farrell, I've been focused yet agile in my work. I excel at recognizing a need or an opportunity to change, adapting quickly, and redirecting my attention to my new endeavor.

Since childhood, I've been highly focused. Whether in school, in outside activities, or at my jobs, I've been conscientious and perseverant. Even so, I've become more determined and diligent since going out on my own. My clients have witnessed my energetic approach in action. I help managers eliminate unnecessary activities and concentrate on the actions that are essential to their goals and, by doing so, I assist them in achieving their objectives.

My agility has enabled me to respond to both difficulties and possibilities. Because I'm resourceful, I regularly spot problems that aren't being addressed, which, in turn, become opportunities I pursue. For example, because I observed that teams often weren't sure how to execute their strategies, I began providing hands-on assistance to these groups. Owing to my quickness, I've also been able to detect problems in my own work and, as a result, adjust my course of action. Here's an illustration. My original topic for this book was how managers could operate more effectively—a subject I was knowledgeable about because of my business. My game plan for this endeavor involved interviewing managers and executives at various companies. Based on the initial interviews I conducted (and those I wasn't able to arrange), I diverted from my strategy and analyzed why I was having trouble and, by doing so, drew two conclusions. Executives hired me to address their firms' challenges but didn't want to publicize these difficulties. Managers were more interested in improving their careers than solving the problems of big business. Thanks to this assessment, I changed to a different topic—how to reinvent your work—and, in turn, revised my plan.

My ability to maintain the proper balance between staying focused and being agile could be better. When I undertake a new endeavor, such as transitioning from employee to entrepreneur, I appropriately devote more energy to my new situation, but if I'm trying to complete a task and also launch a new initiative, I sometimes have difficulty pursuing these divergent paths simultaneously. I'm working to enhance my skill in juggling two efforts at the same time.

My performance in anticipating and preparing for potential implementation hurdles also could be improved. For example, if I had foreseen how difficult it would be to find a literary agent or a publisher, I might have sought an experienced writer as my book's coauthor. Yet, in fairness to myself, predicting the challenges you might have during your plan's execution is hardly an exact science. As is true in many areas of your life, it's a matter of trial and error and, therefore, learning from your mistakes.

CHAPTER EIGHT

STEP SEVEN
Manage Your Attitude

Blow your own horn—subtly.[1]

—CARL SEWELL, AUTHOR AND THE LEADING LUXURY-CAR DEALER IN THE UNITED STATES

Genius is nothing but a greater aptitude for patience.[2]

—GEORGES-LOUIS LECLERC DE BUFFON, FRENCH NATURALIST

An arrogant CEO refuses to listen to his managers' ideas on improving customer service and recognizing and rewarding employees and, over time, his company loses important clients and talented workers. A complacent manager declines to make any enhancements to his business' offerings and, within six months, a competitor displaces this firm as the market leader. Fearful about her future, a businessperson is paralyzed—unable to improve her situation. Envious of another entrepreneur's good fortune, an owner is distracted and doesn't finish his company's reinvention. A professional who's not self-assured has difficulty changing jobs. By alienating his workers, an intolerant leader makes his firm's transformation more difficult. Panicked that she's falling behind her peers, an individual accepts a position that she dislikes and can't perform.

Do these scenarios sound familiar? If so, you understand that your manner or feelings can undermine or even defeat you or your company. Managing your attitude doesn't sound that difficult. Yet, what if you don't seek to reinvent your career or business even though you should? Your smugness may keep you from improving your situation and, as a result, you or your business may fall behind. What if you can't bring yourself to reinvent? Your disappointment, fear, or negative mind-set may be holding you back. What if you can't stay focused on reshaping your work? You may be preoccupied with a peer's good fortune. What if you have trouble reshaping your job, department, or company? Your pretentiousness may be irritating your coworkers or your lack of assurance about your (or your organization's) skills may be slowing your progress. What if you don't attain your goal of advancing your career or improving your business? Your intolerant behavior toward your employees or colleagues may have thwarted your effort. Or, what if you bring about the wrong reinvention? Your impatience may have led you to employ an unproductive idea or approach.

A proper attitude is an essential tool in achieving your reinvention ideal. (Of course, if your goal is to revitalize your attitude, this instrument also becomes the result.) Business professionals view themselves and their businesses objectively—neither overrating nor undervaluing their accomplishments, abilities, or potential. These folks keep the proper perspective on their situation. That is to say, these workers aren't so upbeat that they're self-satisfied and not motivated to improve, nor are they so negative that they've given up any hope of bettering their circumstances. These managers aren't controlled by their feelings—depressed about their setbacks, frightened about their futures, or consumed with envy over others' success. The sensible aren't in a hurry or desperate and, therefore, don't panic—making ill-considered choices or taking irrelevant or even dangerous actions. Instead, these individuals remain composed throughout their reinvention journey and, consequently, attain the goals they've set instead of results they don't expect or want. Practical men and women are also humane in their treatment of colleagues and, that way, don't alienate their coworkers, which could complicate or even endanger their reinventions.

This chapter will help you to manage your attitude. Step Seven will show you how to remain (or become) humble. You won't adversely affect your reinvention by being haughty, nor will you fail to reinvent because you're smug. You'll learn how to stay confident and not let your outlook or feelings keep you from reshaping your job or business. You'll examine how to be patient with your reinvention strategy. That is to say, you won't pursue unrelated or unsound ideas and, in turn, bring about the wrong reinvention. You'll also discover how to be tolerant of your colleagues so that you won't estrange them and, thereby, slow or even derail your reinvention. You'll next assess how your situation lines up with various reinvention options and you'll select the alternative that best fits your circumstances.

You'll then read about two businesspeople who have effectively managed their attitudes during their career and business reinventions.

BE HUMBLE

Colleagues don't allow an overbearing manager to participate in their projects. An aloof manager ignores her customers' ideas on how to improve her firm's service. A pompous executive doesn't involve his workers in his company's reinvention and, as a result, fails in his efforts. A smug entrepreneur declines to enhance his delivery process, even though several competitors have already done so. Despite her mediocre performance, a self-satisfied business professional decides against bettering her skills.

The individuals in these scenarios have let their overblown opinions of themselves or their businesses impede the reshaping of their work, but you've been pretty unassuming your entire career and don't envision that being humble will be that difficult. Yet, what if you have trouble reinventing your position or business and don't know why? Your colleagues or employees may consider you pretentious. What if you're not completely pleased with how you've rejuvenated your role or enhanced your firm's offerings? Because you weren't receptive to others' ideas, you may have missed a chance to catapult your career or business to star status. Or, what if you don't remodel your job or company and, as a result, lose out on becoming a senior manager or your industry's leading firm? Your complacency may have prevented you from capitalizing on an attractive opportunity. In other words, thanks to your smugness, you may not have been agile.

While they're not meek, sharp businesspeople are humble because they realize that being arrogant is an unproductive approach. (In Step Five, Be Practical, you read about this and other ineffective approaches.) Because they're realistic about themselves and their businesses and, therefore, accept that there's usually room for improvement, these managers are also open to others' ideas and approaches, which they use to make career or business changes that are necessary or even desirable. That is to say, these professionals aren't complacent and, therefore, if it's appropriate, they respond nimbly. Now let's consider two illustrations of this important attribute.

Imagine that you're a manager who wants to create a new role for yourself in your company. For the past two decades, you've performed well and could remain in your current position, but because you're not smug about your situation, you'll provide yourself with a new challenge. You visualize moving from your job as a sales manager to a role in which you'd train younger managers on how to develop new business and interact with customers. Because you're humble, you'll discuss your idea with your mentor before you approach your supervisor or your company's senior management. If your advisor provides suggestions on how to improve your concept, you'll be receptive to his recommendations and possibly incorporate these thoughts into your proposal. When you're ready to broach your idea with your supervisor or your company's executives, you'll use a low-key method, such as suggesting that your sales experience might enhance your company's course offerings.

On the other hand, if you're self-satisfied, you may not opt to change jobs. If you're supercilious, you may not be open to your mentor's recommendations and, therefore, may not solicit his input. Even though you should speak with your supervisor, you may bypass this individual and speak directly with your company's president.

Now let's say that you run a company that intends to transition into a new line. Your firm leads the market with its current products and, consequently, could continue its present strategy, but because you and your colleagues aren't complacent about your status, you'll look for new growth opportunities. You envision launching items that will round out your offerings. Because you and your workers are appropriately modest, you'll explore your strategy with several customers. You'll be open to these clients' input and will possibly include their feedback in your plan. When you inaugurate your new line, you'll utilize a subtle approach, for example, stating that even though your products are new, your track record is established.

Conversely, if you and your managers are self-contented, you may not make the effort to introduce a new line. If you and your team are presumptuous, you may not be receptive to customer input and, consequently, may not obtain such feedback. When you launch your new offerings, you may employ a pretentious marketing technique, for example, advocating that customers push aside the current inferior items and purchase your new products.

Here are some questions to help you remain (or become) appropriately modest.

- How would you assess your humility? Have you generally avoided being arrogant or complacent? If not, how often have you been pretentious or smug? What have been the results of this behavior?

- Have you witnessed others' humility (or lack of it)? For example, has an immodest colleague had trouble rejuvenating his role because his peers won't choose him for their projects? Did a co-worker who wasn't receptive to her mentor's ideas fail to create a new role for herself? Have arrogant managers irritated your company's clients? Are you aware of a self-satisfied worker who let his performance or attitude deteriorate? Does a once-smug colleague now regret missing out on a unique opportunity? Have you observed a complacent organization that didn't introduce new products and, as a result, fell behind its competitors?

- During your reinvention journey, will you remain (or become) humble? That is to say, will you avoid being self-important and closed to others' ideas or self-satisfied and unwilling to improve your career or business?

But can you be too humble? Let's consider how to prevent becoming unsure of yourself.

BE CONFIDENT

Depressed by her lack of career progress, a worker is unable to act. Hearing reports of slower economic growth and corporate layoffs, a gloomy manager declines to improve his career. A businessperson who's racked with fear can't make decisions about her work. An entrepreneur who envies his peers is distracted from growing his business. A leader who's unsure of his people's abilities doesn't transition his business into a new market sector. By postponing an interview with her firm's CEO, an insecure professional doesn't obtain the management role she wants.

If these examples sound familiar, you perceive that your mind-set can keep you from pursuing and attaining your goals, but when you're discouraged, pessimistic, afraid, jealous, or insecure, you talk to your spouse, parents, best friend, or mentor, who usually help you cope with your feelings. Yet, what if you can't shake your negative thoughts or fears? You may immobilize yourself or your business and, as a result, be incapable of addressing your problems or opportunities. What if you become fixated on another person's or your business' rapid rise or visibility and can't finish reinvigorating your job or enhancing your business? You may later regret that you expended your energy agonizing over a situation that you couldn't control. Or, what if you have such serious reservations about your (or your workers') abilities that you can't complete the reinvention of your career, department, or company? As you observe other businesspeople proceed confidently, you may wish that you had resolved your doubts.

Rational managers put their disappointments in perspective. These people understand that even if they haven't been successful in a previous endeavor, they can still fulfill their future objectives. They realize that, whatever the existing economic climate, companies are not irrevocably headed downward. These folks have lived through business cycles and, therefore, understand that market conditions change regularly. In any event, perceptive individuals recognize that even as some workers and businesses suffer, others identify and pursue attractive opportunities. Brave professionals come to grips with their fears by analyzing whether their feelings are hindering or even blocking their work reinvention. If they determine that to be the case, these professionals adjust their attitudes. Astute business types don't spin their wheels by obsessing over circumstances they can't control. The realistic don't dwell upon why some people or businesses are more fortunate than others or why a particular event or result occurs. Instead, these sensible workers and owners focus on what they can manage. Bold employees and entrepreneurs also don't lack confidence in their capabilities. If a businessperson thinks that she's unprepared for the new position she wants, she bolsters her skills by obtaining additional training. If an executive or owner has concerns about his people's abilities, he provides the instruction or assistance his workers need to achieve their company's objectives. Let's return to the previous examples and see how the individual and the business owner remain confident.

The first scenario describes a manager who wants to create a new position for himself so that he can move from his sales job to a role in which he'd train younger colleagues. Several years earlier, this individual tried and failed in a similar effort. Rather than letting his prior experience discourage him, this professional assesses this defeat and determines that, at the time, the conditions at his company weren't favorable to establishing his new position. Even though some companies in his industry are laying off workers, this businessperson doesn't infer that his firm won't allow him to develop his new job. Dealing directly with his fear about leaving his current department and jeopardizing his future, this sensible professional concludes that if he performs well in his new role, he'll be more attractive to other areas of his company than if he had remained in sales. This experienced worker doesn't ruminate incessantly about a sales colleague who became a top executive, nor does he obsess about his company's future moves. To enhance his self-assurance, this employee completes a train-the-trainer program conducted by a local coaching firm.

Conversely, if this manager isn't confident, he may assume that because he slipped before, he may founder again and, consequently, may not attempt to create a new role for himself. Concluding that economic conditions might not be conducive to undertaking his initiative, this businessperson may decline to pursue his work ideal. Permitting his fear about his future to dominate his thoughts, this professional may stay in his current position. This experienced worker may become preoccupied with concerns that he can't control, such as why a peer had a chance that he didn't have or whether his company might acquire another firm and, as a result, postpone unrelated endeavors. This individual may also allow his doubts about his talents weaken his commitment to his goal.

In the second example, a business owner intends to launch a new line. This person puts an earlier failure in perspective, concluding that her firm had selected the wrong offerings or used a faulty approach to market them. Although she's read that new item introductions in her industry can be risky, this entrepreneur decides that the demand for her imaginative new line will be strong and might even displace existing products. Acknowledging her fear of failing in this endeavor, this leader reasons that, even if she's not successful, she'll still be able to sell her current offerings. This businessperson doesn't dwell upon the good fortune of a colleague, who parlayed a modest investment in a new line into a multimillion-dollar operation, nor does this manager constantly think about whether the economy will regain its prior momentum or, conversely, continue to grow. In order to be completely confident of her workers' abilities, this owner hires a manager who has extensive experience in inaugurating new industry offerings.

On the other hand, if she isn't confident, this entrepreneur may not understand her prior failure and, therefore, assume that future efforts will also fall through. Concluding that new product introductions usually flop, this businessperson may decide to stay with her current line. Fearing that an unsuccessful launch might damage her firm, this individual may be paralyzed by this possibility. This businessperson may become consumed with issues over which she has no control, such as whether a competitor might inaugurate a new line. This manager may also let her concerns about her people's skills cause her to delay or even cancel the launch of her new offerings.

If you're like most folks, you've probably experienced similar fears and doubts on more than one occasion. Hopefully, the preceding scenarios have helped you understand how to become (or stay) confi-

dent throughout your reinvention journey. The following questions
will further assist you.

- How would judge your confidence? Have you handled failure
  effectively? Have you also maintained a positive outlook, dealt
  with your fears and what you can't control, and remained sure
  of your abilities?

- What have you observed about others' confidence (or lack of
  it)? Has a colleague's depression about her setbacks crippled her
  efforts to improve her career? Did a fellow business owner become so discouraged by an earlier failure that he shut down his
  firm? Has a peer's negative mind-set kept her from pursuing a
  new job? Did an organization's pessimism prevent this company
  from starting a new venture? Was a friend so afraid of failure that
  he didn't even try to advance his career? Did a businessperson
  who was fearful of change cancel an initiative to improve her
  firm's processes? Do you know someone who was intensely jealous of a coworker and, consequently, became distracted from
  reinvigorating her job? Have you met an entrepreneur who's so
  jealous of a colleague's visibility that he's devoted his energy to
  obtaining media exposure for himself and his firm? Has a coworker who was uncertain of his abilities stayed in his current
  position, even though he wanted to change jobs? Did another
  business owner decline to introduce a new offering because he
  didn't think that his workers possessed the skills needed to develop and market this new item?

- During your reinvention, will you put your disappointments in
  the proper perspective? Will you maintain a positive outlook?
  With others' help or on your own, will you come to grips with
  your fears? Will you aim your attention on what you can control and not what you can't? Whether you're reinventing your
  career or business, will you remain assured about your ability to
  attain and perform your ideal work? In other words, will you
  manage your attitude so that you'll remain confident throughout your reinvention?

But even if you strike the right balance—being neither too humble nor too confident—you may undermine your reinvention by your
restlessness or intolerance.

BE PATIENT

Unwilling to wait for a freeze on new positions to end, a worker abandons her effort to create a new role for herself and remains in her current job. In a hurry to introduce a new product, a business owner uses a slipshod method to test this offering and, subsequently, because of customer complaints, has to pull this item from the market. A reckless leader transitions his organization into a new sector that he knows nothing about and, after losing a good deal of time and money, returns to his firm's former focus. Desperate to change jobs, an employee obtains a position that doesn't match his skills or motivations. Afraid that she might fall behind her peers, a young professional panics and accepts a job that she doesn't really want. A quick-tempered entrepreneur alienates his workers and, as a result, delays his firm's establishment of a new venture. Because of her intolerant attitude, an executive fails to transform her organization.

Perhaps the individuals in these examples resemble people you know. You understand that being anxious or brusque can slow the reinvention of your work or even cause it to fail, but most times, you're easygoing and even-tempered. Yet, what if because there's an unexpected delay in your reinvention, you abandon your initiative and accept a less desirable alternative? You may later lament your inability to wait for your ideal. What if you're in a rush to reshape your business and, therefore, adopt quick fixes or surefire schemes before you fully investigate whether or not these strategies are workable? You may not achieve your reinvention and, in turn, waste time and money as you regroup. What if you're frantic to change positions and, because of your hastiness, end up with a job that's no better than the one you had? You may deplore your impetuousness. Or, what if your unforbearing behavior toward your people causes them to react spitefully—slowing your business' launch of a new product? If a competitor gets its offering to market before you do, you may regret your irascible demeanor.

Practical managers and entrepreneurs curb their anxiety so that they don't act rashly. Recognizing that their edginess can lead to unexpected and even disastrous results, prudent businesspeople carefully assess the pros and cons before they try a quick fix, shortcut, or supposedly foolproof plan and, that way, these individuals ensure that they achieve the reinventions they want. Savvy executives and owners also realize that they facilitate their reinventions by treating their colleagues fairly. In other words, these leaders usually control their tempers and make allowances for mistakes—assuming that these errors aren't grave. Let's examine how the manager and the business owner cited earlier remain patient.

In the first example, a manager wants to create a new position for himself so that he can move from his sales job to a role in which he'd train younger colleagues. This individual will maintain his cool. If his mentor is out of town and won't be back for several weeks, this manager will wait for his return. If his supervisor is busy developing his annual plan and temporarily won't schedule unrelated meetings, this experienced worker will bide his time. Or, if his company's senior management takes three months to approve his new position, this seasoned salesperson will remember that his goal probably isn't his president's top priority and, in any case, creating a new position can require considerable discussion. To keep himself occupied, this worker will focus on his current role. Because he won't want to alienate his colleagues, this businessperson will also act professionally, especially toward those involved in his job change.

On the other hand, if this manager isn't patient, he may panic if he can't proceed as quickly as he hoped and, consequently, may decide to remain in his existing position. This individual may also become demanding and short-tempered with colleagues in his current department or with members of senior management.

The second scenario involves a business owner who seeks to introduce a new line. This entrepreneur will stay composed. If her people require a certain amount of time to test the safety of their new offerings, this owner won't force her workers to take dangerous shortcuts. If, however, this individual learns of prudent ways to expedite her business change, she'll evaluate these ideas before she employs such methods. Meanwhile, this leader and her organization will continue to satisfy their customers with their existing offerings. To ensure that she fulfills her objective, this sensible person will also treat her employees with forbearance.

Conversely, if this owner isn't patient, she may become desperate if there's any delay in introducing her new line and, in turn, irritable with her customers, suppliers, and workers. If she becomes overly restless, she may act recklessly and, as a result, jeopardize the launch of her new line.

Being collected and tolerant during the reinvention of your career or business is vital. Here are some questions that will help you improve your patience.

- How would you evaluate your patience? Do you typically make prudent decisions? Are you reasonable with your colleagues?

- What have you observed about other people's patience (or lack of it)? Have you known a coworker who was in a hurry to reinvigorate his job and, as a result, joined a project to which he couldn't contribute? Was a business so desperate to start a new venture that it didn't learn about the prerequisites of such an endeavor and, consequently, failed to establish this unit? For whatever reason, did a colleague panic and accept a job he wasn't able to perform? Did a firm near you adopt an allegedly surefire scheme and, as a result, achieve the wrong reinvention? Did a hot-tempered manager anger his colleagues and, over time, derail his career? Has an irritable leader alienated his workers and, in turn, brought about the demise of his corporate transformation?

- Will you curb your restlessness? That is to say, will you avoid making hasty decisions, taking unproductive shortcuts, or pursuing half-baked approaches? In other words, will you be patient enough to reach your work ideal? Will you also maintain an even temper with your colleagues?

Now that you've examined how to manage your attitude, you need to pinpoint where you might have problems.

IDENTIFY YOUR ATTITUDINAL DIFFICULTIES

Attaining her work ideal sooner than planned, a once-humble leader becomes arrogant. Thanks to the national coverage his firm receives, an owner is no longer motivated to improve his business. A manager suffers a setback in her reinvention journey and, as a result, loses her confidence. Because a new line sells only modestly, an entrepreneur fears that he won't achieve his five-year plan. Under intense pressure to turn around his organization, a usually composed executive becomes edgy. Working for a quick-tempered supervisor, a formerly calm employee becomes abrupt with her colleagues.

You get the message of these examples. Because of your circumstances, you can become less humble, confident, or patient. Perhaps you think it's unlikely that you'd be arrogant, insecure, or restless. You're generally able to manage your attitude. Yet, what if because of a particular result, you change how you think about yourself or your business? A sudden or overwhelming success may cause you to become conceited or smug, while a reversal or defeat may lead you to become insecure, pessimistic, or fearful. What if your surroundings adversely affect your behavior? Absent a significant challenge, you may become self-satisfied or if you're faced with urgent demands, constant deadlines, or a hectic work schedule, you may become anxious and even intolerant of your coworkers. Or, what if someone who doesn't have a proper attitude adversely affects your outlook or demeanor? You may emulate this person's haughty or brusque behavior or you may react to this individual's assuming or irritable disposition by becoming unsure.

Levelheaded managers and entrepreneurs determine where they might have problems with their attitude so that they can avoid these difficulties. These people make sure that a successful outcome doesn't inflate their self-image and a negative result doesn't devastate them. These professionals don't let their situations govern their outlook or approach. That is to say, even in a pressure cooker, they avoid becoming overly edgy or unforbearing or, in a slower-paced environment, becoming complacent. These businesspeople also don't let another individual negatively mold their actions or outlook. Let's look at how the manager and the business owner discussed earlier identify their potential attitudinal obstacles.

The first scenario describes a manager who wants to create a new position for himself so that he can move from a sales job to a role in which he'd train younger colleagues. This individual decides that if he's unable to obtain his new position, he may have difficulty staying confident. On the other hand, if he gets his ideal, this professional is concerned that he may become smug because there will be less pressure associated with his new role than with his current job. To help him cope, this individual will note these potential hindrances and discuss them periodically with his mentor.

In the second example, a business owner seeks to introduce a new line. This person concludes that if she and her people are successful, they may have trouble remaining humble. This entrepreneur is also apprehensive that with the demands of this effort, she may become less tolerant. To assist her and her workers, this individual will document these possible hazards and review them quarterly with her firm's advisory board.

Now it's time for you to identify your potential attitudinal impediments. The following questions will help you do so.

- Have you ever become arrogant because of a recent success or unsure because of a setback or failure? Or, have your employees become pretentious because of the publicity they've received or become less self-assured because of their lack of visibility?

- Has a high-pressure situation caused you to become restless or quick-tempered? Or, did a relaxed atmosphere lead you to let down your guard?
- Because of a pompous supervisor, did you become aloof? Or, has an overbearing boss browbeat you and, as a result, you have become insecure?

Go back to the previous sections of this chapter and review your answers to the questions concerning your humility, confidence, and patience. Identify where you might have a problem and write down this possible difficulty and how you'll address it. Before you kick off your reinvention, you'll review this information.

APPLY YOUR PROPER ATTITUDE

Let's examine how your situation lines up with various reinvention options. You'll learn why you might choose a particular option to fulfill your objective. As was true in the previous chapters, your situation won't match precisely with the attributes in the following scenarios, nor will it include all of these characteristics.

REINVIGORATE YOUR JOB

Your work may incorporate the following components:

- *Be humble.* Once in a while, you're self-satisfied. Or, you're usually willing to improve.
- *Be confident.* You're often depressed about your career. Or, you're sometimes positive about your situation.
- *Be patient.* Occasionally, you're in a hurry and, as a result, make mistakes. Or, you're usually calm.
- *Identify your attitudinal difficulties.* You have trouble putting your past mistakes in perspective. You'll speak with a trusted colleague about this concern.

If the above aspects describe your ideal, here are a couple of reasons you may want to reinvigorate your job:

- You're ready to improve your work.
- You won't let your disappointment or negative thinking get in your way. In other words, you'll use a positive attitude as a tool to achieve a result—an improved attitude.

CHANGE JOBS IN YOUR COMPANY

Your status may reflect the following components:

- *Be humble.* Occasionally, you're aloof and not open to new ideas. Or, you're typically modest and receptive to others' suggestions.
- *Be confident.* Frequently, you're insecure. Or, you try to be self-assured.
- *Be patient.* Once in a while, you become desperate and, therefore, make poor decisions. Or, you're usually composed and carefully assess your options.
- *Identify your attitudinal difficulties.* You have difficulty remaining confident. You'll seek your mentor's support.

If the preceding factors resemble your situation, here are a few reasons you may opt to change jobs:

- You're determined to advance your career.
- You'll make sure that your confidence reflects your abilities.

 ENHANCE YOUR BUSINESS' OFFERINGS OR APPROACH

Your business may include the following components:

- *Be humble.* You and your workers are sometimes complacent. Or, you and your people are generally open to making improvements.
- *Be confident.* Once in a while, you and your team are negative about your prospects or economic conditions. Or, you and your organization are usually upbeat.
- *Be patient.* Frequently, you and your people panic and utilize whatever quick fixes and allegedly surefire schemes are available. Or, you and your staff attempt to evaluate supposedly foolproof plans before you use them.
- *Identify your attitudinal difficulties.* You have trouble remaining patient. You'll regularly review your progress with your advisory board so that you'll avoid hasty decisions.

If the preceding elements describe your circumstances, here are some reasons you may choose to enhance your business:

- You are committed to improving your firm's offerings or approach.
- You won't sacrifice quality in order to obtain a fast result.

TRANSITION YOUR BUSINESS

Your business' situation may be based upon the following components:

- *Be humble.* You and your personnel are sometimes arrogant and not receptive to new concepts. Or, you and your people are typically unpretentious and open to your customers' or suppliers' ideas.
- *Be confident.* Occasionally, you and your managers are apprehensive about fulfilling your objectives. Or, you and your team aren't usually worried about the future.
- *Be patient.* You and your executives are often intolerant of your workers' mistakes, even when these errors are small. Or, you and your direct reports try to keep your cool.
- *Identify your attitudinal difficulties.* You have difficulty maintaining your forbearance toward your employees. You and your executives will get a coach to help you modify your behavior.

If some or most of the above sound familiar, here are some reasons you may choose to transition your business:

- You've pledged to your board that you'll transform your organization.
- You won't beat your workers into submission in order to meet your goal.

START A NEW BUSINESS WITHIN YOUR COMPANY

Your status may embody the following components:

- *Be humble.* You and your managers are often smug. Or, you and your people aren't always self-satisfied.

- *Be confident.* Sometimes, you and your executives are distracted by other companies' achievements. Or, you and your team admire but aren't usually preoccupied with other firm's accomplishments.

- *Be patient.* Periodically, you and your people are in a hurry to reach your goals. Or, you and your workers are generally collected.

- *Identify your attitudinal difficulties.* You have trouble avoiding complacency. You'll speak with other leaders about how they continually improve themselves and their businesses.

If the above sounds like your situation, here are a couple of reasons you may elect to start a new venture:

- You've committed to the market that you'll establish a new venture.

- Your efforts won't be limited to launching this new business. You'll also enhance this unit and the rest of your company.

Now let's read about two people who've stayed humble, confident, and patient throughout their reinventions.

LIVE YOUR PROPER ATTITUDE

Albert Black embodies effective attitude management and, as such, is a rare blend of humility, confidence, and patience.[3] This entrepreneur is founder, president, and CEO of On-Target Supplies & Logistics, a $40 million company that provides office products and supply chain management services to major companies throughout the central United States.

Despite his success, Black never forgets his roots and, therefore, avoids becoming arrogant. This fortyish businessman still remembers the large white trucks—symbols of LBJ's war on poverty—that delivered free lunches to his inner city neighborhood. By simultaneously helping his business and assisting the less fortunate—he's established warehouses and logistics centers in minority neighborhoods in four Texas cities—this businessman has remained humble. Thanks to his philosophy of self-improvement, Black also remains open to others' ideas and, consequently, isn't complacent. For example, this businessman has established a board of advisors that he consults about his firm's progress and before he makes major decisions.

This entrepreneur rarely becomes depressed by his failures, negative or fearful about his firm's prospects, or consumed with others' good fortune. Instead, Black is confident about his abilities because he knows what makes him tick—an unshakable belief in free enterprise. He traces his conviction to his family. His father, a doorman at a downtown Dallas hotel, wanted his youngest son to become a businessman like the ones he served. His mother urged him to compete, while his grandmother stressed that the best way to have a good life is to make life better for others. With an insatiable drive to control and direct, Black has built a business that enables others to enjoy the rewards of capitalism.

This savvy professional is also patient or, as he says, "You take the job you can get until you obtain the job you want." Calmly yet persistently, Black has transformed his company—from custodial service firm and office products vendor to a major corporate supplier of both products and services. Years earlier, Black worked the night shift at a large utility company, first as a doorman and later as a computer operator. When he left work at 1:00 AM, the young man mopped floors at a convenience store and then went home to sleep a few hours. During the day, Black worked for himself, at first, cleaning offices and, subsequently, delivering office supplies. When his business partner abruptly ended their relationship, this entrepreneur experienced the darkest day of his career. Overnight, the 27-year-old businessman was short-handed and confronted with thousands of dollars of debt, but the composed Black revamped his company and, two years later, signed a multimillion-dollar contract with a Fortune 500 corporation. Although he has high expectations of his people, this leader also shows tolerance toward his staff.

As is true with Albert, I'm seldom, if ever, haughty or closed to others' ideas. In fact, my humility has helped me to work effectively with my clients. Unlike consultants who act pretentiously, I approach my engagements with a collegial attitude. In part, I attribute my modesty to my upbringing. During the Depression, my father put himself through Yale University and Harvard Dental School by playing the accordion in a popular band, while my mother worked and completed law school at the same time. Consequently, my parents have imbued me with the mind-set that, whatever their backgrounds, individuals are worthy of respect.

In the past, my lack of confidence sometimes impeded my career or business progress. Once in a while, I became preoccupied with past disappointments or pessimistic about circumstances I couldn't control, such as a client's plans or the prevailing economic conditions.

Periodically, I spent too much time thinking about other people's good fortune. I also frequently questioned whether I possessed the talents necessary to achieve whatever work ideal I was pursuing and, because of these doubts, I sometimes became fearful about my future. Over the past several years, thanks to the success of my various reinventions, I've become far more confident of my abilities.

My patience is also improving. I used to become anxious if my actions weren't producing the desired results as quickly as I planned. More recently, I've recognized that my anxiety often resulted from my frustration with not being able to manage certain circumstances. By reflecting on my prior successes, I've come to realize that, sometimes, not being completely in control can lead to a better outcome. For example, while writing this book, I was anxious to interview a particular person but, because I met one of Jim Farrell's managers on an airplane, I ended up profiling Farrell—an individual who's far more relevant to reinventing your work than the one I originally planned to interview. Despite my occasional impatience with myself, I'm usually tolerant toward others, especially my clients.

I've also identified my potential attitudinal difficulties. To deal with a rare crisis in confidence or a bout of impatience, I seek others' feedback, or I review my situation in light of my past career and business successes. As I can attest, without the proper attitude, you can be your own worst enemy. On the other hand, by being humble, confident, and patient, you can help yourself achieve the reinvention you need or want.

CHAPTER NINE

Implement Your Reinvention

As we make and keep commitments . . . we begin to establish an
inner integrity that gives us the awareness of self-control and
the courage and the strength to accept more
of the responsibility for our own lives.[1]

—STEPHEN R. COVEY, AUTHOR AND BUSINESS COACH

After verifying his work ideal, a manager chooses to transition his business. An entrepreneur who wants to maintain his company's competitive edge appropriately opts to enhance his firm's offerings. Before he starts his career reinvention, a worker learns about the associated requirements and prepares to satisfy them. An employee decides to reinvigorate his job and enhance his department's approach simultaneously.

Most likely, the individuals in these examples will carry out their reinventions, but you'll probably be able to put your plan into action. Yet, what if you're not ready to execute your reinvention strategy? You may find implementing difficult and, consequently, you may struggle or even abandon your effort. What if you select the wrong reinvention option? You may not be able to complete the reshaping of your career or business and, even if you finish this initiative, you may not like the result. What if you're unaware of the requirements associated with the reinvention option you've chosen? You may fail to reach your goal. Or, what if you don't know how to undertake two reinventions at the same time? You may lose out on an opportunity to improve your career or business.

Successful businesspeople make sure that they're fully prepared before they start their reinventions. These sensible people select the remodeling option that best fits their work situation. Astute professionals learn about the requirements associated with their chosen alternative and determine whether they'll be able to satisfy these conditions. These pragmatic individuals also discover how to engage in concurrent work transformations. By their efforts, these people make their reinventions easier or quicker to accomplish and also ensure that the options they pursue lead to their career and business ideals.

You've gotten this far. Don't let a faulty implementation derail your efforts. This critical chapter will show you how to kick off your reinvention. So that you'll be ready, you'll assemble the materials you'll need. By reexamining why you might select a particular reinvention option, what actions this alternative involves, and how you'll complete these activities, you'll finalize your choice. To ensure that you make the right decision, you'll also answer pointed questions. Before you begin your endeavor, you'll learn about the requirements associated with your choice. Then you'll discover why you might engage in two reinventions simultaneously and how to carry out this feat. Let's first make sure that you have what you'll require for your journey.

ASSEMBLE YOUR MATERIALS

Sensing his timing, a worker decides to reinvigorate his job. An employee visualizes her ideal position and verifies that her skills and motivations match her goal. Seeking to enhance his firm's products, an entrepreneur develops a game plan that ingeniously applies the input he's received from his customers. A leader anticipates the execution challenges her people might face as they launch a new line. A businessperson identifies the attitudinal difficulties he might have as he changes jobs.

Maybe you admire how the people in these scenarios have utilized this book's seven steps, but you think that you'll be ready to implement your reinvention whenever you decide to do so. Yet, what if you're not sure whether you're really satisfied with your work? You may opt to do nothing and later regret your decision. What if you don't envision your ideal job or business? You may accept an alternative that doesn't reflect your (or your people's) abilities and interests. What if you fail to validate whether you (or your business) and your ideal match? You (or your workers) may be unable to perform your chosen work or be miserable doing so. What if you aren't able to respond skillfully and promptly to your situation? You may slow your reinvention or be less satisfied with its outcome. What if you shirk developing a strategy? You may be confused about which actions to take or what approach to use and, therefore, give up your reinvention, or you may pursue the wrong activities and, consequently, not meet your objective. What if you don't assess how you (or your team) will stay focused yet agile during your endeavor? By not following through, dodging problems, or missing out on opportunities, you may delay your reinvention or even fail to realize your aim. Or, what if you ignore the obstacles that you might encounter because of your outlook or demeanor? Your reinvention may falter because of your lack of humility, confidence, or patience.

Sharp employees and leaders make sure that before they begin their reinventions, they're completely prepared. That is to say, these people have answered the questions concerning their approach that appear in Steps One through Seven. These individuals have determined their timing, visualized and verified their ideal, developed a game plan that includes resourceful moves, and determined how they'll execute and also manage their attitude. As a result, these folks are ready to finalize their option choices and, in turn, implement their reinventions.

To confirm whether or not you're ready, answer the following questions before you proceed to the next section of this chapter.

- Have you sensed your (or your business') timing? If so, have you decided to change your work? Conversely, if you've chosen to do nothing, are you sure that this is a wise decision? If you haven't concluded whether or not you're satisfied with your job or business, settle this issue.

- Did you visualize your reinvention? If you've imagined your goal, are you pleased with this picture? If not, refine your visualization. On the other hand, if you haven't determined your ideal, craft this image.

- Have you verified that you (or your business) and your work ideal correspond well? If you've confirmed that your objective lines up with your situation, how close is this match? If this isn't a good pairing, revise your ideal. Conversely, if you haven't validated your goal, do so now.

- Did you use your resourcefulness to set your reinvention goal and did you identify resourceful moves to incorporate in your reinvention strategy? If not, backtrack and get this done.

- Have you devised an integrated and easy-to-follow game plan? If so, are you confident about the strategy you've developed? If not, modify your course of action. On the other hand, if you haven't completed this step, lay out your plan.

- Did you determine whether you might have trouble staying focused yet being agile? If you haven't identified your execution challenges, pinpoint these concerns.

- Have you analyzed whether you might experience problems with your attitude? If not, assess your humility, confidence, and patience.

Write down and assemble the above information so that it will be handy as you evaluate the various reinvention options. Now you're ready to continue. Let's move on to assess the first career option.

 ## REINVIGORATE YOUR JOB

A manager realizes it's time to rejuvenate her performance, revitalize her attitude, or enhance her prospects for advancement. An employee envisions keeping his job but making a modest change. A worker thinks that reenergizing her performance correlates well with her abilities and inclinations. A resourceful professional finds new ways to improve his attitude. Recognizing that reinvigorating her job is her first milestone, an aspiring executive develops a practical plan to guide her actions. A businessperson determines why he might have trouble improving his outlook. A leader foresees her attitudinal difficulties in enhancing her performance.

These examples reflect various aspects of reinvigorating your job. As you read through the "Apply" sections of Steps One through Seven, you may have concluded that your circumstances correspond— more or less—to the attributes associated with this option. Yet, even if there isn't a perfect match, you may select this alternative. At a minimum, your situation and career goal must line up with the sense of timing, visualization, and verification that typify this option. In other words, concerning three steps—Sense Your Timing, Visualize Your Reinvention, and Verify Your Ideal—your circumstances and objective and those related to this alternative must align. But because being resourceful is helpful in reinvigorating your job, it's suggested that your ideal also reflect the inventiveness often associated with this option. In any event, if you're ready to rejuvenate your performance, revitalize your attitude or interest, or enhance your prospects for advancement (you sense your timing) and you decide to make a modest change (you visualize your reinvention) and also validate that you're able and willing to take the necessary actions (you verify your ideal), you may elect to reinvigorate your job. Now let's consider three suboptions of this alternative and how to carry out these choices.

Maybe you're aware that you're not living up to your potential or that your work has deteriorated or isn't acceptable and, as a result, you decide to improve how you do your job. You picture rejuvenating your performance by taking corrective action. You verify that your abilities and motivations match your goal or determine that, to match your ideal, you need to bolster your skills, reorder what's important to you, or both. Because you're sharp, you identify an approach, such as obtaining a mentor or speaking with a colleague who solved a similar problem, to help you progress toward your aim. To assist your journey, you develop a simple course of action. You also recognize what may hold you back, such as not staying focused on the steps in your plan, searching for a new position before you resolve your dilemma, or being depressed about your status.

Perhaps you perceive that you're not as satisfied with your work as you had been or hoped to be or that your interest in your work has waned and, therefore, you elect to improve your outlook. You envision revitalizing your attitude by taking on additional responsibilities, such as getting involved in a company project, teaching a class at your firm, or mentoring colleagues, or by creating a new challenge for yourself, like a project to improve one of your company's processes. You confirm that your skills and inclinations correspond closely with your objective. Skillfully, you network with colleagues in order to learn about existing projects or activities in which you can participate, to identify a problem that you can solve, or discern an opportunity on which you can capitalize. To keep your reinvention on track, you formulate a game plan. You also determine that not juggling your job and additional activities, indiscriminately pursuing possibilities, or being aloof may impede your progress.

Or, you realize that you seek greater challenge or responsibility and, consequently, you decide to improve your visibility and build your reputation. By maximizing your performance, assuming new or additional responsibilities, or both, you visualize enhancing your prospects for advancement. You substantiate that your talents and ambitions correlate well with your purpose. You use your inventiveness to refine your goal. You lay out an integrated strategy. You also identify your potential stumbling blocks—not effectively balancing your job and additional activities or becoming consumed with others' success.

Now let's consider the requirements associated with reinvigorating your job. Before you undertake this option, you have to be certain of your objective. For example, if you receive negative feedback about your work, you may feel less positive about your position. That is to say, your performance problem may be adversely affecting your attitude. In this case, while your goal must be to improve how you do your job, by fulfilling this objective, you may also enhance your outlook. On the other hand, if you've become less pleased with your job, your performance may suffer. Under these circumstances, your primary aim has to be to adjust your perspective, which, in turn, may improve your performance. Or, if by participating in a project you also helped enhance your firm's offerings or approach, this outcome signifies that you engaged in two reinventions simultaneously. In this case, your main purpose was to reinvigorate your job. (You'll learn more about concurrent reinventions later in this chapter.)

If you're revitalizing your attitude or interest or improving your visibility by taking on additional responsibilities, you need to make sure that your performance in your regular job doesn't deteriorate. In other words, you must effectively manage your existing and new duties. Otherwise, you may create a new problem for yourself—unacceptable performance—which would require a different game plan from the one you're using.

Or, if you're pursuing projects or responsibilities that involve your coworkers' areas or even their jobs, you have to use finesse in dealing with your colleagues. That is to say, if you don't tactfully handle their concerns about your intrusion on their turf, you may alienate these individuals and, therefore, find it difficult, if not impossible, to engage in your chosen project or activity. For example, if you participate in a high-profile project to design a unique new line, don't be arrogant toward those coworkers whose job is developing new products.

Will you reinvigorate your job? The following questions will help you decide.

- In the Apply sections of Sense Your Timing, Visualize Your Reinvention, and Verify Your Ideal, reexamine the part called Reinvigorate Your Job. Now reevaluate the sense of timing that you identified (or attempted to identify) and also the visualization that you developed and verified (or tried to develop and verify). Do your situation and ideal line up with the circumstances and goal described? If there isn't a close correspondence, are you sure that this alternative is right for you?

- In the Apply sections of Be Resourceful and Be Practical, reassess the part dealing with this option. Then reevaluate the game plan, which includes resourceful moves, that you devised (or tried to devise). How do the components of your strategy and those of the hypothetical plan compare? In other words, will your course of action enable you to carry out this option? If not, how will you revamp your strategy?

- In the Apply sections of Execute Flawlessly and Manage Your Attitude, reread the part relating to this alternative. Then review your assessment of your ability to execute and manage your attitude, including the execution challenges and attitudinal difficulties you anticipated (or attempted to anticipate). Do your data and the theoretical information correspond? If not, how will you revise your evaluation and the obstacles you've identified?

- Can you handle the requirements associated with this option? That is to say, are you sure about your purpose? Will you be able to juggle your current job and the activities related to your reinvention? How will you pursue projects or responsibilities that involve your colleagues' areas or positions without irritating these individuals or incurring their hostility?

After reinvigorating your job, you may decide to make a more substantial change. As you'll learn in Chapter 10, rejuvenating your performance or attitude can be a springboard for a subsequent career move.

CHANGE JOBS IN YOUR COMPANY

A worker senses that he wants new colleagues, a position that better suits his abilities or motivations, a job in a more exciting or higher-profile area, or a new or greater challenge. A manager visualizes changing jobs to reach her potential. A leader confirms that moving into a new position matches his talents and ambitions. An ingenious entrepreneur finds a way to create a new role for herself. Deciding that changing jobs is his initial goal, an executive crafts a sensible strategy. A professional anticipates that if she doesn't juggle her current position and job-change activities, she might not achieve her career objective. By identifying that being impatient may impede his transition, a manager eases the creation of his new role.

These scenarios illustrate different facets of changing jobs. After reading the Apply sections of Steps One through Seven, you may have determined that your situation correlated—to some extent—to the characteristics associated with this option. Yet, even if there isn't a precise pairing, you may elect this alternative. At the least, your circumstances and career objective must line up with the sense of timing, visualization, and verification that usually characterize this option. But because networking (being resourceful) and a plan (being practical) are often critical to changing jobs, it's desirable that your goal also includes the ingenuity and pragmatism that are related to this alternative. In any case, if you desire a position that's more suitable or challenging or that involves new colleagues or is located in another area (you sense your timing) and you set an objective of changing jobs, areas, or roles (you visualize your reinvention) and also confirm that you possess the skills and inclinations to attain your goal (you verify your ideal), you may choose this option. Now let's examine three suboptions and how to implement these choices.

Maybe you perceive that you'd like a job that's a better match with your skills or what drives you. You imagine changing positions within your current department, for example, moving from a role in which you interact primarily with your coworkers to one in which you regularly speak with customers. You establish that your capabilities and interests fit your ideal. By being inventive—you arrange a customer forum—you demonstrate to your supervisor and colleagues that you relate well to clients. You prepare a simple plan for obtaining your new position. You also infer that being too focused on your current role or having a pessimistic outlook might hurt your effort.

Perhaps you appreciate that you want different colleagues or seek to work in a faster-paced or more visible department. You picture changing areas within your company, for instance, transitioning from finance into sales or operations into strategic planning. You make certain that what you're able to do and what's important to you correspond well with your objective. To facilitate your move, you cleverly reposition your image and skillfully draw on the contacts you've made. You craft a strategy to ensure that you take the right actions and use the most productive approach. You also surmise that not striking the right balance between your present position and reinvention effort or losing confidence in your abilities might negatively impact your result.

Or, you discern that you're looking for a new or greater challenge. You visualize creating a new role for yourself, such as moving from sales manager to corporate sales strategist or business leader to technology visionary. You verify that your abilities and ambitions match those associated with your dream position. Imaginatively, you employ a concept you've read about to shape your new job or a technique you've observed to convince your management (or board) to establish this position. To expedite your endeavor, you design a carefully thought-out course of action. You also anticipate that being inflexible or impatient might derail your reinvention.

Let's turn to the requirements that are related to this brand of reinvention. As was true with reinvigorating your job, you have to continue to perform well in your current position. If you fail to maintain your strong track record or reputation, you might be viewed less favorably and, as a result, not be able to switch jobs, areas, or roles. In other words, changing jobs is the quintessential career balancing act. You must remain a highly valued, if not indispensable, part of your team while you actively pursue membership elsewhere.

In order to change areas or create a new role for yourself, you need to network skillfully with your colleagues. By doing so, you learn about opportunities that interest you and cultivate people who can help you pursue these possibilities—whether or not they're established positions. But even if you're moving to a different job within your department, building business relationships throughout your company (and elsewhere) makes sense. A strong support system can facilitate both your current and future reinventions.

As you read in Be Resourceful, to change areas, you often have to transform how others view you. That is to say, you must articulate convincingly that you possess abilities and motivations that are similar or complementary to those of professionals in the department you hope to join. But even if you build a strong case for your move, you might have problems with colleagues who envy your ingenuity and agility. If a coworker's jealousy might hamper your reinvention, be aware of this fact and, if possible, try to develop a collegial relationship with this individual.

Will you choose to change jobs? To assist you with your decision, here are some questions.

- In the Apply sections of Sense Your Timing, Visualize Your Reinvention, and Verify Your Ideal, reread the part called Change Jobs in Your Company. Then reconsider the sense of timing that you determined (or attempted to determine) and the visualization that you crafted and confirmed (or tried to craft and confirm). Do your circumstances and goal correspond with those described? If not, are you certain that this option is appropriate for you?

- In the Apply section of Be Resourceful and Be Practical, review the part dealing with this option. Then reexamine the strategy, which incorporates resourceful moves, that you developed (or attempted to develop). Do the components of your strategy and those of the theoretical plan line up? That is to say, will your plan help you achieve this option? If not, how will you revise your course of action?

- In the Apply sections of Execute Flawlessly and Manage Your Attitude, reassess the part relating to this alternative. Then reevaluate your assessment of your ability to execute and manage your attitude, including the implementation hurdles and behavioral problems you foresaw (or tried to foresee). Does your information correlate with that cited? If not, how will you revamp your analysis and the impediments you've listed?

- Will you be prepared to deal with the requirements related to this option? That is to say, will you effectively manage your current position as you pursue a new role? Will you be adept at networking with colleagues throughout your company? If you're changing areas, will you know how to reposition your image? If not, can your mentor assist you or can you learn from a colleague's experience? Will you also be able to prevent envious coworkers from hampering your reinvention?

Even if you succeed in changing jobs, you may opt to reinvent a second time. As you'll learn in the next chapter, if you're disappointed with your new position or want a new or greater challenge, you may again reshape your work. Your next reinvention may involve improving your department's (or company's) products, services, or processes.

ENHANCE YOUR BUSINESS' OFFERINGS OR APPROACH

An owner realizes that he needs to maintain his firm's market leadership, upgrade his offerings, or keep his people stimulated. A leader envisions making changes to her department's processes. An entrepreneur substantiates that his workers' capacity for and commitment to continuous improvement correlate well with enhancing his business. By listening to her clients, a quick-witted manager discovers ways to improve her division's services. To ensure that his reinvention is completed on time, an executive develops a pragmatic course of action. A businessperson predicts that if her team isn't diligent yet nimble, she might have trouble achieving her department's improvement. A professional determines that if his organization is unreceptive to customer input, he might not bring about his business' reinvention.

These scenarios depict various features of enhancing a business. By perusing the Apply sections of Steps One through Seven, you may have decided that your circumstances somewhat correspond to this option's usual features. Yet, even if your match isn't perfect, you may select this alternative. As you've seen already, at a minimum, your business situation and reinvention aim must correlate with the sense of timing, visualization, and verification that are usually associated with this option. But because obtaining and applying input is important to enhancing your business, it's advisable that your ideal also embody the resourcefulness that's related to this alternative. In any event, if you seek to maintain your business' competitive edge, elevate its status, or keep your workers motivated (you sense your timing) and you establish an objective of enhancing your products, services, or processes (you visualize your reinvention) and also certify that you and your workers have the abilities and inspiration to fulfill this objective (you verify your ideal), you may opt to enhance your area or firm. Let's look at two suboptions and how to carry out these choices.

Perhaps you recognize the need to hold onto your business' competitive edge or even elevate your firm's status. You envision making improvements to your firm's offerings. You validate that your employees' collective talents and ambitions match those related to your ideal. To reach your aim, you and your people solicit and inventively apply input from your current and potential customers. You create a clear course of action to make certain that you attain your goal on time and within your budget. You also expect that if you and your team aren't conscientious, don't serve your customers with your existing products or services, or aren't receptive to others' ideas, you might undermine your endeavor.

Or, you perceive a chance to keep your workers challenged. You visualize streamlining or modernizing your business' approach, for example, to selling or hiring, or your firm's processes, such as procurement, production, or fulfillment. You confirm that your staff's skills and interests correspond closely to your objective. In order to bring about the right changes, you and your reports seek your suppliers' feedback, speak with colleagues at other companies, and, in turn, cleverly parlay what you learn. To ensure that you take the right actions in the proper order, you lay out a practical plan. You also anticipate that if you and your employees aren't selective about the improvements you undertake, become consumed with these efforts and ignore your regular business, or are impatient to launch a new process, you might endanger your existing business and its reinvention.

Now let's consider the requirements associated with this type of reinvention. As you discovered in the two career reinvention options, you and your people must stay on an even keel concerning your regular work and business transformation. That is to say, you need to make improvements in your offerings or approach while you manage your current operation. If you don't satisfy your customers, work well with your suppliers, or retain your workers, you might damage your area or firm and, as a result, be unable to capitalize on the improvements you make.

You and your organization need to be sure that you're making the right enhancements at the appropriate time. That's why it's critical to obtain input from a variety of sources, both in and outside your area or company. Customers frequently make valuable suggestions, which, in turn, lead to increased sales. Suppliers who sell to various businesses are usually aware of which processes or approaches are effective and which aren't. Employees—especially those on the front line—often understand what customers want, and workers who use a firm's existing processes are typically well acquainted with the pros and cons of these methods.

You also have to be capable of completing the improvements you pursue. If you have doubts about whether you and your people have the collective talents and inclinations to accomplish such enhancements, you need to resolve your concerns by bolstering your organization's skills or making trade-offs in what's important to you. If you and your employees don't perform such adjustments, you may end up wasting time and money or even fail to reach your reinvention goal.

Is enhancing your business' offerings or approach the right option for your area or company? The following questions will help you decide.

- In the Apply sections of Sense Your Timing, Visualize Your Reinvention, and Verify Your Ideal, review the part called Enhance Your Business' Offerings or Approach. Then reassess the sense of timing that you realized (or tried to realize) and the visualization that you created and certified (or attempted to create and certify). Do your business' conditions and objective mirror those discussed? If not, are you sure that this alternative is the right one for your area or firm?

- In the Apply sections of Be Resourceful and Be Practical, reread the part dealing with this alternative. Then reevaluate the plan, which includes resourceful actions, that you designed (or tried to design). Are your strategy's components and those of the hypothetical plan similar? In other words, will your game plan enable you to achieve this option? If not, how will you modify your strategy?

- In the Apply sections of Execute Flawlessly and Manage Your Attitude, revisit the part relating to this option. Then reexamine your evaluation of your ability to execute and manage your attitude, including the obstacles to execution and the attitudinal problems you predicted (or attempted to predict). How do your facts compare to those described? If there's not a good comparison, how will you revise your assessment and the hurdles you've identified?

- Will you be ready to handle the requirements associated with this option? That is to say, will you manage your reinvention and existing business? Will you be certain that you're doing the right improvements at the appropriate time? In addition, will you be confident that your people are capable of undertaking this alternative?

Even if you achieve this brand of reinvention, you may again reshape your business. As you'll read in Chapter 10, if you have a chance to introduce a new offering or line, you may transition your business.

TRANSITION YOUR BUSINESS

A leader recognizes the urgency of overhauling his company, while a peer sees a propitious market for taking advantage of opportunities and, in turn, enhancing his firm's growth and reputation. An entrepreneur dreams of transforming her organization and, subsequently, introducing a new product, launching a new line, or even acquiring other firms. An executive makes sure that his people have the talents and ambitions to make a significant change, like moving into a new market sector. By listening to her clients and employees and learning from colleagues at other firms, a manager imaginatively reshapes her business. A CEO puts together an integrated strategy for restructuring his company. A seasoned manager assumes that if his employees don't finish the right actions, his business might fail to inaugurate a new line. A president anticipates that if her reports are impatient for results or she's intolerant of their mistakes, her firm's reengineering might miscarry.

These scenarios represent various aspects of transitioning a business. After reading the Apply sections of Steps One through Seven, you may have concluded that your situation matches relatively well to those described. Yet, even if there isn't a perfect correspondence, you may choose this option. As you've read before, at the least, your business' circumstances and reinvention objective must line up with the sense of timing, visualization, and verification that typify this alternative. But because skillfully securing and utilizing input and employing a pragmatic plan are often essential to launching new offerings, moving into a new sector, refocusing an organization, or expanding a business, it's recommended that your ideal also incorporate the resourcefulness and practicality associated with this option. In any case, if you intend to overhaul or reposition your operation or, conversely, take advantage of opportunities (you sense your timing) and you establish an aim of refocusing your firm, launching new offerings, making acquisitions, or moving into a new market sector (you visualize your reinvention) and also prove that you and your employees have the skills and drive to attain this milestone (you verify your ideal), you may elect this alternative. Let's examine three suboptions and how to implement these choices.

Perhaps you're convinced that your company isn't performing acceptably or up to its potential and, consequently, you envision restructuring your business, refocusing your organization, and, in turn, rebuilding your firm. You attest that you and your employees have the collective abilities and motivation to accomplish this sweeping change. You inventively apply the positive practices that you observe at other companies and cleverly encourage communication and collaboration among your people. Spelling out the specific actions and approach necessary to produce the desired outcome, you construct a detailed strategy. You also predict that if you and your workers fail to stick with your plan or become complacent about progress, your transformation might flop.

Maybe you feel that market conditions are conducive to expanding your business and, in turn, improving its standing in the marketplace. You picture introducing a new offering or line. You check that you and your staff have the capabilities and predisposition to complete such a launch. Through speaking with your current and potential clients and consulting with a market expert, you imaginatively devise new products or services and a new technique for delivering these items. You institute a sound plan to guide your organization's activities. You also foresee that if you and your workers don't juggle your ongoing business and this effort, are overconfident because of your prior accomplishments, or become edgy if your new offerings don't perform well immediately, your firm's evolution might flounder.

Or, you sense that it's time to reposition your firm and move it from a slow-growing or low-margin market segment. Conversely, you see a chance to expand your already-thriving business into a new area. In either case, you visualize transitioning your company into a new market sector. You validate that you and your people possess the requisite talents and ambition to carry out this substantial endeavor. To lead your firm's initiative, you ingeniously hire an executive who's been successful in this segment. You establish a game plan so that you'll attain your goal before market conditions become less favorable. You also identify that if you and your employees don't effectively manage your current business and transition, lose confidence, or become anxious for quick results, your reinvention might fail.

Let's now examine the requirements associated with this type of reinvention. Whichever suboption you pursue, you must maintain an equilibrium between your existing operation and business remodeling. That is to say, during a corporate transformation, it's not uncommon for managers to focus inward and neglect their customers. When launching a new offering or line, workers sometimes ignore fixing problems with their existing products or services or miss out on opportunities to enhance these items. Or, when employees and their leaders become wrapped up in learning about a new sector, these individuals often forget that their current business is still paying the bills or even financing their firm's transition.

If you're turning around your business, you need to be certain about the problems you'll address and how you'll solve these dilemmas. Otherwise, you might spend time and money working on concerns or using methods that don't help you reach your business ideal. As a result, you may lose credibility with your customers, employees, and investors and find it difficult, if not impossible, to generate enthusiasm about or confidence in regrouping.

If you're inaugurating a new offering or line, you have to be sure that you're introducing the appropriate items and at the right time. As was true with enhancing your products or services, you must get feedback from both your workers and your marketplace and also verify that your organization has the ability and drive to undertake this substantial effort. Occasionally, a business that's been successful in the past wrongly presumes that it will achieve its goal—regardless of its offerings or the prevailing market conditions.

If you're moving your firm into a new market sector, you need to understand this segment and also be positive that this transition makes sense for your business. In other words, even if a particular area is growing rapidly, this phenomenon doesn't signify that this sector will continue to expand at this rate. Or, even if many of your company's competitors are jumping into this segment, their actions don't guarantee that such a move is either prudent or feasible for your business.

Will you choose to transition your business? To assist you in making this decision, here are some useful questions.

- In the Apply sections of Sense Your Timing, Visualize Your Reinvention, and Verify Your Ideal, revisit the part called Transition Your Business. Then reexamine the sense of timing that you perceived (or tried to perceive) and the visualization that you crafted and validated (or attempted to craft and validate). Do your business' circumstances and reinvention ideal correspond to those described? If not, are you sure that this option is appropriate for your area or firm?

- In the Apply sections of Be Resourceful and Be Practical, review the part dealing with this alternative. Then reassess the strategy, which includes resourceful moves, that you shaped (or tried to shape). Do your plan's features resemble the theoretical components cited? That is to say, will your plan enable you to complete this option? If not, how will you revamp your strategy?

- In the Apply sections of Execute Flawlessly and Manage Your Attitude, reread the part covering this option. Then reevaluate your assessment of your ability to execute and manage your attitude, including the impediments to implementation and the demeanor dilemmas you identified (or attempted to identify). How does your information compare to that cited? If there's not a close correlation, will you amend your analysis and the obstacles you've identified?

- Will you be prepared to deal with the requirements related to this option? However you're transitioning your business, will you balance your reinvention and existing business? If you're transforming your firm, will you be sure about your problems and how to fix them? If you're introducing new items, will you be certain that you're launching the appropriate new offerings at the right time and that your people will be able to carry out this significant effort? If you're segueing into a new market sector, will you be informed about this segment and be confident that such a move is the correct one for your firm?

Even if you successfully transition your business, you might reinvent again in the future. If your company excels at something, such as providing a particular service, you may launch a new unit that focuses exclusively on this capability.

START A NEW BUSINESS WITHIN YOUR COMPANY

An entrepreneur senses that he and his workers are ready to parlay their knack for managing global projects. A CEO visualizes establishing a new unit that will solidify her company's competitive edge, generate additional revenues, and enhance her firm's reputation. A leader verifies that his employees have the requisite abilities and mind-set to undertake an entrepreneurial venture. Exploiting what she's learned from other companies, an enterprising manager launches a new business. In order to minimize the risk associated with his new venture, an owner develops a sensible plan. An executive predicts that if she and her reports don't strike the right balance between their new venture and existing business, their entrepreneurial pursuit might founder. A businessperson anticipates that if his personnel grow impatient, they might lose confidence in themselves or in their new business.

The preceding examples portray different facets of starting a new business within a company. From reading the Apply sections of Steps One through Seven, you may have decided that your circumstances are similar to those discussed. Yet, even if there isn't a flawless match, you may elect this option. At a minimum, your business' conditions and reinvention goal must correspond well with the sense of timing, visualization, and verification that characterize this choice. But because cleverly utilizing feedback, employing a practical plan, executing flawlessly, and having the proper attitude are often vital to accomplishing this option, it's prudent that your ideal also include most—if not all—of these other attributes. That is to say, if the various aspects of your reinvention line up with the components cited in the seven steps, you're more likely to succeed in starting a new venture than if there's not such a correlation. In any event, if you seek to parlay one or more of your business' capabilities (you sense your timing) and you set a goal of establishing a new business within your company (you visualize your reinvention) and also confirm that you and your people have the talents and ambition to achieve this aim (you verify your ideal), you may choose this option. Let's look at an example of this alternative.

Because there's strong demand for the services at which your business excels, you perceive it's time to capitalize on your competitive edge. You envision creating a new unit that will generate additional revenues and also enhance your firm's stature. Although smaller, an earlier endeavor shows that you and your managers have the capabilities and drive to reach your goal. By learning from and partnering with another firm, you ingeniously minimize the risk associated with your new venture. You devise a realistic strategy to ensure that you fulfill your objective without exceeding your budget. You also expect that if you and your colleagues don't maintain an equilibrium between the rest of your business and your new unit, become arrogant about your inventiveness, or are restless for quick results, your venture might come to naught.

Now let's assess the requirements related to this type of reinvention. As you learned in the other options, you have to manage your ongoing business and reinvention. That is to say, until your new business is self-sustaining, you must not endanger your firm's current customer base, revenues, or earnings. When (or if) your new venture is self-supporting, you may elect to shut down your other divisions and focus exclusively on this business.

Your organization must have demonstrated the talent that your new business will parlay. Let's say that, by joining forces, workers from different departments have managed international projects for your firm's customers. If your employees were successful in these initiatives, you may be comfortable capitalizing on this capability and, in turn, setting up a business that's devoted to such undertakings. On the other hand, if such endeavors have sometimes turned out badly, you may want to delay forming this new unit until your personnel work the kinks out of their approach.

You and your people also need to have the appropriate mind-set to launch and manage an entrepreneurial venture. In other words, starting a new venture within a company isn't business as usual. Such an endeavor is usually risky and difficult. If your managers have prior experience in establishing and running new businesses and, consequently, the disposition to handle an entrepreneurial opportunity, you may feel confident pursuing this alternative. But if your reports don't have such a track record and, as a result, aren't inclined to operate like small businesspeople, you may want to choose another option.

Despite these requirements, will you opt to start a new business within your company? Before you do, you'll want to answer the following questions.

- In the Apply sections of Sense Your Timing, Visualize Your Reinvention, and Verify Your Ideal, reread the part called Start a New Business within Your Company. Then reevaluate the sense of timing that you realized (or attempted to realize) and the visualization that you shaped and tested (or tried to shape and test). Do your situation and reinvention objective resemble those discussed? If not, are you positive that this alternative is suitable for your business?

- In the Apply sections of Be Resourceful and Be Practical, revisit the part dealing with this option. Then reexamine the plan, which incorporates resourceful activities, that you developed (or attempted to develop). Do your plan's components correlate well to the hypothetical features listed? In other words, will your course of action allow you to finish this option? If not, how will you redraft your plan?

- In the Apply sections of Execute Flawlessly and Manage Your Attitude, review the part concerning this option. Then reconsider your analysis of your ability to execute and manage your attitude, including the execution hurdles and attitudinal difficulties you anticipated (or tried to anticipate). How does your information line up with the cited theoretical data? If these items aren't similar, how will you redo your assessment and the list of obstacles you've developed?

- Will you be ready to handle the requirements associated with this option? That is to say, will you maintain an equilibrium between your business and reinvention journey? Will you be fully confident that your people possess both the ability and mind-set necessary to start up and run an entrepreneurial venture?

As you read earlier, you may undertake this reinvention and another at the same time.

DO TWO OPTIONS SIMULTANEOUSLY

As he reinvigorates his job, a worker also enhances one of his company's processes. While introducing a new offering, a businessperson rejuvenates his performance. In order to refocus his organization, a chief executive first revitalizes his attitude. A manager helps her firm launch a new business and, because of her entrepreneurial know-how, her CEO asks her to change jobs and run this new venture.

The individuals in these examples have reinvented their jobs and businesses—simultaneously or almost so—but you think that, if it's necessary, you'll be able to do likewise. Yet, what if you don't recognize that a particular reinvention depends upon or leads to a different transformation? You may not accomplish your objective or you may be unprepared to pursue the reinvention that arises from your initial endeavor. What if you're not fully aware of the various reinvention combinations? You may miss out on an opportunity to reshape your career or company. Or, what if you don't know about the requirements associated with undertaking two reinventions at the same time? You may fail to accomplish one or both of these initiatives.

Savvy businesspeople recognize that one reinvention is sometimes contingent upon or results in another. That is to say, professionals are knowledgeable about the numerous job-business reinvention alternatives. These prudent folks are also wise to the requirements associated with these blends and, therefore, are able to complete their career and corporate transformations. Now let's examine the various reinvention combos.

If you're reinvigorating your job by engaging in a project, you may also enhance your company's approach or help your firm launch a new offering or line. Conversely, if your area is enhancing its offerings, by your involvement, you may revitalize your attitude about your job. If you're a leader who's transforming your organization, before you begin, you may need to reenergize your performance. Or, thanks to a successful reinvention, you may renew your attitude. If you're an executive who's starting a new business within your company, through this significant undertaking, you may also reinvigorate your role.

If you change jobs and, as a result, become involved in improving an area's offerings or approach or launching a new product or line, you may engage in concurrent reinventions. On the other hand, if your management asks you to assume a new role—improving your company's processes, leading a transition into a new market sector, or establishing a new venture—you may simultaneously advance your company and career.

Whatever the combination, there are two requirements associated with performing contemporaneous reinventions. You need to identify the primary initiative, which may lead to a second reinvention. For example, if you're the leader who's refocusing your organization but need to rejuvenate your performance before you start, your corporate transformation is the principal endeavor. If this corporate overhaul leads to reenergizing your attitude, the latter is a by-product of the former. Once you recognize the main reinvention, you must also be willing to make certain trade-offs. If you're the manager who's responsible for spearheading the transition into a new sector or launch of a new venture, until you complete your assignment, this task is your priority and, consequently, you may have to make compromises that involve your career or personal life. But after you complete this effort, you're free to make career advancement your predominant concern.

Will you undertake two reinventions concurrently? If so, prepare yourself by answering the following questions.

- Will you reinvigorate your job and enhance your (or your company's) business at the same time? Or, will you revitalize your attitude and simultaneously introduce a new offering or start a new venture within your firm?

- Will you change jobs, areas, or roles and also enhance your (or your company's) business? Or, will you assume a new role or move to another department and, at the same time, lead the launch of a new line or venture?

- Whatever the concurring reinventions, will you recognize which one is primary? Will you also be prepared to make any related trade-offs?

This chapter has shown you how to implement your reinvention. Yet, what if after you reinvent, you want to reinvent again? In other words, what if you're unhappy with the result of your career change or business improvement, need to address a problem, want to take advantage of an opportunity, or seek a new challenge? Chapter 10 will help you handle such situations.

CHAPTER TEN

Reinvent Your Work Again

Looking back may be tempting, but it's terribly counterproductive. . . .
Pour your energy, every bit of it, into adapting to your new world. . . .[1]

—ANDREW GROVE, AUTHOR AND CHAIRMAN, INTEL CORPORATION

Six months after he rejuvenates his performance, a worker moves to a new department of his company. After a year in a new position, a manager revitalizes her attitude. Having successfully enhanced his firm's existing products, an owner introduces a new offering. Acknowledging that his department's move into a new market sector failed, a leader retrenches and refocuses his organization. Following the establishment of a new venture, an executive changes roles in her company.

The businesspeople in these examples have again reinvented their work. After you complete your reinvention, you don't think that another change will be necessary. Yet, what if you're not pleased with the result of your reinvention? Your new position may not be as exciting as you thought it would be or your new offerings may not be selling briskly. What if you'd like to work in a higher-profile department or your people seek a new challenge? You may have to change jobs and your employees may need to enhance your firm's offerings or launch new ones. Or, what if you spot a problem you didn't expect or discern an opportunity you can't miss? You may need to upgrade a critical process or initiate a project to inaugurate a new line.

You grasp the intent of these questions. You may need or want to reinvent your work again and, therefore, you have to know how to accomplish this feat. As you may surmise, astute professionals are able to reinvent anew. Based on their assessment of their situation, these managers determine whether or not they'll reinvent again and, if they decide to do so, these workers choose the right option(s) for reinventing their jobs, businesses, or both.

With this final chapter, you'll come full circle. In other words, you'll restart the reinvention process. You'll examine why you might need or want to change your job or business again and, if so, which option you'll employ. You'll also discover the caveats associated with your alternative and, that way, you'll be fully prepared to step into your future.

To begin, let's consider a key reason you might reinvent another time.

REVIEW YOUR MISSION AND MILESTONES

After enhancing his division's products, a leader consecutively introduces new offerings and establishes a new venture within his company. Having bolstered her skills, a businessperson changes jobs and subsequently creates a new role for herself in her firm. A manager determines whether a reinvention is consistent with his business' long-term objective.

Do you remember reading about mission statements and milestones in Step Five, Be Practical? Most likely, the individuals in these scenarios are using these tools to direct their actions, but you don't think you'll need such mechanisms. Besides, you want to be as flexible as possible so that you (or your business) can respond to a change in your circumstances. Yet, what if after numerous reinventions, you're unsure whether you're going in the right direction? You may wish you had a road map for your career or business. What if you aren't ready to assume a new role or your business isn't prepared to launch a new line? You may miss out on an attractive opportunity. Or, what if you have a chance to switch to a different position or your business has an opportunity to introduce a new product or service but you aren't sure whether to take advantage of this situation? Without a standard by which you can judge a potential change, you may not know whether a particular reinvention makes sense for your job or company.

As you read in Step Five, business professionals recognize that they may pursue several job or business reinventions, which, over time, lead to their highest goal. That being the case, these people create customized mission statements and develop the key milestones that they must attain to reach their ultimate aim. In turn, executives, entrepreneurs, and employees use these instruments to prepare themselves for an upcoming event or stage. Along the way, if these managers discern a problem or opportunity, they utilize these tools to decide whether (or not) they'll respond to their circumstances. In other words, equipped with these mechanisms, workers have a benchmark against which to evaluate a potential reinvention. Let's consider two examples that will help you refine (or shape) your mission statement and milestones and also make sure that your reinvention is consistent with these tools.

Perhaps you're an experienced manager who now wants a more significant challenge. You envision moving from your job, which involves selling to your firm's clients, to a role in which you manage an entire division. You've confirmed that your abilities—selling, industry know-how, and leading others—and what's important to you—money and recognition—correlate well with your reinvention objective. Your long-term aim is to become one of your company's top executives. In this case, your mission may be to capitalize on your skill-strengths to help build the premier firm in your industry and, by accomplishing this aim, you'll earn the respect and compensation you're looking for. Your milestones may involve becoming the manager of a moderately sized division and, if you perform well, a global division and, ultimately, your company's chief operating officer or even its president and CEO. Because your reinvention goal is your initial milestone, the job change you're considering fits your purpose and, therefore, it makes sense to proceed.

Or, you manage a business that you seek to transform and, therefore, you visualize restructuring your firm. You've verified that your employees' capabilities—analytical skills and ingenuity—and their motivations—being challenged and personal wealth—correspond with your reinvention aim. Your company's ultimate objective is to inaugurate numerous new products and services. Your business' mission may be to parlay your workers' talents in order to provide the most comprehensive range of offerings in your industry and, by doing so, your people will be fulfilled and will share in your company's financial success. Your milestones may include reengineering your business, introducing a new product, and, if this item sells, additional new products, and, eventually, services that complement these items. Because your reinvention aim is your first milestone, this corporate overhaul is consistent with your long-term goal and, consequently, it's logical to move forward.

If, however, in either of these cases, your reinvention didn't correspond to your mission and milestones, you'd need to reassess your work reshaping relative to your long-term objective. Based on this reexamination, if you decide to proceed with your reinvention, you'd have to adjust your mission and milestones. Conversely, if you choose to abandon your reinvention, you'd craft a new reinvention goal. Either way—as you learned in Execute Flawlessly—you'd be agile.

Before you move on to the next section, review and revise (or develop) your mission statement and milestones. That way, you'll be able to evaluate this chapter's information relative to these tools. Here are a few questions to assist you in refining (or shaping) these mechanisms.

- Does (or will) your mission statement reflect your or your business' capabilities, motivations, and ultimate aim?

- Do (or will) your or your business' milestones build logically upon one another? Will you use these stages to prepare your or your people's skills?

- Before you undertake another reinvention, will you evaluate this move against your purpose and related work events? That is to say, will you avoid reinventing haphazardly?

Let's now examine why and how you might reinvent after a modest career change.

REINVENT AFTER YOU REINVIGORATE YOUR JOB

Because she didn't fully reenergize her outlook, an employee is disappointed by the outcome of her reinvention. A year after he rejuvenates his performance, a worker recognizes the need to improve his work again. An executive revitalizes her attitude and, subsequently, senses that she wants a new challenge. Having reinvigorated his role, a businessperson detects a problem that might impede his department's progress.

The individuals in these examples may reinvent a second time. Let's look at three examples of how you might reinvent after you reinvigorate your job.

A few months ago, you rejuvenated your performance but, at this point, you see that this change won't suffice. You visualize reviving your attitude by getting involved in projects and confirm that your skills and inclinations correspond to this goal. You skillfully employ your network of contacts to identify relevant opportunities and use a simple game plan to guide your effort. You also anticipate that if you don't follow through or become anxious about finding a project, you might undermine your new reinvention.

Although you recently reenergized your perspective, you realize that you're ready to take on a more challenging role. Picturing your new position, you verify that you and your ideal match. You cleverly convince your management that you'll be able to handle this assignment and, with their approval, lay out a practical plan to facilitate your job change. You also foresee that if you don't juggle your current position and reinvention or lose confidence in your abilities, you might jeopardize your latest career reshaping.

Or, even though you're pleased with how you've revived your role, you discover a problem, like a product flaw, or an opportunity, such as demand for a new offering. In response, you envision fixing the defect or launching the new item. You ingeniously initiate a task force to address this situation and devise a sound course of action so that you and your colleagues will meet your objective. You also predict that if you and your coworkers don't apply the necessary energy to your effort or become impatient for results, your business reinvention might break down.

Let's turn to the caveats associated with reinventing again after you reinvigorate your job. Some workers hold that once you've rejuvenated your performance or attitude, you must next switch jobs. Such a progression is often logical but, if this move isn't right for you, don't feel compelled to make this change. Further, if you want to kick off a business reinvention, don't be intimidated by this prospect. You don't have to be the boss or owner to initiate an improvement or addition to your department's or company's offerings or processes. Frequently, a less senior employee spots a problem or discerns an opportunity that his colleagues miss.

To help you determine whether you'll reinvent again after you rejuvenate your performance or revitalize your attitude, here are some questions to ask yourself.

- Have you assessed your situation? Are you dissatisfied with the result of your reinvention? Do you seek new colleagues, a higher-profile or faster-paced department, or a new challenge?

Or, have you identified a problem with your company's offerings or processes or discovered an opportunity to grow your (or your employer's) business?

- Will you respond to your (or your company's) circumstances? If so, how will you reinvent anew? Will you again refresh your performance or reenergize your outlook? Instead, will you change jobs, departments, or roles within your company? Will you create a task force or project to solve a problem or capitalize on an opportunity? Or, will you reinvigorate your job and help your company at the same time? In any case, will you use your mission statement and milestones to determine whether you'll make this change?

- Will you remember the caveats related to your next reinvention? Will you accept that after you reinvigorate your job, you aren't obliged to change positions? In addition, will you grasp that you don't need to be the leader or owner of a business to bring about a worthwhile improvement or addition?

Now let's consider how you might reinvent after you change positions, departments, or roles.

REINVENT AFTER YOU CHANGE JOBS

A manager who switched positions is dissatisfied with his new work. A year after a job change, a professional seeks a new challenge. Having assumed a new role, a businessperson realizes that she has to refresh her perspective. In a new department, a worker spots a problem with his department's offerings.

The people in these examples may reinvent anew. Let's evaluate three examples of why and how you might reinvent again after you've changed jobs.

Having recently changed jobs or departments, you're miserable in your new position because you don't enjoy your colleagues, don't like your new assignment, or resent having to sacrifice time with your family. Perhaps your new role is more than you bargained for. Or, you'd prefer to work in a more exciting department or have more demanding duties. Whatever your situation, you sense it's time for another job change. You imagine moving to a new position that will meet your objectives and confirm that your abilities and motivations fit this ideal. By networking skillfully, you identify the job you want and, in turn, develop a clear strategy for reaching your goal. You also acknowledge that if you don't manage your current position and reinvention or become discouraged about your progress, you might doom your latest career maneuver.

After you switched jobs, you became complacent, but thanks to your mentor's feedback, you now discern the need to improve. You visualize revitalizing your perspective by taking on additional responsibilities and validate that you'll be able and willing to make such a change. By using your resourcefulness, you aptly pinpoint where and how you can play a role and, using this information, craft a plan to achieve your aim. You also expect that if you don't strike the right balance between your regular work and new activities or become closed to new ideas, you might undermine your job reinvigoration.

Or, even though you're content with your new job, you spot a way to help your company solve a problem or pursue an opportunity. You envision starting a project that will correct a faulty process or introduce a new line and verify that you and your goal match. Cleverly persuading your management to back this initiative, you present a sensible course of action. You also anticipate that if you and your project team don't stick with this plan or become intolerant of each other's mistakes, your business reinvention might fizzle.

Let's consider the cautions associated with reinventing anew after you've changed jobs. That you switched jobs before doesn't signify that you must do so again. If a more modest career change, such as taking on additional duties or participating in projects, is what you require, don't force yourself to do more. Besides, if you continually switch positions or roles, take jobs that aren't right for you and then drop them, or hop from department to department, your management and colleagues may view you as fickle or unreliable and, therefore, an undesirable leader or coworker. Think carefully about another job change and also discuss this action with your mentor and trusted colleagues.

Will you reinvent again after you've changed jobs? If so, what will you do? To help you decide, here are some questions to consider.

- Have you evaluated your circumstances? Are you displeased with your new job, department, or role? Do you want to change positions, departments, or both? Have you become self-satisfied or sloppy and need to adjust your attitude or performance? Or, have you spotted a problem with your department's (or company's) offerings or approach or a chance to inaugurate a new item?

- Will you react to your (or your company's) situation? If so, how will you reinvent again? Will you switch positions or reinvigorate the one you have? Will you initiate a project whose aim is to resolve a dilemma or take advantage of an opportunity? Or, will you undertake a career and business reinvention simultaneously? In any event, will you employ your mission statement and milestones to decide whether (or not) your next move makes sense?

- Will you be attentive to the warnings associated with your next reinvention? That is to say, will you make the career change that's appropriate, even if it involves only a modest improvement? Will you also change jobs prudently so that your management and colleagues won't see you as volatile and, consequently, an unacceptable leader or coworker?

Let's now turn to how you'll reinvent after you've made a modest improvement to your business.

REINVENT AFTER YOU ENHANCE YOUR BUSINESS

An executive questions whether a recent product enhancement was effective. An entrepreneur who's pleased with her firm's improved approach chooses to revamp her offerings. With the success of his division's enhanced service, a manager decides to launch a new item. After remodeling their business' products, a group of workers becomes complacent and, as a result, their leader elects to refocus his people. Seeking to parlay his company's knack for continuous improvement, a CEO plans to establish a new venture. An owner who's completed the reengineering of her firm's processes opts to create a new role for herself.

The professionals in these scenarios may follow their business' enhancement with another reinvention. Let's examine four examples of how you might reinvent again after you've enhanced your business.

You're not happy with how your revamped approach is working. On the other hand, you're thrilled with how your enhanced offering is selling and want to remodel your other items. In either case, you perceive a need or an opportunity to enhance your business again. You picture reengineering your processes or, instead, recreating your products or services and confirm that your workers have the skills and drive to complete such an initiative. You and your quick-witted team seek feedback from your suppliers concerning the best approaches or suggestions from your customers about the improvements they'd like to see and, using this information, develop a pragmatic plan to lead you. You also figure that if you don't balance your ongoing business and reinvention or become unreceptive to new concepts and methods, your latest business enhancement might break down.

Even after enhancing your offerings, your firm's growth is stalled, or your business' profitability hasn't improved. On the other hand, because of your enhanced products or services, your business has turned around its performance and, consequently, your customers are demanding new items. Under either of these conditions, you feel obliged to undertake a more sweeping reinvention. You visualize transitioning your firm into a new sector or, conversely, introducing one or more new items and you verify that your employees have the abilities and motivation to finish such an effort. You aptly solicit advice from a market guru or, conversely, skillfully obtain input from your current and potential clients and, in turn, shape a sensible strategy to guide your journey. You also project that if you and your team don't follow through or become impatient for quick results, your newest business transformation might founder.

You've successfully enhanced your business numerous times and, as a result, other firms regularly seek your company's advice on how they can similarly improve their operations. Consequently, you think it's appropriate to set up an entrepreneurial unit. Imagining this new venture, you attest that you and your people possess the talent and mind-set required to launch this business. You ingeniously minimize the risk of this effort by partnering with a firm that's created several such operations and, together, you create an integrated plan. You also foresee that if you and your colleagues don't maintain an equilibrium between your existing operation and new business or become arrogant about your inventiveness, your current reinvention might fail.

Or, you're drained from continuously improving your business and, therefore, seek to restore your vigor. You envision creating a new role for yourself, and you're sure that what you're able to do and what's important to you match your ideal. Because you're sharp, you apply ideas from managers outside your company and, in turn, you develop a realistic plan to advance your aim. You also surmise that if you become complacent or distracted by another business enhancement, you might not attain your goal.

Let's examine the admonitions associated with reinventing anew after enhancing your business. Sometimes, workers become consumed with revamping their processes or offerings and, as a result, fail to discern problems or opportunities that affect the rest of their business. If you've previously enhanced your business, stay alert. That way, you'll be able to respond promptly to your situation—before a difficulty becomes impossible to resolve or favorable circumstances change. Further, if you decide to engage in a more ambitious business reinvention, such as refocusing your organization, launching new offerings, or starting a new venture, the appropriate businessperson has to lead such an effort. A businessperson who's skilled in improving an item or approach may not be effective in a more sweeping endeavor. Whether you're the leader of a division or company or the manager who initiates a change, you must choose the right person to lead your reinvention—even if that means selecting someone other than yourself.

After you enhance your business, will you reinvent again? If you're uncertain, here are some questions that will help you decide on your next reinvention.

- What is your situation? Are you dissatisfied with the recent enhancement of your firm's offerings or approach? Conversely, are you pleased with the outcome of your prior reinvention and, therefore, seek to make additional improvements? Despite your enhancement effort, has your firm been unable to generate acceptable revenues or earnings? Are your customers requesting new products or services? Can you parlay your company's knack for continuous improvement? Or, would you like to enliven your mood, change jobs, or create a new role for yourself within your company?

- Will you respond to your circumstances? If so, will you again enhance your business and, if so, what will you improve? Will you transition your firm into a new sector or introduce new offerings? Will you establish a new business within your company? Will you reinvigorate your performance or attitude or change jobs, departments, or roles within your firm? Or, will you undertake career and business reinventions at the same time? In any case, will you utilize your mission statement and milestones to assess a potential course of action?

- Will you be mindful of the caveats related to your next reinvention? That is to say, will you avoid being preoccupied with making improvements to your business? If you choose to launch a more extensive reinvention, such as inaugurating a new product or service, moving in or out of a market sector, or starting a new venture, will you select the appropriate individual to lead this effort?

Let's now assess how you'll reinvent after you've made a more substantial improvement to your business.

REINVENT AFTER YOU TRANSITION YOUR BUSINESS

With the failure of his company's turnaround, an executive decides to move his firm into a new sector. Because her firm's new product didn't meet customer expectations, an owner opts to reposition and, in turn, relaunch this item. A leader who successfully refocused her organization subsequently elects to introduce a new service, while a peer decides to make an acquisition. After launching several new products, a businessperson chooses to inaugurate a new line. Because her company's new offerings have been well received, a professional considers enhancing these items. Reacting to the market's demand for his firm's new services, a CEO commits to establishing a new venture that will provide combinations of these offerings. An entrepreneur who's devoted himself to introducing new products perceives the need to reanimate his role.

The people in these scenarios may undertake another reinvention. Let's evaluate four examples of how you might reinvent anew after you've transitioned your business.

Perhaps you're dissatisfied with your recent business transition. Your business transformation hasn't resulted in improved revenues or earnings or your new offerings aren't delivering the results you expected. On the other hand, maybe you're pleased with your inauguration of a new product or service and seek to launch additional items. In either case, you recognize a need or an opportunity to transition your business again. You visualize moving into a new sector or relaunching your new product or service or, conversely, introducing new offerings. Regardless of how you again transition your business, you verify that your people's skills and motivations correspond with your objective. For such an extensive reinvention, you resourcefully obtain and apply input from your marketplace and also develop and follow a detailed plan. In addition, you anticipate that if you and your people don't strike the right balance between your current business and reinvention or become impatient for a quick turnaround or an offering that will skyrocket your firm to success, your reinvention might meet with disaster.

You're delighted that your firm's new products are selling well, but you see a way to make these items even better. You picture enhancing your company's offerings and feel confident that your workers have the abilities and inclination to achieve this goal. Ingeniously incorporating feedback from your current and potential clients, you and your employees lay out a simple plan to fulfill your aim. You also predict that if your people become consumed with making enhancements and neglect their customers or become unreceptive to new ideas and approaches, your reinvention might fall short.

You've observed that your customers often purchase several of your business' new offerings simultaneously. That being the case, you perceive an opportunity to establish a new unit within your firm. Envisioning an entrepreneurial venture that will provide product and service packages, you assert that your people possess the talent and drive to undertake this endeavor. To make sure that you accomplish your goal, you survey companies who've taken a similar route and inventively employ what you learn to craft your game plan. You also project that if you and your managers don't stay alert to the rest of your business or become arrogant about your innovative new venture, your reinvention might negatively impact your company.

Or, for the past two years, you've been involved in overhauling your department or company and, consequently, you're ready for a different challenge. You imagine taking on a new role, such as designing new offerings, and you're confident that you have the capability and ambition to meet this goal. Cleverly repositioning your image with your management and colleagues, you put together a sensible plan to attain your ideal. You also suspect that if you don't follow through or become pessimistic about the market for new products or services, you might doom your job change.

Let's look at the cautions related to reinventing anew after transitioning your business. If you previously transformed your department or company and now seek to launch a new offering, line, or venture, most likely, you'll require a different leader for this endeavor. Similarly, if your last reinvention entailed introducing new offerings and, this time, you plan to overhaul your business, you'll probably need a new manager for this initiative. Growing an existing business or establishing a new venture involves different skills from restructuring or refocusing a company. A second warning concerns continually engaging in extensive changes. Businesses that keep their people in a perpetual state of flux often find that, over time, productivity and morale decline. Consequently, if you've recently reengineered your department or company, inaugurated numerous new offerings, or both, you need to consider carefully how and when—or even whether—you'll again reinvent your business. If you're unsure about your next step, speak with colleagues in and outside your firm.

Having completed the transition of your business, will you reinvent anew? If so, you'll want to answer the following questions.

- What are your circumstances? Were you successful in overhauling your department or company, moving into a new sector, or introducing a new offering or line? Or, did your effort fail? If your new offerings are performing well, do you want to improve these items? Do you seek a way to capitalize on the demand for your new offerings? Or, do you need to revitalize your attitude or improve your performance or seek a new department or challenge?

- Will you react to your situation? If so, will you again transition your firm and what will you do? Will you enhance your department's or company's new offerings or refine its new structure or new processes? Will you launch a new unit within your business that will parlay your new products or services or a particular capability? Will you reinvigorate your role or change jobs? Or, will you participate in simultaneous career and business reinventions? In any event, will you use your mission statement and milestones as a benchmark against which you'll judge a potential reinvention?

- Will you heed the warnings associated with your subsequent reinvention? Will you choose the right person to lead your business' next transition? That is to say, if you're transforming your organization or launching new offerings, will your leader have the appropriate skills? How will you ensure that you're not involving your department or business in too much change?

Now let's evaluate how you'll reinvent after you've created a new venture.

REINVENT AFTER YOU START A NEW BUSINESS WITHIN YOUR COMPANY

Because his new business failed to parlay his firm's competitive edge, an owner chooses to shut down this unit and refocus his organization. A new operation is running smoothly and, as a result, its leader opts to introduce a new offering. Having established a success-ful entrepreneurial venture, a CEO decides to start another new busi-ness. Pleased with their new unit, managers elect to enhance this business' approach. An executive who's launched a new business senses it's time to change jobs in his company.

The folks in these examples may engage in a subsequent reinven-tion. Let's look at four examples of how you might reinvent again after you've started a new business within your company.

Your new venture is a disaster and, consequently, you need to close this unit. On the other hand, your new unit is so successful that customers are demanding additional offerings. In either case, you realize that, at this point, you have to transition your business. You envision refocusing your organization on the rest of your business or, conversely, launching a new product or service. Whether you're retrenching or expanding, you confirm that your employees' skills and interests correlate well with your aim. If you're refocusing, you ingeniously motivate your personnel and if you're introducing new items, you imaginatively incorporate your clients' input. Using a game plan to guide your efforts, you also assume that if your people don't adhere to their strategies or become depressed about their fail-ure or, conversely, haughty about their success, your reinvention might go astray.

You're ecstatic about the progress of your new venture and think it's time to start another. You picture starting another new business and you're confident that your people will be able and willing to han-dle such an endeavor. Because you're enterprising, you implement a new compensation package and you and your people create a realistic plan. You assume that if your managers don't apply the requisite energy to this new effort or become smug about their prior success, you might not establish your new unit.

You and your colleagues are pleased with your new business but sense that there's room for improvement. Visualizing the enhance-ment of your new venture's approach, you're certain that your work-ers' abilities and motivations match this objective. You and your quick-witted team apply input from your suppliers and follow a simple plan. You also predict that if you and your employees become engrossed in these enhancements and neglect the rest of the business or become closed to new methods, your reinvention might miss its goal.

Or, as a manager who's started several new businesses, you're ready for a different challenge. Imagining a new job in a different department within your company, you're comfortable that your tal-ents and ambitions line up well with your ideal. You skillfully utilize your network of contacts to find your new position and employ a practical plan to guide your actions. You also project that if you don't stick with your strategy or become conceited about your entrepreneurial experiences, you might not obtain your new role.

There are two cautions associated with reinventing again after starting a new business. Just because you previously established a new venture, you're not obliged to launch another entrepreneurial operation. If a more limited change, such as introducing a new offering or enhancing the new unit's approach, is fitting, undertake the simpler reinvention. Moreover, if you start too many unrelated businesses, you may end up with an unwieldy or unfocused collection of entities. That being the case, whether you're an executive who leads a company or an employee who's recommending the creation of a new unit, you must make sure that starting another new venture is a wise move.

Will you reinvent anew after you start a new business? To help you with this important decision, here are some useful questions.

- What is your situation? Were you successful in starting a new venture or did your initiative flop? Do you want to start another new business? Or, do you seek a different pace or challenge?

- Will you react to your circumstances? If your venture failed to meet expectations, will you shut down your new unit? Conversely, if your new entity is a success, will you start another new operation? Instead, will you introduce new offerings or enhance the new business' offerings or approach? Or, will you revive your mental outlook or switch to another department of your company? In any case, will you employ your mission statement and milestones to determine your next move?

- Will you be attentive to the caveats associated with your subsequent reinvention? If it's appropriate, will you engage in a more modest reinvention? Will you also avoid establishing too many unrelated businesses?

Now you're ready to proceed.

STEP INTO YOUR FUTURE

Through this book, you learned how to reinvent your work. You discovered how to use your awareness to decide whether or not to make a change in your career or business and, if you opt to do so, how to parlay this knowledge to craft your work ideal, which embodies your skills—such as selling, managing people, or financial know-how—and motivations, such as wealth, power, prestige, or personal fulfillment. You found out how to use your resourcefulness to discern and address problems or opportunities, shape or refine your reinvention objective, and go after your aim. You recognized how to employ your practicality to reach your goal. You learned how to execute your reinvention flawlessly and also how to manage your attitude throughout your journey. You explored various options for undertaking your reinvention, which involve modest efforts or more extensive endeavors, and how to implement these alternatives. Most likely, you concluded that every aspect of your reinvention—whether or not you reinvent and why you might do so, your work ideal, your approach, and your choice of option—will be unique to you or your business. In addition, you probably deduced that reinventing your work is an intuitive yet logical process that's repeatable over the life of a career or business.

You should now perceive whether (or not) you need or want to change your job or business. You understand how to develop an image of your work ideal and confirm that your abilities and ambitions match this goal. You realize how to incorporate resourcefulness in your job or business. You recognize how to develop a mission statement and milestones to guide your career or business and how to use a game plan to direct your reinvention. You grasp how to stay focused yet be agile and maintain your humility, confidence, and patience. You know how to choose a reinvention alternative and, in turn, implement this option. You also appreciate that others have used—and are using—this book's approach to reinvent their careers and businesses. In other words, you are—or have the power to become—a success in your eyes. Keep this handbook within reach. You never know when you might need or want to reinvent (again).

Troubleshoot Your Reinvention

If you're having trouble and don't know why, this guide, which includes the ten most common problems and their related solutions, will help you get back on track.

PROBLEM 1: You're not sure whether or not it's time to reinvent your career or business.

SOLUTION: Make sure that you've thoroughly and objectively assessed the industry you work in, the company you work for or own, your performance, and your attitude toward your work. When you pull together a picture that incorporates these elements, you'll probably find that you're either basically satisfied with your work, somewhat satisfied but need or want something more or different, or miserable and need to do something about it. If the last two descriptions sound like your situation, most likely, you're ready to reinvent. If you need further assistance, refer to Chapter 2, Step One: Sense Your Timing.

PROBLEM 2: You don't know how to craft your reinvention goal.

SOLUTION: Fully and honestly examine your preferences, interests, skills and strengths, and motivations. Then pull together an integrated picture that includes these factors. The image of your ideal work should incorporate your preferences and interests, reflect what you're able to do, and be consistent with what's important to you. If you need more help, refer to Chapter 3, Step Two: Visualize Your Reinvention.

PROBLEM 3: You're not certain that your work ideal fits you or your business.

SOLUTION: You must evaluate whether your abilities and motivations correspond with those typically associated with your ideal work. If there's not a match, you may abandon your reinvention. Conversely, if there's a correlation, you may proceed. Or, if this pairing could be closer, you may revise your reinvention goal or make adjustments, such as bolstering your skills or making trade-offs in what's important to you. If you require additional assistance, refer to Chapter 4, Step Three: Verify Your Ideal.

PROBLEM 4: You don't understand how to become resourceful or how to use this capability in your job or business.

SOLUTION: You become resourceful by being aware of your (or your business') situation, being informed about your marketplace, and being receptive to new ideas and approaches. To be resourceful in your work, you may initiate a project to deal with a problem or go after an opportunity. You may ingeniously apply input from your customers, suppliers, or employees. You may experiment with a new technology. You may also emulate another manager's modus operandi. To learn more about being resourceful, refer to Chapter 5, Step Four: Be Resourceful.

PROBLEM 5: You're having trouble developing your mission, milestones, or reinvention game plan.

SOLUTION: Your mission statement has to reflect your (or your people's) skills, motivations, and highest goal. The milestones required to reach this long-term goal need to build logically upon one another. Your game plan must include the actions you'll take to fulfill your reinvention aim and also your approach, which has to be as efficient and effective as possible. Overall, your course of action needs to be integrated and easy to follow and stick with. For more help in devising these tools, refer to Chapter 6, Step Five: Be Practical.

PROBLEM 6: You're having difficulty executing your reinvention.

SOLUTION: You may be having trouble staying focused, being agile, or both. If you're not concentrating or applying the necessary energy, you may not be adequately focused. If you're not dealing with your problems or taking advantage of opportunities, you may not be sufficiently agile. Or, you may not be able to strike the right balance between your diligence and nimbleness. In order to diagnose your problem(s), you may want to review Chapter 7, Step Six: Execute Flawlessly.

PROBLEM 7: Your reinvention is proceeding more slowly than planned or your work reshaping is more difficult than you anticipated.

SOLUTION: Your attitude may be impeding your progress. Your arrogance may be irritating your coworkers or, because you're not open to new ideas, you may be missing out on approaches that might expedite your reinvention. Conversely, your lack of confidence, regrets about the past, fear about the future, negative perspective, or jealousy of others may be holding you or your business back. Your impatience may be causing you to experiment with unsound ideas or your intolerance may be alienating your colleagues. To be sure of the source of your problems, you may want to reread Chapter 8, Step Seven: Manage Your Attitude.

PROBLEM 8: You're not certain how to select a reinvention option.

SOLUTION: At a minimum, your situation and work ideal must line up with the sense of timing, visualization, and verification that typify the option you choose. More extensive work reinventions—such as changing jobs, restructuring and refocusing your organization, launching new offerings, making acquisitions, moving into new sectors, or establishing new ventures—require stronger matches. You also need to understand the requirements associated with the alternative you elect. Chapter 9, Implement Your Reinvention, examines why you might select a particular option, what actions this alternative involves, and how to complete these activities. You'll also learn why you might engage in two reinventions simultaneously and how to carry out this feat.

PROBLEM 9: You've reinvented but need or want to make another change. What should you do?

SOLUTION: You may reinvent again. Chapter 10, Reinvent Your Work Again, explains how to make sure that your next move is consistent with your mission and milestones. This section also discusses why you might reinvent again after a particular reinvention, what actions you'd take to accomplish your next work reshaping, and the caveats associated with this subsequent change.

PROBLEM 10: Reinvention sounds good, but you're not positive that it really works.

SOLUTION: The stories at the end of Chapters 2 through 8 illustrate how businesspeople have used the seven steps to reinvent their careers, businesses, or both—often at the same time. By reading these anecdotes, you'll learn how other people have applied this book's approach and you'll appreciate that you're not alone in rejuvenating, revamping, or recreating your work. You'll also be more confident that reinventing your work is possible—whoever you are and whatever your situation or work ideal.

Read the Bios

You've read about eight people who've used the seven-step approach to reinvent their jobs, their businesses, or both. Here are these professionals' biographical sketches.

ALBERT C. BLACK, JR.

Black grew up in a housing project in South Dallas. He graduated from the University of Texas at Dallas with a degree in business and political science and also has an M.B.A. from Southern Methodist University's Cox School of Business.

In 1982, while working the night shift at a utility company, Black started his own business, On-Target Industrial Maintenance. Seven years later, with a large contract from Texas Instruments, On-Target transitioned from custodial service and office supplies vendor to corporate supplier.

Today, On-Target Supplies & Logistics provides both products and logistical and supply chain management services to major corporations located in Texas, Oklahoma, Louisiana, Arkansas, and Missouri. The company's clients include Alcatel, Raytheon, Texas

Instruments, TXU (formerly Texas Utilities), Electronic Data Systems (EDS), and SBC Communications (formerly Southwestern Bell Telephone).

In 2000, Black served as chairman of the board of the Greater Dallas Chamber of Commerce. He also sits on other corporate, civic, and educational boards, including Chase Bank of Texas, Dallas Assembly, Dallas Citizens Council, Dallas Leadership Foundation, Dallas Together Forum, Texas Southern University, and Baylor University's Hankamer School of Business. Black has also won numerous awards: the Dallas mayor's Top Talent professional, Ernst & Young's Southwest Entrepreneur of the Year, the Black Chamber of Commerce's Quest for Success award, and the 30th Congressional District's Award for outstanding business achievement. PBS profiled Black and his company in its *Small Business 2000* series.

Living in his hometown, Black is married with three children.

NELSON CARBONELL

Carbonell grew up in Rockville, Maryland, a Washington, D.C., suburb. He graduated from George Washington University with a degree in electrical engineering.

In 1985, Carbonell joined TRW as an electrical engineer, although the company used him to program computers. A year later, he returned to the Washington Consulting Group, where he had worked during college. In 1990, Carbonell left the consulting firm and went to work for Oracle, a software company. The following year, he left Oracle and joined PRC, Inc. (now a subsidiary of Litton Industries), which built document imaging systems for the federal government. In 1993, Carbonell and a colleague founded their own company, Alta Software. Five years later, Alta built Cisco's Internetworking Product Center—the world's largest (at the time) e-commerce system. In 1999, the company, which changed its name to Cysive, went public.

Today, Reston, Virginia–based Cysive designs and builds highly reliable systems that support large-scale e-businesses. The company's customers include AT&T, Qualcomm, Cisco Systems, Daimler-Chrysler, First Union, and the Tribune Company. The company has additional offices in Atlanta, Chicago, Dallas, New York, and Mountain View and in Southern California.

In 1998, Cysive was a finalist for the Computerworld/Smithsonian Technology Award and, the next year, the company received the Blue Chip Enterprise Award and was named one of Washington Technology's 50 Fastest Growing Companies and *Red Herring*'s Top 100 IPOs. In 2000, Deloitte & Touche honored Cysive with its Technology Fast 500 and its Virginia Technology Fast 50 awards, and Carbonell was a finalist for Ernst & Young's Entrepreneur of the Year Award. Currently, this CEO serves on the Executive Committee of the Washington-Baltimore chapter of the Young President's Organization.

Residing in Northern Virginia, Carbonell is married with four children.

GREGG ENGLES

Born in Durant, Oklahoma, Engles grew up in Denver. He graduated from Dartmouth College with a degree in economics, attended Yale's School of Management, and graduated from Yale Law School in 1982.

After a clerkship for U.S. Court of Appeals Judge Anthony Kennedy (now a Supreme Court Associate Justice) and an unsuccessful attempt to start his own business, he joined a small, Dallas-based investment firm in 1983. Subsequently, Engles and a colleague started their own real estate company, but with the collapse of their Texas marketplace, they shut down their business. In 1988, Engles purchased Reddy Ice Company from the Southland Corporation and, for the next five years, he and a partner acquired other ice and food businesses. In late 1993, Engles purchased Suiza Dairy of Puerto Rico and also teamed up with the former head of Southland's dairy business. The two events led to the creation of Suiza Foods, which went public in 1996. From the beginning, Suiza has made acquisitions and consolidated them: regional dairies across the country, Morningstar, a national company with branded products, and Southern Foods.

Today, Suiza, a Fortune 500 and *Forbes'* Platinum 400 List company, is also a leader in product innovation. In 1999, *Dairy Foods* magazine named Suiza Foods Processor of the Year. In April 2001, Suiza Foods agreed to acquire Dean Foods in a deal valued at $1.5 billion. This transaction is expected to close before the end of 2001. Engles would serve as CEO of the combined firm.

Engles serves on the board of the Milk Industry Foundation and the International Dairy Foods Association and is also active in other organizations, including Young President's Organization, Yale Law School Association, Dallas Citizens Council, and Boy Scouts of America Council. In 1999, Engles won *Dairy Field* magazine's Executive of the Year award.

Engles and his wife live in Dallas.

W. JAMES FARRELL

Farrell grew up in Buffalo, New York. He graduated from the University of Detroit with a degree in electrical engineering and served in the U.S. Army from 1965 to 1967.

After the Army, Farrell joined Illinois Tool Works (ITW) on a full-time basis, first working as a sales representative in Dayton and Detroit and, in 1972, becoming the general manager of an Illinois-based start-up division. Four years later, he advanced to executive vice president of the fastener group, which, at the time, represented 30 percent of the company's revenues. In the late 1970s and the 1980s, Farrell ran the largest part of ITW and, during this period, also promoted the company's 80/20 philosophy. In 1994, Farrell became president and, the following year, CEO. He assumed his current position as CEO and chairman in 1996.

Today, ITW, a manufacturer of engineered products and systems, has more than 500 businesses that operate in 40 countries with approximately 53,000 employees. In addition to being a Fortune 500 company, ITW is on *Forbes'* Platinum 400 List.

Farrell is a director of UAL Corporation; Allstate Insurance Company; Sears, Roebuck, and Company; and the Federal Reserve Bank of Chicago. He is affiliated with numerous business groups: the Business Council, the Chicago Club, the Commercial Club of Chicago, the Economic Club of Chicago, the Illinois Business Roundtable, and the Mid-America Committee. Farrell is a director of the Chicago Public Library Foundation, Junior Achievement of Chicago, the Lyric Opera of Chicago, the United Way/Crusade of Mercy, and the Big Shoulders Fund. He is a trustee of Northwestern University, the Chicago Symphony Orchestra, and the Rush Presbyterian–St. Luke's Medical Center, and chairman of the board of trustees of the Museum of Science and Industry. Farrell also serves on the advisory board of the J.L. Kellogg Graduate School of Management.

Residing in the Chicago area, Farrell is married with five children.

EVELYN GRANVILLE

Born in a segregated Washington, D.C., Granville was one of five valedictorians of her high school class. In 1945, with a major in mathematics, she graduated summa cum laude and Phi Beta Kappa from Smith College and, four years later, as one of the first two African-American women in the United States to obtain a doctorate in mathematics, she graduated from Yale University.

Granville spent three years in academia, first as a research assistant and part-time math instructor at New York University and then at Fisk University as an Associate Professor of Mathematics. In 1952, Granville took a government job, working on problems involving missile fuses at the National Bureau of Standards, later known as the Diamond Ordinance Fuse Laboratories of the Department of the Army. Joining IBM in 1956, Granville entered the business world and, in what was the highlight of her years at the company, she was part of a team that formulated orbit computations and computer procedures for NASA's Vanguard and Mercury projects. After moving to Los Angeles, she left IBM and joined Space Technology Laboratories and, subsequently, North American Aviation Company, where she continued to support NASA projects. In 1963, she returned to IBM, joining the company's Federal Systems Division. Four years later, Granville left IBM and returned to academia, this time as a professor at California State University in Los Angeles, where, for the next 17 years, she taught computer programming, numerical analysis, and a mathematics course—new math—for elementary school teachers. Granville and a colleague also published a textbook on teaching this new discipline. Granville moved to East Texas in 1984 to begin her first of three so-called retirements but, instead, became a professor of mathematics and computer science at Texas College and, from 1990 through 1997, a mathematics professor at the University of Texas at Tyler. During 1998 and 1999, Granville participated in Dow Chemical Company's Pioneers in Science Program, through which she conducted workshops for students, their parents, and their teachers.

Today, Granville conducts federally sponsored Eisenhower workshops, which are designed to improve the teaching of mathematics.

In 1989, Granville received an honorary doctor of science degree from Smith College, which, a decade later, recognized her as one of 27 Remarkable Women alumnae. In 1999, the National Academy of Sciences also honored her. In 2001, Granville received an honorary doctor of science degree from Yale University.

Granville is married and lives in Texas.

PAULA MADISON

Madison grew up in Harlem, New York. She attended Cardinal Spellman High School, graduated from Vassar College with a degree in history and black studies, and attended Syracuse University's Newhouse School of Journalism.

In 1976, she began her career as a reporter for the *Syracuse Herald Journal* in Syracuse, New York. Moving to Texas in 1980, she became an investigative reporter at the *Fort Worth Star Telegram* and, subsequently, assistant city editor at the *Dallas Times Herald*. Madison made the transition to television news in 1982, joining Dallas' WFAA-TV. From 1986 to 1987, she was news director at KOTV-TV in Tulsa, Oklahoma and, from 1987 to 1989, executive news director at KHOU-TV in Houston. In 1989, moving back to her native New York, Madison became assistant news director of WNBC-TV, NewsChannel 4. By 1996, she was vice president and news director—one of the few African-American women news directors in the country and the first in that position in the intensely competitive New York market. Under her direction, *NewsChannel 4 at 11 PM* became a top-rated news program and WNBC became the number-one-rated affiliate for late news in the United States. NewsChannel 4 received the prestigious George Foster Peabody award for its 1996 report "Passport to Kill."

In 2000, Madison became president and general manager of KNBC, NBC-TV's Los Angeles–based affiliate.

Madison sits on several boards, including Vassar College's board of trustees, National Medical Fellowships, Inc., the Center For Public Integrity, and the Maynard Institute for Journalism Education. She also serves on the executive committee of the Campaign to Save Cardinal Spellman High School. Madison has won numerous awards, including the APPLE Institute award, the National Association of Black Journalists' Ida B. Wells Award, Support Network's Ninth Annual Community Service Award, and the Tri-State Catholic Committee on Radio and Television's TRISCOURT Award. In addition, New York City and various organizations, including the YMCA, *Crain's New York Business,* and General Electric, NBC's parent company, have recognized her achievements.

Residing in the Los Angeles area, Madison is married with one daughter.

JIMMY R. RIDINGS

Ridings was born and raised in Meridian, Texas, a small town near Waco. He attended Baylor University.

Dropping out of college after two years, Ridings went to work as a forklift operator for a mobile home company and, shortly thereafter, transitioned into selling plumbing supplies to the mobile home industry. For the next 15 years, he worked for two different companies, both of which regularly cut his commissions. In 1985, frustrated by the limitations on his earning ability, Ridings left his employer and became an independent sales representative. After his main client no longer needed his services, Ridings started his own company. For the next five years, the Texan struggled to grow his business. In 1990, he took Craftmade International, his $12.5 million ceiling fan company, public. In 1998, Craftmade acquired Trade Source International (TSI), a wholesale distributor of outdoor lighting fixtures to mass merchandisers, and, as a result, Craftmade added a new distribution channel and also doubled its revenues.

Today, Craftmade is a market leader in the design, distribution, and marketing of superior quality ceiling fans, light kits, and related accessories, including bathstrip and outdoor lighting. The company sells products through a network of more than 1,600 lighting showrooms and wholesalers that cater to the home construction, remodeling, and upscale commercial building markets. Craftmade is also pursuing cross-marketing opportunities with its TSI subsidiary in the mass merchandiser market. Two other Craftmade subsidiaries assemble lamps and distribute telecommunications cable and components.

Four times in the past decade, *Forbes* has named Craftmade International to its annual list of America's 200 Best Small Companies. In 1999, because of the company's excellent customer relations, the magazine profiled Craftmade as one of 12 to Watch.

Married with two grown children, Ridings lives in the Dallas area.

FELICIA A. ZIMMERMAN

Zimmerman was born in Hartford, Connecticut. She graduated from Smith College with a degree with honors in history and also has a master's degree from the Johns Hopkins School of Advanced International Studies.

After college, Zimmerman worked for Hartford National Bank (now part of Fleet Bank) and later for an executive recruiting firm.

Subsequently, while attending graduate school in Washington, D.C., she worked part-time on Capitol Hill as an assistant to a Senate Appropriations subcommittee. Moving to New York in 1977, Zimmerman served as executive assistant to the Citibank's Senior Adviser for International Operations and, in 1981, she joined TransWorld Corporation's corporate planning staff. In 1982, Zimmerman moved to Dallas, where she became part of Frito-Lay's internal consulting group and, subsequently, a national sales manager and sales strategist. Five years later, Zimmerman launched her own business and became a communication coach to corporate managers and executives. In 1993, after transitioning her firm into consulting, she began helping corporate managers operate more effectively by rejuvenating, revamping, or recreating their approach. Over the past 14 years, Zimmerman has worked with thousands of managers at various companies, including Corning, ExxonMobil, American Airlines, Texas Instruments, Electronic Data Systems (EDS), and PricewaterhouseCoopers.

Today, Zimmerman speaks before corporate groups and also appears as a guest on local TV and radio programs. Serving on the associate board of Southern Methodist University's Cox School of Business, she also mentors MBA students.

Zimmerman resides in Dallas.

NOTES

CHAPTER 1. REINVENT YOUR WORK

1. Mark Albion, *Making a Life, Making a Living* (New York: Warner Books, 2000), 19.

CHAPTER 2. STEP ONE: SENSE YOUR TIMING

1. James Champy and Nitin Nohria, *The Arc of Ambition* (Cambridge, MA: Perseus Books, 2000), 197.

2. Andrew S. Grove, *Only the Paranoid Survive,* paperback ed. (New York: Currency Doubleday, 1999), 193.

3. Gregg Engles, interview by author, tape recording, Dallas, TX, 19 December 1999.

4. Gerry Clark, "Think Nationally, Act Locally," *Dairy Foods,* December 1999, 36.

CHAPTER 3. STEP TWO: VISUALIZE YOUR REINVENTION

1. Michael Useem, *The Leadership Moment* (New York: Times Business, 1998), 281.

2. Grove, *Only the Paranoid Survive,* 195.

3. Paula Madison, interview by author, tape recording, Mount Vernon, NY, 10 October 1999.

CHAPTER 4. STEP THREE: VERIFY YOUR IDEAL

1. Jack Trout with Steve Rivkin, *The Power of Simplicity* (New York: McGraw-Hill, Inc., 1999), 91.

2. Evelyn Granville, interview by author, tape recording, Ben Wheeler, TX, 4 October 1999.

CHAPTER 5. STEP FOUR: BE RESOURCEFUL

1. Robert Slater, *Jack Welch and the GE Way* (New York: McGraw-Hill Companies, Inc., 1999), 5.

2. Nelson Carbonell, interview by author, tape recording, Reston, VA, 9 December 1999.

CHAPTER 6. STEP FIVE: BE PRACTICAL

1. Ram Charan, *What the CEO Wants You to Know* (New York: Crown Business, 2001), 134.

2. Jimmy Ridings, interview by author, tape recording, Coppell, TX, 23 November 1999.

CHAPTER 7. STEP SIX: EXECUTE FLAWLESSLY

1. Noel M. Tichy with Eli Cohen, *The Leadership Engine* (New York: HarperBusiness, 1997), 128.

2. Steven L. Goldman, Roger N. Nagel, and Kenneth Preiss, *Agile Competitors and Virtual Organizations* (New York: Van Nostrand Reinhold, 1995), 42.

3. W. James Farrell, interview by author, tape recording, Glenview, IL, 21 December 1999.

CHAPTER 8. STEP SEVEN: MANAGE YOUR ATTITUDE

1. Carl Sewell and Paul B. Brown, *Customers for Life* (New York: Currency Doubleday, 1990), 66.

2. Georges-Louis Leclerc de Buffon, quoted in *Bartlett's Familiar Quotations,* Justin Kaplan, ed., 16th ed. (Boston: Little, Brown and Company, Inc., 1992), 311.

3. Albert Black, interview by author, tape recording, Dallas, TX, 4 December 1999.

CHAPTER 9. IMPLEMENT YOUR REINVENTION

1. Stephen R. Covey, *The Seven Habits of Highly Effective People,* paperback ed. (New York: Fireside/Simon & Schuster, 1990), 92.

CHAPTER 10. REINVENT YOUR WORK AGAIN

1. Grove, *Only the Paranoid Survive,* 197-98.

The following books and periodicals may help you in your reinvention journey.

PERIODICALS

The Wall Street Journal
The gold standard for keeping up with business—no matter what you do or where you work. Front-page stories may give you ideas for your job or business.

The New York Times
If you don't read this newspaper during the week, enjoy it on Sundays. The business section may provide you with concepts that you can apply to your work.

Industry Standard
If you're involved in technology, you're probably reading this publication, but even if you're not, you may find this magazine's analysis of the new economy insightful.

Forbes
In this magazine's regular feature on entrepreneurs, you may pick up useful ideas or approaches for your business.

Fortune
Using this publication's articles about corporate trends, you may better assess your industry or company.

Business Week
If you don't have time to read a daily newspaper, you may want to peruse this periodical.

Harvard Business Review
You may benefit by examining this periodical's case studies.

Fast Company
Occasionally, you may appreciate a story about an entrepreneur or corporate manager.

BOOKS

CORPORATE REINVENTION

Grove, Andrew. *Only the Paranoid Survive*. Paperback ed., New York: Currency Doubleday, 1999.
> How the executive dealt with Intel's "strategic inflection points." Includes an excellent final chapter, Career Inflection Points.

Hamel, Gary. *Leading the Revolution*. Boston: Harvard Business School Press, 2000.
> How companies, especially large ones, transform themselves.

CAREER REINVENTION

Butler, Timothy, and James Waldroop. *Discovering Your Career in Business*. Reading, MA: Perseus, 1997.
> From the Directors of MBA career development programs at Harvard Business School, psychological insights on pursuing your career.

Champy, James, and Nitin Nohria. *The Arc of Ambition*. Cambridge, MA: Perseus Books, 2000.
> Includes an excellent chapter, Reinvention is the Key to Longevity.

Hunt, Christopher, and Scott Scanlon, eds. *Navigating Your Career*. New York: John Wiley & Sons, 1997.
> Essays by headhunters on choosing and changing your career.

Peters, Tom. *Reinventing Work: The Brand You 50*. New York: Alfred A. Knopf, 1999.
> Although somewhat superficial, includes 50 ways to transform yourself into an "independent contractor-in-spirit" or a "brand."

AWARENESS

Breathnach, Sarah Ban. *Something More*. New York: Warner Books, Inc., 1998.
> Beautifully written sketches about why "searching for something more is settling for nothing less than you deserve."

Lao-tzu. *Tao Te Ching.* Translated by Stephen Mitchell. New York: Harper & Row, 1988; first HarperPerennial ed., New York: HarperPerennial, 1991.
>Timeless wisdom, especially about knowing what you can and can't control.

RESOURCEFULNESS, PRACTICALITY, AND EXECUTION

Charan, Ram. *What the CEO Wants You to Know.* New York: Crown Business, 2001.
>A quick read that provides down-to-earth wisdom.

Gerber, Michael. *The E-Myth Manager.* New York: HarperBusiness, 1998.
>Told through an imaginary conversation, how to develop an entrepreneurial mind-set.

Slater, Robert. *Jack Welch and the GE Way.* New York: McGraw-Hill Companies, Inc., 1999.
>How Welch (now the former CEO) and his company remained focused yet agile.

Trout, Jack, with Steve Rivkin. *The Power of Simplicity.* New York: McGraw-Hill, Inc., 1999.
>Practical advice from a marketing guru.

INSPIRING STORIES

Albion, Mark. *Making a Life, Making a Living.* New York: Warner Books, 2000.
>Stories about individuals who pursue their passions while they balance their work with the rest of their lives.

Brinker, Norman, and Donald Phillips. *On the Brink.* Arlington, TX: Summit Publishing Group, 1996.
>About Norm Brinker, a restaurant entrepreneur and the chairman emeritus of Brinker International.

Marcus, Stanley. *Minding the Store.* Dallas, TX: Stanley Marcus, 1974; facsimile ed., Denton, TX: University of North Texas, 1997.
>About the retailing legend and his world-famous store, Neiman Marcus.

Useem, Michael. *The Leadership Moment.* New York: Times Business, 1998.
>Nine true stories, including those of Roy Vagelos, former CEO of Merck, and John Gutfreund, former head of Salomon Inc.

INDEX

Reinvent Your Company!

For special discounts on 20 or more copies of *Reinvent Your Work: How to Rejuvenate, Revamp, or Recreate Your Career,* please call Dearborn Trade Special Sales at 800-621-9621, extension 4307.

Dearborn™
Trade Publishing
A **Kaplan Professional** Company